C-1459 CAREER EXAMINATION SERIES

This is your
PASSBOOK for...

Safety Security Officer

Test Preparation Study Guide
Questions & Answers

NATIONAL LEARNING CORPORATION®

COPYRIGHT NOTICE

This book is SOLELY intended for, is sold ONLY to, and its use is RESTRICTED to individual, bona fide applicants or candidates who qualify by virtue of having seriously filed applications for appropriate license, certificate, professional and/or promotional advancement, higher school matriculation, scholarship, or other legitimate requirements of education and/or governmental authorities.

This book is NOT intended for use, class instruction, tutoring, training, duplication, copying, reprinting, excerption, or adaptation, etc., by:

1) Other publishers
2) Proprietors and/or Instructors of "Coaching" and/or Preparatory Courses
3) Personnel and/or Training Divisions of commercial, industrial, and governmental organizations
4) Schools, colleges, or universities and/or their departments and staffs, including teachers and other personnel
5) Testing Agencies or Bureaus
6) Study groups which seek by the purchase of a single volume to copy and/or duplicate and/or adapt this material for use by the group as a whole without having purchased individual volumes for each of the members of the group
7) Et al.

Such persons would be in violation of appropriate Federal and State statutes.

PROVISION OF LICENSING AGREEMENTS – Recognized educational, commercial, industrial, and governmental institutions and organizations, and others legitimately engaged in educational pursuits, including training, testing, and measurement activities, may address request for a licensing agreement to the copyright owners, who will determine whether, and under what conditions, including fees and charges, the materials in this book may be used them. In other words, a licensing facility exists for the legitimate use of the material in this book on other than an individual basis. However, it is asseverated and affirmed here that the material in this book CANNOT be used without the receipt of the express permission of such a licensing agreement from the Publishers. Inquiries re licensing should be addressed to the company, attention rights and permissions department.

All rights reserved, including the right of reproduction in whole or in part, in any form or by any means, electronic or mechanical, including photocopying, recording, or by any information storage and retrieval system, without permission in writing from the Publisher.

Copyright © 2025 by
National Learning Corporation

212 Michael Drive, Syosset, NY 11791
(516) 921-8888 • www.passbooks.com
E-mail: info@passbooks.com

PASSBOOK® SERIES

THE *PASSBOOK® SERIES* has been created to prepare applicants and candidates for the ultimate academic battlefield – the examination room.

At some time in our lives, each and every one of us may be required to take an examination – for validation, matriculation, admission, qualification, registration, certification, or licensure.

Based on the assumption that every applicant or candidate has met the basic formal educational standards, has taken the required number of courses, and read the necessary texts, the *PASSBOOK® SERIES* furnishes the one special preparation which may assure passing with confidence, instead of failing with insecurity. Examination questions – together with answers – are furnished as the basic vehicle for study so that the mysteries of the examination and its compounding difficulties may be eliminated or diminished by a sure method.

This book is meant to help you pass your examination provided that you qualify and are serious in your objective.

The entire field is reviewed through the huge store of content information which is succinctly presented through a provocative and challenging approach – the question-and-answer method.

A climate of success is established by furnishing the correct answers at the end of each test.

You soon learn to recognize types of questions, forms of questions, and patterns of questioning. You may even begin to anticipate expected outcomes.

You perceive that many questions are repeated or adapted so that you can gain acute insights, which may enable you to score many sure points.

You learn how to confront new questions, or types of questions, and to attack them confidently and work out the correct answers.

You note objectives and emphases, and recognize pitfalls and dangers, so that you may make positive educational adjustments.

Moreover, you are kept fully informed in relation to new concepts, methods, practices, and directions in the field.

You discover that you are actually taking the examination all the time: you are preparing for the examination by "taking" an examination, not by reading extraneous and/or supererogatory textbooks.

In short, this PASSBOOK®, used directedly, should be an important factor in helping you to pass your test.

SAFETY SECURITY OFFICER

DUTIES
As a Safety and Security Officer Trainee, you would be required to complete comprehensive one-year training program. During this period, you would be trained to protect persons and property, to prevent and detect crime and to maintain peace, order and security in a State agency, facility or community residence. While serving your traineeship, you might be assigned, on a fixed or rotating shift, to mobile or foot patrol, dispatch desk post, fire post or to fire and safety inspections.

SUBJECT OF EXAMINATION
The written test will be designed to test for knowledge, skills, and/or abilities in such areas as:
1. Applying written information in a security services setting;
2. Preparing written material;
3. Understanding and interpreting written material; and
4. Understanding and interpreting graphs, charts, tables and diagrams.

INTRODUCTION

This test guide provides a general description of the most common subject areas which will be tested and an explanation of the different types of questions you may see on the test.

Not all subject areas tested in the Safety and Security Series are covered in this test guide. The Examination Announcement will list the subject areas that will be included on the particular test you will be taking. Some of these subject areas may not be covered in this test guide.

The most common subject areas included in the Safety and Security Series are:

1. **APPLYING WRITTEN INFORMATION IN A SAFETY AND SECURITY SETTING:** These questions evaluate your ability to read, interpret and apply rules, regulations, directions, written narratives and other related material. You will be required to read a set of information and to appropriately apply the information to situations similar to those typically experienced in a public safety and security service setting. All information needed to answer the questions is contained in the rules, regulations, etc. which are cited.

2. **FOLLOWING DIRECTIONS (MAPS):** These questions test your ability to follow physical/geographic directions using street maps or building maps. You will have to read and understand a set of directions and then use them on a simple map.

3. **PREPARING WRITTEN MATERIAL:** These questions test for the ability to present information clearly and accurately, and to organize paragraphs logically and comprehensibly. For some questions, you will be given information in two or three sentences, followed by four restatements of the information. You must then choose the best version. For other questions, you will be given paragraphs with their sentences out of order. You must then choose, from among four choices, the best order for the sentences.

4. **PRINCIPLES AND PRACTICES OF SAFETY AND SECURITY:** These questions test for a knowledge of the proper principles and practices in the field of safety and security. The questions will cover such areas as selecting the best course of action to take in a safety or security related situation.

5. **SAFETY AND SECURITY METHODS AND PROCEDURES:** These questions test for knowledge of the methods and procedures utilized in safety and security related positions. The questions cover such areas as principles and practices of safety and security precautions in a building or grounds setting, accident prevention, proper response to safety or security related incidents, the investigation of incidents, and the inspection of buildings or grounds for potential safety and/or security problems.

INTRODUCTION – CONTINUED

6. **UNDERSTANDING AND INTERPRETING WRITTEN MATERIAL:** These questions test how well you comprehend written material. You will be provided with brief reading selections and will be asked questions about the selections. All the information required to answer the questions will be presented in the selections; you will not be required to have any special knowledge relating to the subject areas of the selections.

7. **SUPERVISION:** These questions test for knowledge of the principles and practices employed in planning, organizing, and controlling the activities of a work unit toward predetermined objectives. The concepts covered, usually in a situational question format, include such topics as assigning and reviewing work; evaluating performance; maintaining work standards; motivating and developing subordinates; implementing procedural change; increasing efficiency; and dealing with problems of absenteeism, morale, and discipline.

8. **ADMINISTRATIVE SUPERVISION:** These questions test for knowledge of the principles and practices involved in directing the activities of a large subordinate staff, including subordinate supervisors. Questions relate to the personal interactions between an upper level supervisor and his/her subordinate supervisors in the accomplishment of objectives. These questions cover such areas as assigning work to and coordinating the activities of several units, establishing and guiding staff development programs, evaluating the performance of subordinate supervisors, and maintaining relationships with other organizational sections.

The remainder of this test guide explains how you will be tested in each subject area listed above. A **TEST TASK** is provided for each subject area. This is an explanation of how a question is presented and how to correctly answer it. Read each explanation carefully. This test guide also provides at least one **SAMPLE QUESTION** for each subject area. The sample question is similar to the type of questions that will be presented on the actual test. This test guide provides the **SOLUTION** and correct answer to each sample question. You should study each sample question and solution in order to understand how the correct answer was determined.

At the end of this test guide we have included a **PRACTICE TEST** which includes additional examples of the types of questions you may see on your written test. Answers are provided in the Practice Test Key so that you can see how well you have done.

SUBJECT AREA 1

APPLYING WRITTEN INFORMATION IN A SAFETY AND SECURITY SETTING: These questions evaluate your ability to read, interpret and apply rules, regulations, directions, written narratives and other related material. You will be required to read a set of information and to appropriately apply the information to situations similar to those typically experienced in a public safety and security service setting. All information needed to answer the questions is contained in the rules, regulations, etc. which are cited.

TEST TASK: You will be given a set of rules, regulations, or other written information to read. You will then be asked a question which requires you to apply the rule to a given situation.

SAMPLE QUESTION:

RULE: While patrolling your grounds or building, keep a notebook and pencil with you. Keep the following emergency phone numbers in the notebook: police, fire department, nearby hospitals, alarm company, your supervisor, and the head of your building.

When you observe something out of the ordinary, take notes. Describe what is unusual, people who are unfamiliar, and any suspicious activity. If a crime or offense takes place, record what happened, who was involved, physical appearance of the suspect, clothing worn by the suspect, time and date, names and phone numbers of witnesses, where suspect was last seen, and any physical evidence found.

SITUATION: While you are doing your rounds at 11:20 p.m. you notice a door that has been left ajar. The door opens to the office of the Assistant Director of your facility. The door is typically closed and locked for the day when the Assistant Director leaves, usually between 5:00 and 6:00 p.m. The office is dark and no one is there.

QUESTION: Based solely on the above Rule and Situation, what, if anything, should be recorded in your notebook?

A. The office was dark when you entered it.
B. No one was in the office.
C. The door was open at 11:20 p.m.
D. No entry needs to be made.

The correct answer to this sample question is choice C.

SOLUTION: The Situation states that while doing your rounds at 11:20 p.m., you notice a door left ajar. This door is typically closed and locked for the day between 5:00 and 6:00 p.m. by the Assistant Director. The question asks what, if anything, you should record about this incident in your notebook. To answer the question, evaluate all of the choices.

Solution continued on next page.

SUBJECT AREA 1 – CONTINUED

Choice A *states that you should record in your notebook the fact that the office was dark when you entered it. The Rule states that you should take notes when you observe something out of the ordinary. It is not out of the ordinary for the Assistant Director's office to be dark at 11:20 p.m. since the Assistant Director usually leaves for the day between 5:00 and 6:00 p.m. Choice A is incorrect.*

Choice B *states that you should record in your notebook the fact that no one was in the office. The Rule states that you should take notes when you observe something out of the ordinary. It is not out of the ordinary for the Assistant Director's office to be unoccupied at 11:20 p.m. since the Assistant Director is not usually at work after 6:00 p.m. Choice B is incorrect.*

Choice C *states that you should record in your notebook the fact that the door was open at 11:20 p.m. The Rule states that you should take notes when you observe something out of the ordinary. It is out of the ordinary for the Assistant Director's office door to be open at 11:20 p.m. because the door is typically closed and locked when the Assistant Director leaves for the day, usually between 5:00 and 6:00 p.m. Choice C is the correct answer.*

Choice D *states that you should make no entry in your notebook. The Rule states that you should take notes when you observe something out of the ordinary. It is out of the ordinary for the Assistant Director's office door to be open at 11:20 p.m. because the door is typically closed and locked when the Assistant Director leaves for the day, usually between 5:00 and 6:00 p.m. Choice D is incorrect.*

SUBJECT AREA 2

FOLLOWING DIRECTIONS (MAPS): These questions test your ability to follow physical/geographic directions using street maps or building maps. You will have to read and understand a set of directions and then use them on a simple map.

TEST TASK: You will be provided with street maps or building maps. You will then be asked questions which require you to refer to the given maps and related information.

SAMPLE QUESTION:

DIRECTIONS: Base your answer to the following question on the sample information and sample map below. The map below shows a section of a city. The circled numbers are starting points and stopping points. Buildings are shown with letters. A roadblock is shown as a dark circle. One-way blocks are shown with an arrow pointing in the direction that you may travel on that block. For example:

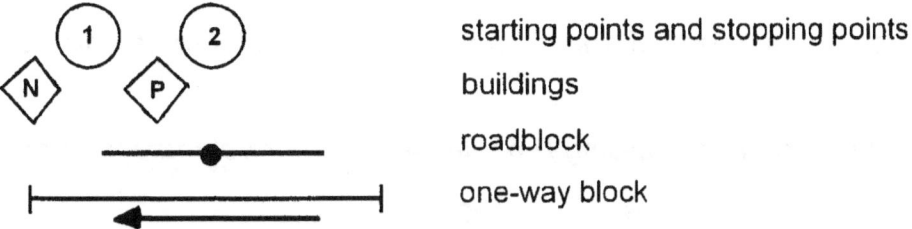

starting points and stopping points

buildings

roadblock

one-way block

You may not go through a roadblock or travel in the wrong direction on a one-way block. You are to answer the question by finding and following the SHORTEST CORRECT route between the two locations given. All blocks are equal in length.

NOTE 1: Blocks may be traveled in either direction UNLESS only one direction is shown by an arrow for that block.

NOTE 2: You "pass" a building when you travel the block NEAREST the building.

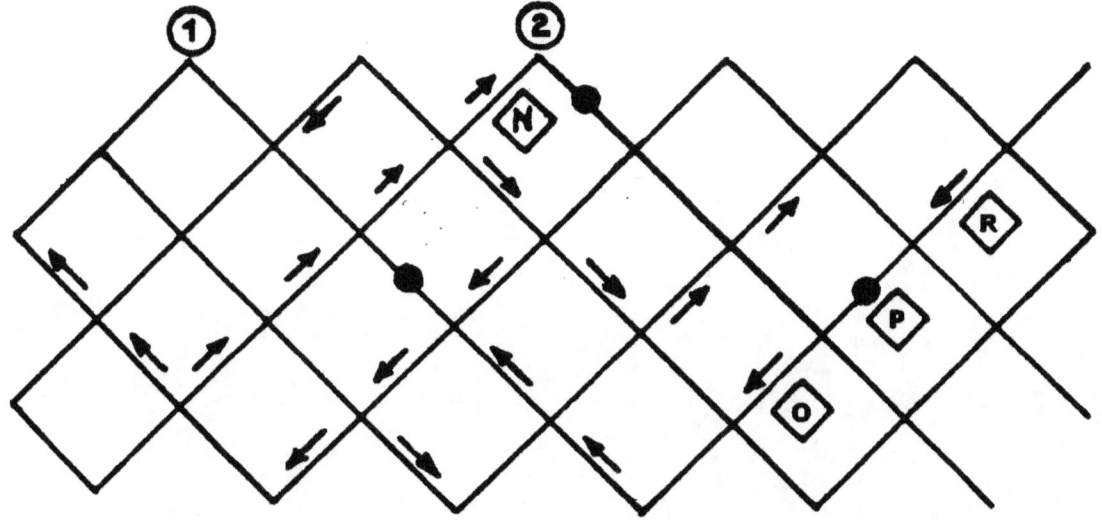

SUBJECT AREA 2 – CONTINUED

QUESTION: Which one of the following is a building you pass on the shortest correct route from point 1 to point 2?

A. N
B. O
C. P
D. R

The correct answer to this sample question is choice A.

SOLUTION:

Choice A *is the correct answer to this question. The shortest correct route from point 1 to point 2 is four blocks and passes only building N.*

Choice B *is not correct. You do not pass building O on the shortest correct route from point 1 to point 2.*

Choice C *is not correct. You do not pass building P on the shortest correct route from point 1 to point 2.*

Choice D *is not correct. You do not pass building R on the shortest correct route from point 1 to point 2.*

SUBJECT AREA 3

PREPARING WRITTEN MATERIAL: These questions test for the ability to present information clearly and accurately and for the ability to organize paragraphs logically and comprehensibly.

TEST TASK: There are two separate test tasks in this subject area.

- For the first, **Information Presentation**, you will be given information in two or three sentences, followed by four restatements of the information. You must then choose the best version.

- For the second, **Paragraph Organization**, you will be given paragraphs with their sentences out of order, and then be asked to choose, from among four choices, the best order for the sentences.

INFORMATION PRESENTATION SAMPLE QUESTION:

Martin Wilson failed to take proper precautions. His failure to take proper precautions caused a personal injury accident.

Which one of the following best presents the information above?

A. Martin Wilson failed to take proper precautions that caused a personal injury accident.
B. Proper precautions, which Martin Wilson failed to take, caused a personal injury accident.
C. Martin Wilson's failure to take proper precautions caused a personal injury accident.
D. Martin Wilson, who failed to take proper precautions, was in a personal injury accident.

The correct answer to this sample question is choice C.

SOLUTION:

Choice A *conveys the incorrect impression that proper precautions caused a personal injury accident.*

Choice B *conveys the incorrect impression that proper precautions caused a personal injury accident.*

Choice C *best presents the original information: Martin Wilson failed to take proper precautions and this failure caused a personal injury accident.*

Choice D *states that Martin Wilson was in a personal injury accident. The original information states that Martin Wilson caused a personal injury accident, but it does not state that Martin Wilson was in a personal injury accident.*

SUBJECT AREA 3 – CONTINUED

PARAGRAPH ORGANIZATION SAMPLE QUESTION:

The following question is based upon a group of sentences. The sentences are shown out of sequence, but when correctly arranged, they form a connected, well-organized paragraph. Read the sentences, and then answer the question about the best arrangement of these sentences.

1. Eventually, they piece all of this information together and make a choice.

2. Before actually deciding upon a human services job, people usually think about several possibilities.

3. They imagine themselves in different situations, and in so doing, they probably think about their interests, goals, and abilities.

4. Choosing among occupations in the field of human services is an important decision to make.

Which one of the following is the best arrangement of these sentences?

A. 2-4-1-3
B. 2-3-4-1
C. 4-2-1-3
D. 4-2-3-1

The correct answer to this sample question is choice D.

SOLUTION:

Choices A and C present the information in the paragraph out of logical sequence. In both A and C, sentence 1 comes before sentence 3. The key element in the organization of this paragraph is that sentence 3 contains the information to which sentence 1 refers; therefore, in logical sequence, sentence 3 should come before sentence 1.

Choice B also presents the information in the paragraph out of logical sequence. Choice B places the main idea of the paragraph (Sentence 4) in between two detail sentences (Sentences 1 and 3). The logical sequence of the information presented in the paragraph is therefore interrupted.

Choice D presents the information in the paragraph in the best logical sequence. Sentence 4 introduces the main idea of the paragraph: "choosing an occupation in the field of human services." Sentences 2-3-1 then follow up on this idea by describing, in order, the steps involved in making such a choice. Choice D is the best answer to this sample question.

SUBJECT AREA 4

PRINCIPLES AND PRACTICES OF SAFETY AND SECURITY: These questions test for a knowledge of the proper principles and practices in the field of safety and security. The questions will cover such areas as selecting the best course of action to take in a safety or security related situation.

TEST TASK: You will be presented with situations in which you must apply knowledge of the principles and practices of safety and security to answer the questions correctly.

SAMPLE QUESTION:

You are in charge of maintaining order in a room where a large number of people gather to transact business. A woman in the back of one of the lines starts to shout that she has been waiting for an hour and her line "has not moved at all." She continues to protest, and the rest of the crowd is getting restless.

Which one of the following actions would be best to take first in this situation?

A. Escort the woman to the head of the line and make sure her business is transacted promptly.
B. Tell the woman that unless she acts in a more orderly fashion, you will escort her out of the room.
C. Immediately remove the woman from the room.
D. Call the local police and detain the woman until the police arrive.

The correct answer to this sample question is choice B.

SOLUTION:

Choice A *is not correct because escorting the woman to the head of the line and making sure her business is transacted promptly is not the best action to take first in this situation. This action could increase the restlessness of the other people who have also been waiting in the same line and will only serve to reinforce the woman's disruptive behavior.*

Choice B *is the correct answer because telling the woman that unless she acts in a more orderly fashion, you will escort her out of the room is the best action to take first in this situation. This action provides the woman with a clear warning to stop her disruptive behavior and advises her of the consequence should she continue to loudly protest the long wait.*

Choice C *is not correct because immediately removing the woman from the room is not the best action to take first in this situation. This action is too harsh based on the situation and could escalate the woman's disruptive behavior.*

Choice D *is not correct because calling the local police and detaining the woman until they arrive is not the best action to take first in this situation. This action is too harsh based on the situation and could escalate the woman's disruptive behavior.*

SUBJECT AREA 5

SAFETY AND SECURITY METHODS AND PROCEDURES: These questions test for knowledge of the methods and procedures utilized in safety and security related positions. The questions cover such areas as principles and practices of safety and security precautions in a building or grounds setting, accident prevention, proper response to safety or security related incidents, the investigation of incidents, and the inspection of buildings or grounds for potential safety and/or security problems.

TEST TASK: You will be presented with questions in which you must apply knowledge of the methods and procedures utilized in safety and security related positions to answer the questions correctly.

SAMPLE QUESTION:

The most important purpose of patrolling the halls and grounds of a facility is to

A. discourage potential violations of rules or laws
B. give people on site the opportunity to obtain information or advice
C. maintain a routine observation of facility employees and their actions for your records
D. be able to provide assistance to local police authorities by accurately reporting whether unauthorized activity occurs in or near the facility

The correct answer to this sample question is choice A.

SOLUTION:

Choice A *is the correct answer because discouraging potential violations of rules or laws is the most important purpose of patrolling the halls and grounds of a facility. Your presence while patrolling the halls and grounds of a facility may be enough to deter potential rule or law violators.*

Choice B *is not correct because giving people on site the opportunity to obtain information or advice is not the most important purpose of patrolling the halls and grounds of a facility. Although giving people on site the opportunity to obtain information or advice may be an important purpose of patrolling the halls and grounds of a facility, it is not the most important purpose.*

Choice C *is not correct because maintaining a routine observation of facility employees and their actions for your records is not the most important purpose of patrolling the halls and grounds of a facility. Although maintaining a routine observation of facility employees and their actions for your records may be an important purpose of patrolling the halls and grounds of a facility, it is not the most important purpose.*

Choice D *is not correct because being able to provide assistance to local police authorities by accurately reporting whether unauthorized activity occurs in or near the facility is not the most important purpose of patrolling the halls and grounds of a facility. Although being able to provide assistance to local police authorities by accurately reporting whether unauthorized activity occurs in or near the facility may be an important purpose of patrolling the halls and grounds of a facility, it is not the most important purpose.*

SUBJECT AREA 6

UNDERSTANDING AND INTERPRETING WRITTEN MATERIAL: These questions test how well you comprehend written material. You will be provided with brief reading selections and will be asked questions about the selections. All the information required to answer the questions will be presented in the selections; you will not be required to have any special knowledge relating to the subject areas of the selections.

TEST TASK: You will be provided with brief reading passages and then will be asked questions relating to the passages. All the information required to answer the questions will be provided in the passages.

SAMPLE QUESTION: "Increasingly, behavior termed 'road rage' is being viewed as a public health issue, because of the number of deaths and injuries related to it. Such behavior is often a reaction to the feeling that one has been treated unfairly by another driver, and it is much less likely to occur if a driver is treated fairly. 'Fair play' on the road includes the observance not only of traffic regulations but also of the rules of courtesy. Courteous driving is based on common sense consideration for other drivers and a strong desire to make the roads safe for everyone. Good highway manners should become just as much a matter of habit as other kinds of manners."

Which one of the following statements is best supported by the above selection?

A. Courteous driving contributes to road safety.
B. Those who are generally polite are also courteous drivers.
C. Unlike driving courtesy, the observance of traffic regulations is a matter of habit.
D. Being courteous when driving is more important than observing traffic regulations.

The correct answer to this sample question is choice A.

SOLUTION: To answer this question correctly, you must evaluate each choice against the written selection and determine the one that is best supported by the written selection.

Choice A *states, "Courteous driving contributes to road safety." Choice A is supported by the statement in the written selection that, "Courteous driving is based on...a strong desire to make the roads safe for everyone." This is the correct answer.*

Choice B *states, "Those who are generally polite are also courteous drivers." Choice B is not supported by the written selection. The written selection does not mention "those who are generally polite" at all. Choice B is not the correct answer to this question.*

Choice C *states, "Unlike driving courtesy, the observance of traffic regulations is a matter of habit." Choice C is not supported by the written selection. The written selection makes no such bold statement. Instead, the written material mildly suggests that "Good highway manners should become just as much a matter of habit as other kinds of manners." Choice C is not the correct answer to this question.*

Choice D *states, "Being courteous when driving is more important than observing traffic regulations." Choice D is not supported by the written selection. The written selection states, "'Fair play' on the road includes the observance not only of traffic regulations but also of the rules of courtesy." The written selection does not state that being courteous is more important than observing traffic regulations. Choice D is not the correct answer to this question.*

SUBJECT AREA 7

SUPERVISION: These questions test for knowledge of the principles and practices employed in planning, organizing, and controlling the activities of a work unit toward predetermined objectives. The concepts covered, usually in a situational question format, include such topics as assigning and reviewing work; evaluating performance; maintaining work standards; motivating and developing subordinates; implementing procedural change; increasing efficiency; and dealing with problems of absenteeism, morale, and discipline.

TEST TASK: You will be presented with situations in which you must apply knowledge of the principles and practices of supervision in order to answer the questions correctly.

SAMPLE QUESTION:
Assume that the unit you supervise is given a new work assignment and that you are unsure about the proper procedure to use in performing this assignment. Which one of the following actions should you take FIRST in this situation?

A. Obtain input from your staff.
B. Consult other unit supervisors who have had similar assignments.
C. Use an appropriate procedure from a similar assignment that you are familiar with.
D. Discuss the matter with your supervisor.

The correct answer to this sample question is choice D.

SOLUTION:

Choice A is not correct. Since this assignment is new for your unit, your staff would not be expected to be more knowledgeable than you about the proper procedure.

Choice B is not correct. Although discussing this matter with other supervisors may increase your knowledge of the new assignment, similar assignments performed in other units may differ in some important way from your new assignment. Other units may also function differently from your unit, so the procedures used to perform similar assignments may differ accordingly.

Choice C is not correct. Since this assignment is new for your unit, you would have no way of knowing whether the procedure from a similar assignment is appropriate to use. You would need someone with the appropriate knowledge, usually your supervisor, to determine if the procedure from a similar assignment could be used before you actually employed this procedure in the performance of your new assignment.

Choice D is the correct answer to this question. Your supervisor is more likely to be informed about what procedure may be appropriate for work that he or she assigns to you than would other unit supervisors or your staff. Even if your supervisor does not know what procedure is appropriate, a decision regarding which procedure to use should be made with his or her participation, since he or she has the ultimate responsibility for your unit's work.

SUBJECT AREA 8

ADMINISTRATIVE SUPERVISION: These questions test for knowledge of the principles and practices involved in directing the activities of a large subordinate staff, including subordinate supervisors. Questions relate to the personal interactions between an upper level supervisor and his/her subordinate supervisors in the accomplishment of objectives. These questions cover such areas as assigning work to and coordinating the activities of several units, establishing and guiding staff development programs, evaluating the performance of subordinate supervisors, and maintaining relationships with other organizational sections.

TEST TASK: You will be presented with situations in which you must apply knowledge of the principles and practices of administrative supervision to answer the questions correctly. You will be placed in the role of a supervisor of a section, which is made up of several units. Each unit has a supervisor and several employees. All unit supervisors report directly to you.

SAMPLE QUESTION:

You have delegated a work project to two unit supervisors and have asked them to collaborate on it. Later, you observe two employees strongly arguing about which one of them is responsible for a certain activity within the work project. The arguing employees work for different units. Which one of the following actions is most appropriate for you to take in this situation?

A. Intercede in the employees' argument and settle it.
B. Meet with the unit supervisors of the two employees and inform them of the situation you observed.
C. Inform one unit supervisor of the situation and ask this supervisor to take care of it.
D. Set up a meeting that includes both unit supervisors and both employees to resolve the situation.

The correct answer to this sample question is choice B.

SOLUTION:

Choice A is not correct. In your position, you supervise properly by giving direction through your unit supervisors. By taking this choice, you are not allowing your unit supervisors to handle a problem involving their staff members. Also, it is not reasonable that you would be able to settle the employees' dispute. Earlier, you delegated the work project to the two unit supervisors, who would be responsible for assigning activities related to the project. The two unit supervisors must deal with the problem.

Choice B is the correct answer to this question. The two unit supervisors are collaborating on the work project and therefore giving the assignments. You should meet with them and tell them about the employees' argument. The unit supervisors should be informed about the point of contention and the fact that the two employees had a heated argument. The unit supervisors must then work out a way to handle the situation.

Choice C is not correct. Speaking to only one supervisor about the situation means that the second supervisor may be uninformed, or only partly informed, about the situation. You cannot be assured that the first supervisor will include the second supervisor in finding a way to settle the issue. If the first unit supervisor chooses to handle the situation on his own and speak to both employees, this supervisor would be giving direction to one employee from another unit. This is not good supervisory practice. Also, in taking Choice C, you are favoring one supervisor and slighting the other.

Choice D is not correct. The unit supervisors need to come up with a way of handling the situation that you observed. To do this, they must be informed without the employees present. Also, by including the employees in the meeting, you may get a replay of their earlier argument, which is not helpful.

PRACTICE TEST

Below and on the following pages are additional examples of the types of questions that will be on the written test for the Safety and Security Series. The answers are given on page 25. Good luck!

APPLYING WRITTEN INFORMATION IN A SAFETY AND SECURITY SETTING

DIRECTIONS: The following two questions evaluate your ability to read and interpret a specific rule and apply it to a given situation or situations. Each question or set of questions is given with a **RULE** along with a **SITUATION** or situations. You should base your answers to these questions upon the information provided and **NOT** upon any other information you may have on the subject.

1. **RULE:** A security officer is to obey all lawful regulations of the employer and all orders of a police officer in police matters. The security officer is to assist and cooperate with police officers in preserving the peace. Where police are on the scene, on duty and off duty security personnel should identify themselves as security officers and offer assistance. The police officer's directives and judgment shall prevail.

SITUATION: When leaving work for the day, you see that a motor vehicle accident has taken place on the highway near your workplace. You approach the accident in your car and see that a police officer is on the scene. You inform the police officer that you are a security officer. Traffic is stopped.

According to the above Rule, under which one of the following conditions, if any, should you take control of directing traffic in this Situation?

A. The police officer instructs you to direct traffic.
B. You regularly direct traffic as part of your job.
C. You should not direct traffic because you are off duty.
D. You should not direct traffic because the highway is not on facility property.

2. **RULE:** If a law enforcement officer is required to be at a mental health facility, the officer will be required to lock his weapon in a designated gun cabinet and retain the only key. In areas where gun cabinets are not available, the law enforcement officer shall be asked to remove the bullets from his weapon and retain the weapon. The only other allowable option is for the officer to lock the weapon in his patrol car.

SITUATION: During rounds as a security officer in a mental health facility with no gun control cabinets available, you come upon a law enforcement officer whom you know to be a firearms instructor. You allow the officer to enter the building with his weapon.

Based solely on the above Rule and Situation, in which one of the following cases is your action correct?

A. The officer has stated that his police agency prohibits an officer from locking a weapon in his patrol car.
B. The officer has stated that he would be willing to put his weapon in a gun cabinet.
C. The officer has shown you a letter stating he must attend a meeting at the facility today on the topic of firearm instruction.
D. The officer has removed the bullets from his weapon.

FOLLOWING DIRECTIONS (MAPS)

DIRECTIONS: The following map presents a diagram of a floor of an office building. You should become familiar with the map and interpret it with the legend provided. Use the map to answer the questions on the next page.

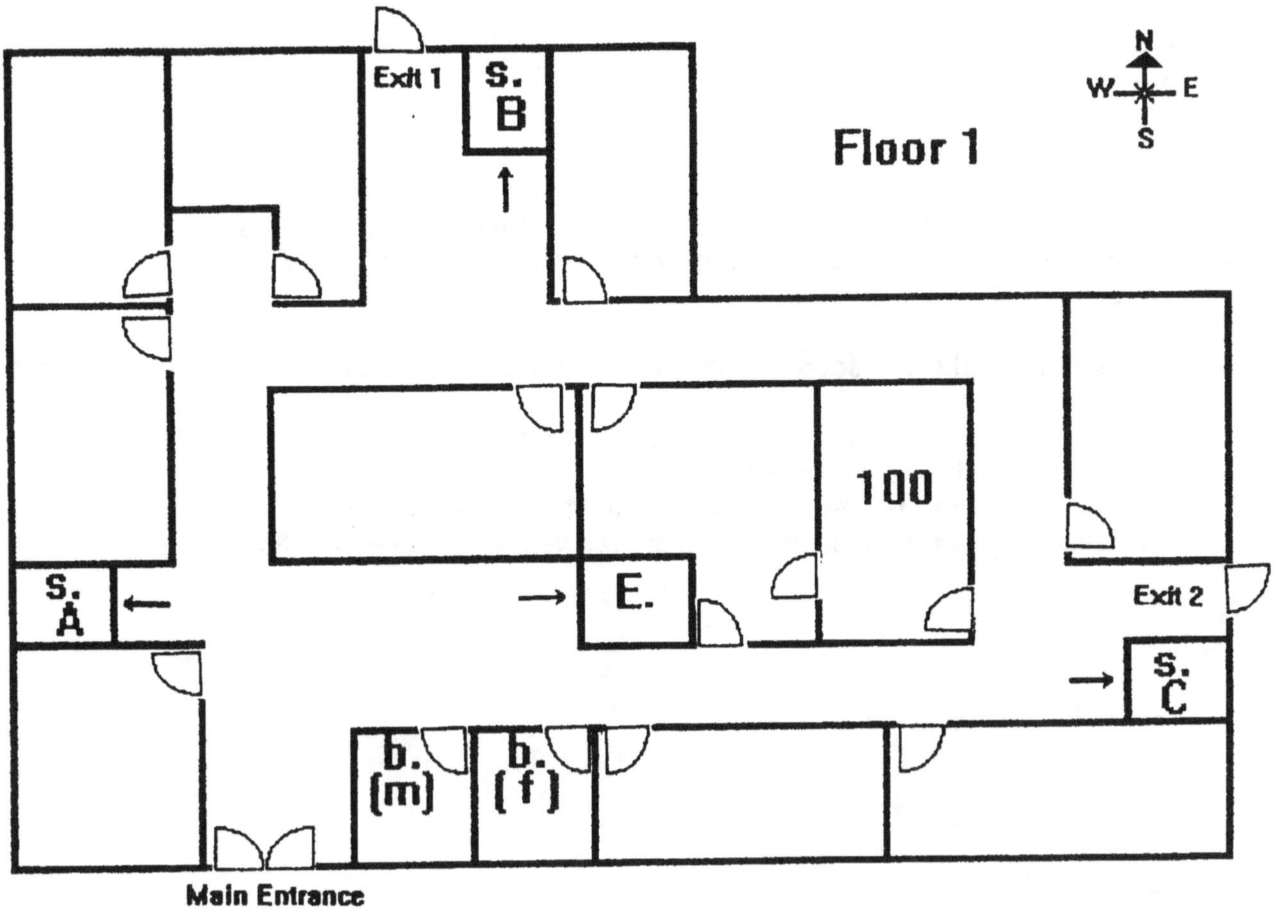

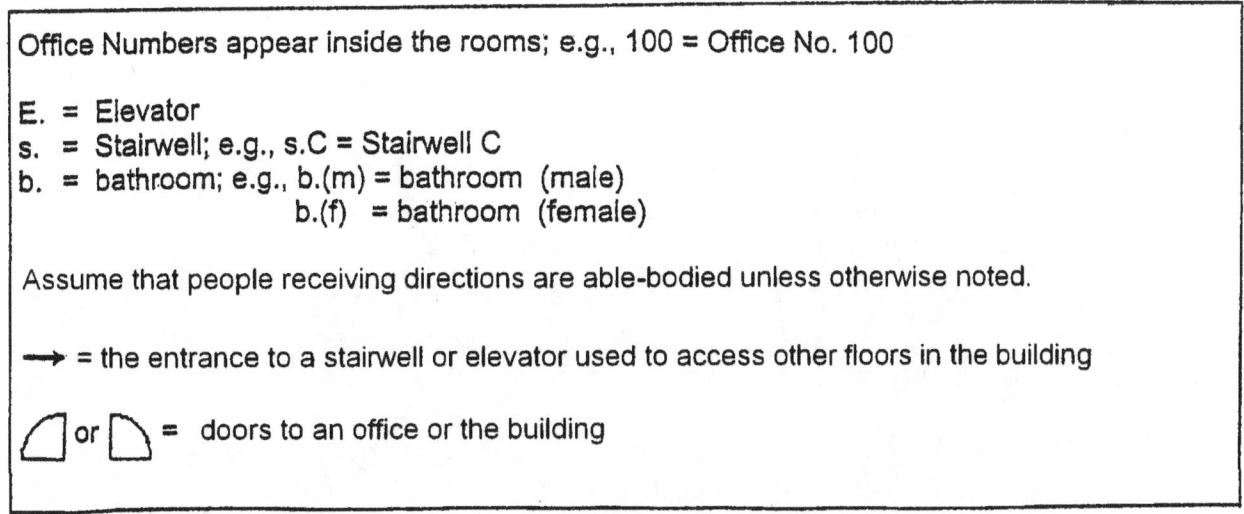

Legend:

Office Numbers appear inside the rooms; e.g., 100 = Office No. 100

E. = Elevator
s. = Stairwell; e.g., s.C = Stairwell C
b. = bathroom; e.g., b.(m) = bathroom (male)
               b.(f) = bathroom (female)

Assume that people receiving directions are able-bodied unless otherwise noted.

→ = the entrance to a stairwell or elevator used to access other floors in the building

◠ or ◡ = doors to an office or the building

FOLLOWING DIRECTIONS (MAPS) (Continued)

3. For a person in Office No. 100, which one of the following is the most direct route to leave the building in an emergency?

A. through exit 1
B. through exit 2
C. through stairwell C
D. through the Main Entrance

4. Which one of the following routes is the best to take if the elevator is out of service and a person standing directly inside the main entrance wants to get from Floor 1 to Floor 2 in the most efficient way?

A. Walk straight, take the second right, take the first left and take stairwell B to the second floor.
B. Walk straight, take the second right, walk straight, take the next right, take the first left and take stairwell C to the second floor.
C. Walk straight, take the first right, walk straight and take stairwell C to the second floor.
D. Walk straight, take the first left and take stairwell A to the second floor.

PREPARING WRITTEN MATERIAL

DIRECTIONS: Read the information given in the following two questions carefully. Then select the choice which presents the information most clearly, accurately, and completely.

5. Senator Martinez met with the county legislature. Then Senator Martinez announced that the meal subsidy program would start in June.

Which one of the following best presents the information given above?

A. After meeting with the county legislature, Senator Martinez announced that the meal subsidy program would start in June.
B. Senator Martinez met with the county legislature and announced that the meal subsidy program would start in June.
C. Senator Martinez announced that the meal subsidy program would start in June after a meeting with the county legislature.
D. Senator Martinez, who met with the county legislature, announced that the meal subsidy program would start in June.

6. Frank Colombe wrote the press release. He sent three copies to the Director. The Director then gave one of the copies to the Commissioner.

Which one of the following best presents the information given above?

A. Frank Colombe sent to the Director three copies of the press release he had written, who then gave a copy to the Commissioner.
B. Frank Colombe sent three copies of the press release he had written to the Director, who then gave one of the copies to the Commissioner.
C. The Director gave the Commissioner one of the three copies of the press release Frank Colombe had written and had been sent to him.
D. Of the three copies of the press release Frank Colombe had written and sent to the Director, one was then given to the Commissioner by him.

PREPARING WRITTEN MATERIAL (Continued)

DIRECTIONS: The following two (2) questions are based upon a group of sentences. The sentences are shown out of sequence, but when they are correctly arranged they form a connected, well-organized paragraph. Read the sentences and then answer the question about what order to arrange them in.

7.
1. The phosphates in detergents are carried into sewage systems, and from there into local rivers and streams, and eventually into large bodies of water.

2. The algae absorb much of the available oxygen that is necessary to sustain marine life.

3. There is no doubt that phosphates damage the environment through a complex chain of events.

4. Phosphates are nutrients, and, as such, they aid the growth of the algae living in the water.

5. This results not only in the death of fish and other aquatic life, but also in the too-thick growth of vegetation in the water.

Which one of the following is the best arrangement of these sentences?

A. 1-3-4-2-5
B. 1-4-2-5-3
C. 3-1-4-2-5
D. 3-4-2-1-5

8.
1. Never before has time been measured at a speed beyond the realm of experience.

2. Just how profound an effect it is having on society is as yet to be determined.

3. The computer has accelerated our sense of time beyond anything we have experienced before.

4. Though it is possible to conceive of an interval that brief and even to manipulate time at that speed, it is not possible to experience it.

5. It works in a time frame in which the nanosecond—a billionth of a second—is the primary measurement.

Which one of the following is the best arrangement of these sentences?

A. 1-2-3-5-4
B. 1-4-3-5-2
C. 3-2-5-4-1
D. 3-5-4-1-2

PRINCIPLES AND PRACTICES OF SAFETY AND SECURITY

9. You are on patrol in a radio-equipped car at night. You discover that a large drum of gasoline near a garage on the property is punctured and is rapidly spilling gasoline on the ground around the building.

Which one of the following actions should you take first in this situation?

A. Submit a written report of the incident to your supervisor.
B. Report the matter to headquarters.
C. Examine the puncture to see if it was accidental or deliberate.
D. Check other drums or containers around the building for punctures.

10. You hear shouting on the second floor of a building where you are on duty. Upon arriving at the scene, you see two building employees engaged in a fist fight in the hall.

Which one of the following actions should you take first in this situation?

A. Report the matter to the supervisors of the two employees.
B. Ask observers how the fight started.
C. Call for assistance.
D. Break up the fight.

SAFETY AND SECURITY METHODS AND PROCEDURES

11. Complaints relating to suspicious activity, especially at night, are often groundless. Which one of the following is the best way of handling such a complaint?

A. Analyze the nature of the complaint to make sure that it is justifiable before dispatching anyone to the scene.
B. Consider the complaint justified only if it corresponds to similar complaints in the same area.
C. Take no action on the complaint, but make a record of it.
D. Attend to the complaint immediately on the assumption that it is justified.

12. In the course of an investigation, you are interviewing a person who is over-talkative. Which one of the following is the best method for you to use in order to obtain the facts which you seek?

A. Tell the witness to talk only about the facts you are interested in.
B. Place a time limit on the witness's answers to your questions.
C. Make it clear that you want only "yes" or "no" answers to your questions.
D. Guide the conversation toward the subject of interest when the witness talks about subjects clearly not relevant to the interview.

UNDERSTANDING AND INTERPRETING WRITTEN MATERIAL

DIRECTIONS: The following two questions are related to the reading selection preceding each question. Base your answer to the question SOLELY on what is said in the selection – NOT on what you may happen to know about the subject discussed.

13. "The increasing demands upon our highways from a growing population and the development of forms of transportation not anticipated when the highways were first built have brought about congestion, confusion, and conflict, until the yearly toll of traffic accidents is now at an appalling level. If the death and disaster that traffic accidents bring throughout the year were concentrated into one calamity, we would shudder at the tremendous catastrophe. The loss is no less catastrophic because it is spread out over time and space."

Which one of the following statements concerning the yearly toll of traffic accidents is best supported by the passage above?

A. It is increasing the demands for safer means of transportation.
B. It has resulted in increased congestion, confusion, and conflict on our highways.
C. It has resulted mainly from the new forms of transportation.
D. It does not shock us as much as it should because the accidents do not all occur at the same time.

14. "Depression is one of the top public health problems in the United States, and its occurrence is on the rise. One in 20 Americans develops a case of depression serious enough to require professional treatment. The incidence of depression has been escalating among Baby Boomers (Americans born in the years 1946 through 1964). The reason for this increase is that the lifestyles of this generation have become increasingly demanding while offering little support. Also, stress and poor eating habits are now more the rule than the exception, and both can disrupt brain chemistry enough to bring on depression."

Which one of the following statements is best supported by the above selection?

A. We can expect a small proportion of the population to require treatment for depression at some time in their lives.
B. Baby Boomers have the highest rate of depression in the United States.
C. Lifestyle demands are the major cause of depression in the current generation.
D. Depression can cause a disruption in the chemistry of the brain.

SUPERVISION

DIRECTIONS: For the following two questions, assume that you are the newly appointed supervisor of a unit consisting of several employees. You report to a section head.

15. You have a suspicion that some of your employees are not working to the best of their abilities. Which one of the following actions should you take first in this situation?

A. Arrange for these employees to take a course in organizing priorities.
B. Determine which employee is the worst offender.
C. Assess the assignments and work methods of these employees.
D. Set up a meeting with these employees to learn about any work problems they are having.

16. As you are giving an employee a certain assignment, she expresses concern that it is too difficult. The employee is reluctant to accept the assignment. Which one of the following actions should you take first in this situation?

A. Insist that the employee take on the assignment.
B. Tell the employee that it is likely she has completed assignments of similar difficulty before.
C. Offer to share the tasks of the assignment with the employee.
D. Ask the employee why she sees the assignment as difficult.

ADMINISTRATIVE SUPERVISION

DIRECTIONS: For the following two questions, assume that you supervise a section composed of several units. Each unit has a supervisor and several employees. All unit supervisors report directly to you.

17. Assume that you are the head of a section made up of four units, each of which is responsible for similar work. The work volume of one of the units of the section has permanently decreased to the point that the supervisor of that unit now is responsible for much less work than any of the other three unit supervisors. Of the following, which determination should you as the section head make first in this situation?

A. Can other or additional tasks be assigned to this unit?
B. Can the unit supervisor function as assistant section head?
C. Can the unit supervisor's position be reclassified or reallocated?
D. Can the section be reorganized into three units?

18. In which one of the following circumstances should you try to reduce turnover in the section you supervise?

A. The turnover is higher than that of other sections.
B. The turnover reduces the number of highly experienced employees.
C. The turnover lowers the efficiency of the section.
D. The turnover requires unit supervisors to spend a moderate amount of time in training new employees.

PRACTICE TEST KEY

(1) A
(2) D
(3) B
(4) D
(5) A
(6) B
(7) C
(8) D
(9) B
(10) C
(11) D
(12) D
(13) D
(14) A
(15) C
(16) D
(17) A
(18) C

HOW TO TAKE A TEST

I. YOU MUST PASS AN EXAMINATION

A. WHAT EVERY CANDIDATE SHOULD KNOW

Examination applicants often ask us for help in preparing for the written test. What can I study in advance? What kinds of questions will be asked? How will the test be given? How will the papers be graded?

As an applicant for a civil service examination, you may be wondering about some of these things. Our purpose here is to suggest effective methods of advance study and to describe civil service examinations.

Your chances for success on this examination can be increased if you know how to prepare. Those "pre-examination jitters" can be reduced if you know what to expect. You can even experience an adventure in good citizenship if you know why civil service exams are given.

B. WHY ARE CIVIL SERVICE EXAMINATIONS GIVEN?

Civil service examinations are important to you in two ways. As a citizen, you want public jobs filled by employees who know how to do their work. As a job seeker, you want a fair chance to compete for that job on an equal footing with other candidates. The best-known means of accomplishing this two-fold goal is the competitive examination.

Exams are widely publicized throughout the nation. They may be administered for jobs in federal, state, city, municipal, town or village governments or agencies.

Any citizen may apply, with some limitations, such as the age or residence of applicants. Your experience and education may be reviewed to see whether you meet the requirements for the particular examination. When these requirements exist, they are reasonable and applied consistently to all applicants. Thus, a competitive examination may cause you some uneasiness now, but it is your privilege and safeguard.

C. HOW ARE CIVIL SERVICE EXAMS DEVELOPED?

Examinations are carefully written by trained technicians who are specialists in the field known as "psychological measurement," in consultation with recognized authorities in the field of work that the test will cover. These experts recommend the subject matter areas or skills to be tested; only those knowledges or skills important to your success on the job are included. The most reliable books and source materials available are used as references. Together, the experts and technicians judge the difficulty level of the questions.

Test technicians know how to phrase questions so that the problem is clearly stated. Their ethics do not permit "trick" or "catch" questions. Questions may have been tried out on sample groups, or subjected to statistical analysis, to determine their usefulness.

Written tests are often used in combination with performance tests, ratings of training and experience, and oral interviews. All of these measures combine to form the best-known means of finding the right person for the right job.

II. HOW TO PASS THE WRITTEN TEST

A. NATURE OF THE EXAMINATION

To prepare intelligently for civil service examinations, you should know how they differ from school examinations you have taken. In school you were assigned certain definite pages to read or subjects to cover. The examination questions were quite detailed and usually emphasized memory. Civil service exams, on the other hand, try to discover your present ability to perform the duties of a position, plus your potentiality to learn these duties. In other words, a civil service exam attempts to predict how successful you will be. Questions cover such a broad area that they cannot be as minute and detailed as school exam questions.

In the public service similar kinds of work, or positions, are grouped together in one "class." This process is known as *position-classification*. All the positions in a class are paid according to the salary range for that class. One class title covers all of these positions, and they are all tested by the same examination.

B. FOUR BASIC STEPS

1) Study the announcement

How, then, can you know what subjects to study? Our best answer is: "Learn as much as possible about the class of positions for which you've applied." The exam will test the knowledge, skills and abilities needed to do the work.

Your most valuable source of information about the position you want is the official exam announcement. This announcement lists the training and experience qualifications. Check these standards and apply only if you come reasonably close to meeting them.

The brief description of the position in the examination announcement offers some clues to the subjects which will be tested. Think about the job itself. Review the duties in your mind. Can you perform them, or are there some in which you are rusty? Fill in the blank spots in your preparation.

Many jurisdictions preview the written test in the exam announcement by including a section called "Knowledge and Abilities Required," "Scope of the Examination," or some similar heading. Here you will find out specifically what fields will be tested.

2) Review your own background

Once you learn in general what the position is all about, and what you need to know to do the work, ask yourself which subjects you already know fairly well and which need improvement. You may wonder whether to concentrate on improving your strong areas or on building some background in your fields of weakness. When the announcement has specified "some knowledge" or "considerable knowledge," or has used adjectives like "beginning principles of…" or "advanced … methods," you can get a clue as to the number and difficulty of questions to be asked in any given field. More questions, and hence broader coverage, would be included for those subjects which are more important in the work. Now weigh your strengths and weaknesses against the job requirements and prepare accordingly.

3) Determine the level of the position

Another way to tell how intensively you should prepare is to understand the level of the job for which you are applying. Is it the entering level? In other words, is this the position in which beginners in a field of work are hired? Or is it an intermediate or advanced level? Sometimes this is indicated by such words as "Junior" or "Senior" in the class title. Other jurisdictions use Roman numerals to designate the level – Clerk I, Clerk II, for example. The word "Supervisor" sometimes appears in the title. If the level is not indicated by the title, check the description of duties. Will you be working under very close supervision, or will you have responsibility for independent decisions in this work?

4) Choose appropriate study materials

Now that you know the subjects to be examined and the relative amount of each subject to be covered, you can choose suitable study materials. For beginning level jobs, or even advanced ones, if you have a pronounced weakness in some aspect of your training, read a modern, standard textbook in that field. Be sure it is up to date and has general coverage. Such books are normally available at your library, and the librarian will be glad to help you locate one. For entry-level positions, questions of appropriate difficulty are chosen – neither highly advanced questions, nor those too simple. Such questions require careful thought but not advanced training.

If the position for which you are applying is technical or advanced, you will read more advanced, specialized material. If you are already familiar with the basic principles of your field, elementary textbooks would waste your time. Concentrate on advanced textbooks and technical periodicals. Think through the concepts and review difficult problems in your field.

These are all general sources. You can get more ideas on your own initiative, following these leads. For example, training manuals and publications of the government agency which employs workers in your field can be useful, particularly for technical and professional positions. A letter or visit to the government department involved may result in more specific study suggestions, and certainly will provide you with a more definite idea of the exact nature of the position you are seeking.

III. KINDS OF TESTS

Tests are used for purposes other than measuring knowledge and ability to perform specified duties. For some positions, it is equally important to test ability to make adjustments to new situations or to profit from training. In others, basic mental abilities not dependent on information are essential. Questions which test these things may not appear as pertinent to the duties of the position as those which test for knowledge and information. Yet they are often highly important parts of a fair examination. For very general questions, it is almost impossible to help you direct your study efforts. What we can do is to point out some of the more common of these general abilities needed in public service positions and describe some typical questions.

1) General information

Broad, general information has been found useful for predicting job success in some kinds of work. This is tested in a variety of ways, from vocabulary lists to questions about current events. Basic background in some field of work, such as sociology or economics, may be sampled in a group of questions. Often these are principles which have become familiar to most persons through exposure rather than through formal training. It is difficult to advise you how to study for these questions; being alert to the world around you is our best suggestion.

2) Verbal ability

An example of an ability needed in many positions is verbal or language ability. Verbal ability is, in brief, the ability to use and understand words. Vocabulary and grammar tests are typical measures of this ability. Reading comprehension or paragraph interpretation questions are common in many kinds of civil service tests. You are given a paragraph of written material and asked to find its central meaning.

3) Numerical ability

Number skills can be tested by the familiar arithmetic problem, by checking paired lists of numbers to see which are alike and which are different, or by interpreting charts and graphs. In the latter test, a graph may be printed in the test booklet which you are asked to use as the basis for answering questions.

4) Observation

A popular test for law-enforcement positions is the observation test. A picture is shown to you for several minutes, then taken away. Questions about the picture test your ability to observe both details and larger elements.

5) Following directions

In many positions in the public service, the employee must be able to carry out written instructions dependably and accurately. You may be given a chart with several columns, each column listing a variety of information. The questions require you to carry out directions involving the information given in the chart.

6) Skills and aptitudes

Performance tests effectively measure some manual skills and aptitudes. When the skill is one in which you are trained, such as typing or shorthand, you can practice. These tests are often very much like those given in business school or high school courses. For many of the other skills and aptitudes, however, no short-time preparation can be made. Skills and abilities natural to you or that you have developed throughout your lifetime are being tested.

Many of the general questions just described provide all the data needed to answer the questions and ask you to use your reasoning ability to find the answers. Your best preparation for these tests, as well as for tests of facts and ideas, is to be at your physical and mental best. You, no doubt, have your own methods of getting into an exam-taking mood and keeping "in shape." The next section lists some ideas on this subject.

IV. KINDS OF QUESTIONS

Only rarely is the "essay" question, which you answer in narrative form, used in civil service tests. Civil service tests are usually of the short-answer type. Full instructions for answering these questions will be given to you at the examination. But in case this is your first experience with short-answer questions and separate answer sheets, here is what you need to know:

1) Multiple-choice Questions

Most popular of the short-answer questions is the "multiple choice" or "best answer" question. It can be used, for example, to test for factual knowledge, ability to solve problems or judgment in meeting situations found at work.

A multiple-choice question is normally one of three types—
- It can begin with an incomplete statement followed by several possible endings. You are to find the one ending which *best* completes the statement, although some of the others may not be entirely wrong.
- It can also be a complete statement in the form of a question which is answered by choosing one of the statements listed.

- It can be in the form of a problem – again you select the best answer.

Here is an example of a multiple-choice question with a discussion which should give you some clues as to the method for choosing the right answer:

When an employee has a complaint about his assignment, the action which will *best* help him overcome his difficulty is to
   A. discuss his difficulty with his coworkers
   B. take the problem to the head of the organization
   C. take the problem to the person who gave him the assignment
   D. say nothing to anyone about his complaint

In answering this question, you should study each of the choices to find which is best. Consider choice "A" – Certainly an employee may discuss his complaint with fellow employees, but no change or improvement can result, and the complaint remains unresolved. Choice "B" is a poor choice since the head of the organization probably does not know what assignment you have been given, and taking your problem to him is known as "going over the head" of the supervisor. The supervisor, or person who made the assignment, is the person who can clarify it or correct any injustice. Choice "C" is, therefore, correct. To say nothing, as in choice "D," is unwise. Supervisors have and interest in knowing the problems employees are facing, and the employee is seeking a solution to his problem.

2) True/False Questions

The "true/false" or "right/wrong" form of question is sometimes used. Here a complete statement is given. Your job is to decide whether the statement is right or wrong.

SAMPLE: A roaming cell-phone call to a nearby city costs less than a non-roaming call to a distant city.

This statement is wrong, or false, since roaming calls are more expensive.

This is not a complete list of all possible question forms, although most of the others are variations of these common types. You will always get complete directions for answering questions. Be sure you understand *how* to mark your answers – ask questions until you do.

V. RECORDING YOUR ANSWERS

Computer terminals are used more and more today for many different kinds of exams.
For an examination with very few applicants, you may be told to record your answers in the test booklet itself. Separate answer sheets are much more common. If this separate answer sheet is to be scored by machine – and this is often the case – it is highly important that you mark your answers correctly in order to get credit.
An electronic scoring machine is often used in civil service offices because of the speed with which papers can be scored. Machine-scored answer sheets must be marked with a pencil, which will be given to you. This pencil has a high graphite content which responds to the electronic scoring machine. As a matter of fact, stray dots may register as answers, so do not let your pencil rest on the answer sheet while you are pondering the correct answer. Also, if your pencil lead breaks or is otherwise defective, ask for another.

Since the answer sheet will be dropped in a slot in the scoring machine, be careful not to bend the corners or get the paper crumpled.

The answer sheet normally has five vertical columns of numbers, with 30 numbers to a column. These numbers correspond to the question numbers in your test booklet. After each number, going across the page are four or five pairs of dotted lines. These short dotted lines have small letters or numbers above them. The first two pairs may also have a "T" or "F" above the letters. This indicates that the first two pairs only are to be used if the questions are of the true-false type. If the questions are multiple choice, disregard the "T" and "F" and pay attention only to the small letters or numbers.

Answer your questions in the manner of the sample that follows:

32. The largest city in the United States is
    A. Washington, D.C.
    B. New York City
    C. Chicago
    D. Detroit
    E. San Francisco

1) Choose the answer you think is best. (New York City is the largest, so "B" is correct.)
2) Find the row of dotted lines numbered the same as the question you are answering. (Find row number 32)
3) Find the pair of dotted lines corresponding to the answer. (Find the pair of lines under the mark "B.")
4) Make a solid black mark between the dotted lines.

VI. BEFORE THE TEST

Common sense will help you find procedures to follow to get ready for an examination. Too many of us, however, overlook these sensible measures. Indeed, nervousness and fatigue have been found to be the most serious reasons why applicants fail to do their best on civil service tests. Here is a list of reminders:

- Begin your preparation early – Don't wait until the last minute to go scurrying around for books and materials or to find out what the position is all about.
- Prepare continuously – An hour a night for a week is better than an all-night cram session. This has been definitely established. What is more, a night a week for a month will return better dividends than crowding your study into a shorter period of time.
- Locate the place of the exam – You have been sent a notice telling you when and where to report for the examination. If the location is in a different town or otherwise unfamiliar to you, it would be well to inquire the best route and learn something about the building.
- Relax the night before the test – Allow your mind to rest. Do not study at all that night. Plan some mild recreation or diversion; then go to bed early and get a good night's sleep.
- Get up early enough to make a leisurely trip to the place for the test – This way unforeseen events, traffic snarls, unfamiliar buildings, etc. will not upset you.
- Dress comfortably – A written test is not a fashion show. You will be known by number and not by name, so wear something comfortable.

- Leave excess paraphernalia at home – Shopping bags and odd bundles will get in your way. You need bring only the items mentioned in the official notice you received; usually everything you need is provided. Do not bring reference books to the exam. They will only confuse those last minutes and be taken away from you when in the test room.
- Arrive somewhat ahead of time – If because of transportation schedules you must get there very early, bring a newspaper or magazine to take your mind off yourself while waiting.
- Locate the examination room – When you have found the proper room, you will be directed to the seat or part of the room where you will sit. Sometimes you are given a sheet of instructions to read while you are waiting. Do not fill out any forms until you are told to do so; just read them and be prepared.
- Relax and prepare to listen to the instructions
- If you have any physical problem that may keep you from doing your best, be sure to tell the test administrator. If you are sick or in poor health, you really cannot do your best on the exam. You can come back and take the test some other time.

VII. AT THE TEST

The day of the test is here and you have the test booklet in your hand. The temptation to get going is very strong. Caution! There is more to success than knowing the right answers. You must know how to identify your papers and understand variations in the type of short-answer question used in this particular examination. Follow these suggestions for maximum results from your efforts:

1) Cooperate with the monitor

The test administrator has a duty to create a situation in which you can be as much at ease as possible. He will give instructions, tell you when to begin, check to see that you are marking your answer sheet correctly, and so on. He is not there to guard you, although he will see that your competitors do not take unfair advantage. He wants to help you do your best.

2) Listen to all instructions

Don't jump the gun! Wait until you understand all directions. In most civil service tests you get more time than you need to answer the questions. So don't be in a hurry. Read each word of instructions until you clearly understand the meaning. Study the examples, listen to all announcements and follow directions. Ask questions if you do not understand what to do.

3) Identify your papers

Civil service exams are usually identified by number only. You will be assigned a number; you must not put your name on your test papers. Be sure to copy your number correctly. Since more than one exam may be given, copy your exact examination title.

4) Plan your time

Unless you are told that a test is a "speed" or "rate of work" test, speed itself is usually not important. Time enough to answer all the questions will be provided, but this does not mean that you have all day. An overall time limit has been set. Divide the total time (in minutes) by the number of questions to determine the approximate time you have for each question.

5) Do not linger over difficult questions

If you come across a difficult question, mark it with a paper clip (useful to have along) and come back to it when you have been through the booklet. One caution if you do this – be sure to skip a number on your answer sheet as well. Check often to be sure that you have not lost your place and that you are marking in the row numbered the same as the question you are answering.

6) Read the questions

Be sure you know what the question asks! Many capable people are unsuccessful because they failed to *read* the questions correctly.

7) Answer all questions

Unless you have been instructed that a penalty will be deducted for incorrect answers, it is better to guess than to omit a question.

8) Speed tests

It is often better NOT to guess on speed tests. It has been found that on timed tests people are tempted to spend the last few seconds before time is called in marking answers at random – without even reading them – in the hope of picking up a few extra points. To discourage this practice, the instructions may warn you that your score will be "corrected" for guessing. That is, a penalty will be applied. The incorrect answers will be deducted from the correct ones, or some other penalty formula will be used.

9) Review your answers

If you finish before time is called, go back to the questions you guessed or omitted to give them further thought. Review other answers if you have time.

10) Return your test materials

If you are ready to leave before others have finished or time is called, take ALL your materials to the monitor and leave quietly. Never take any test material with you. The monitor can discover whose papers are not complete, and taking a test booklet may be grounds for disqualification.

VIII. EXAMINATION TECHNIQUES

1) Read the general instructions carefully. These are usually printed on the first page of the exam booklet. As a rule, these instructions refer to the timing of the examination; the fact that you should not start work until the signal and must stop work at a signal, etc. If there are any *special* instructions, such as a choice of questions to be answered, make sure that you note this instruction carefully.

2) When you are ready to start work on the examination, that is as soon as the signal has been given, read the instructions to each question booklet, underline any key words or phrases, such as *least, best, outline, describe* and the like. In this way you will tend to answer as requested rather than discover on reviewing your paper that you *listed without describing*, that you selected the *worst* choice rather than the *best* choice, etc.

3) If the examination is of the objective or multiple-choice type – that is, each question will also give a series of possible answers: A, B, C or D, and you are called upon to select the best answer and write the letter next to that answer on your answer paper – it is advisable to start answering each question in turn. There may be anywhere from 50 to 100 such questions in the three or four hours allotted and you can see how much time would be taken if you read through all the questions before beginning to answer any. Furthermore, if you come across a question or group of questions which you know would be difficult to answer, it would undoubtedly affect your handling of all the other questions.

4) If the examination is of the essay type and contains but a few questions, it is a moot point as to whether you should read all the questions before starting to answer any one. Of course, if you are given a choice – say five out of seven and the like – then it is essential to read all the questions so you can eliminate the two that are most difficult. If, however, you are asked to answer all the questions, there may be danger in trying to answer the easiest one first because you may find that you will spend too much time on it. The best technique is to answer the first question, then proceed to the second, etc.

5) Time your answers. Before the exam begins, write down the time it started, then add the time allowed for the examination and write down the time it must be completed, then divide the time available somewhat as follows:
    - If 3-1/2 hours are allowed, that would be 210 minutes. If you have 80 objective-type questions, that would be an average of 2-1/2 minutes per question. Allow yourself no more than 2 minutes per question, or a total of 160 minutes, which will permit about 50 minutes to review.
    - If for the time allotment of 210 minutes there are 7 essay questions to answer, that would average about 30 minutes a question. Give yourself only 25 minutes per question so that you have about 35 minutes to review.

6) The most important instruction is to *read each question* and make sure you know what is wanted. The second most important instruction is to *time yourself properly* so that you answer every question. The third most important instruction is to *answer every question*. Guess if you have to but include something for each question. Remember that you will receive no credit for a blank and will probably receive some credit if you write something in answer to an essay question. If you guess a letter – say "B" for a multiple-choice question – you may have guessed right. If you leave a blank as an answer to a multiple-choice question, the examiners may respect your feelings but it will not add a point to your score. Some exams may penalize you for wrong answers, so in such cases *only*, you may not want to guess unless you have some basis for your answer.

7) Suggestions
    a. Objective-type questions
        1. Examine the question booklet for proper sequence of pages and questions
        2. Read all instructions carefully
        3. Skip any question which seems too difficult; return to it after all other questions have been answered
        4. Apportion your time properly; do not spend too much time on any single question or group of questions

5. Note and underline key words – *all, most, fewest, least, best, worst, same, opposite*, etc.
6. Pay particular attention to negatives
7. Note unusual option, e.g., unduly long, short, complex, different or similar in content to the body of the question
8. Observe the use of "hedging" words – *probably, may, most likely*, etc.
9. Make sure that your answer is put next to the same number as the question
10. Do not second-guess unless you have good reason to believe the second answer is definitely more correct
11. Cross out original answer if you decide another answer is more accurate; do not erase until you are ready to hand your paper in
12. Answer all questions; guess unless instructed otherwise
13. Leave time for review

   b. Essay questions
   1. Read each question carefully
   2. Determine exactly what is wanted. Underline key words or phrases.
   3. Decide on outline or paragraph answer
   4. Include many different points and elements unless asked to develop any one or two points or elements
   5. Show impartiality by giving pros and cons unless directed to select one side only
   6. Make and write down any assumptions you find necessary to answer the questions
   7. Watch your English, grammar, punctuation and choice of words
   8. Time your answers; don't crowd material

8) Answering the essay question

Most essay questions can be answered by framing the specific response around several key words or ideas. Here are a few such key words or ideas:

M's: manpower, materials, methods, money, management
P's: purpose, program, policy, plan, procedure, practice, problems, pitfalls, personnel, public relations

   a. Six basic steps in handling problems:
   1. Preliminary plan and background development
   2. Collect information, data and facts
   3. Analyze and interpret information, data and facts
   4. Analyze and develop solutions as well as make recommendations
   5. Prepare report and sell recommendations
   6. Install recommendations and follow up effectiveness

   b. Pitfalls to avoid
   1. *Taking things for granted* – A statement of the situation does not necessarily imply that each of the elements is necessarily true; for example, a complaint may be invalid and biased so that all that can be taken for granted is that a complaint has been registered

2. *Considering only one side of a situation* – Wherever possible, indicate several alternatives and then point out the reasons you selected the best one
3. *Failing to indicate follow up* – Whenever your answer indicates action on your part, make certain that you will take proper follow-up action to see how successful your recommendations, procedures or actions turn out to be
4. *Taking too long in answering any single question* – Remember to time your answers properly

IX. AFTER THE TEST

Scoring procedures differ in detail among civil service jurisdictions although the general principles are the same. Whether the papers are hand-scored or graded by machine we have described, they are nearly always graded by number. That is, the person who marks the paper knows only the number – never the name – of the applicant. Not until all the papers have been graded will they be matched with names. If other tests, such as training and experience or oral interview ratings have been given, scores will be combined. Different parts of the examination usually have different weights. For example, the written test might count 60 percent of the final grade, and a rating of training and experience 40 percent. In many jurisdictions, veterans will have a certain number of points added to their grades.

After the final grade has been determined, the names are placed in grade order and an eligible list is established. There are various methods for resolving ties between those who get the same final grade – probably the most common is to place first the name of the person whose application was received first. Job offers are made from the eligible list in the order the names appear on it. You will be notified of your grade and your rank as soon as all these computations have been made. This will be done as rapidly as possible.

People who are found to meet the requirements in the announcement are called "eligibles." Their names are put on a list of eligible candidates. An eligible's chances of getting a job depend on how high he stands on this list and how fast agencies are filling jobs from the list.

When a job is to be filled from a list of eligibles, the agency asks for the names of people on the list of eligibles for that job. When the civil service commission receives this request, it sends to the agency the names of the three people highest on this list. Or, if the job to be filled has specialized requirements, the office sends the agency the names of the top three persons who meet these requirements from the general list.

The appointing officer makes a choice from among the three people whose names were sent to him. If the selected person accepts the appointment, the names of the others are put back on the list to be considered for future openings.

That is the rule in hiring from all kinds of eligible lists, whether they are for typist, carpenter, chemist, or something else. For every vacancy, the appointing officer has his choice of any one of the top three eligibles on the list. This explains why the person whose name is on top of the list sometimes does not get an appointment when some of the persons lower on the list do. If the appointing officer chooses the second or third eligible, the No. 1 eligible does not get a job at once, but stays on the list until he is appointed or the list is terminated.

X. HOW TO PASS THE INTERVIEW TEST

The examination for which you applied requires an oral interview test. You have already taken the written test and you are now being called for the interview test – the final part of the formal examination.

You may think that it is not possible to prepare for an interview test and that there are no procedures to follow during an interview. Our purpose is to point out some things you can do in advance that will help you and some good rules to follow and pitfalls to avoid while you are being interviewed.

What is an interview supposed to test?

The written examination is designed to test the technical knowledge and competence of the candidate; the oral is designed to evaluate intangible qualities, not readily measured otherwise, and to establish a list showing the relative fitness of each candidate – as measured against his competitors – for the position sought. Scoring is not on the basis of "right" and "wrong," but on a sliding scale of values ranging from "not passable" to "outstanding." As a matter of fact, it is possible to achieve a relatively low score without a single "incorrect" answer because of evident weakness in the qualities being measured.

Occasionally, an examination may consist entirely of an oral test – either an individual or a group oral. In such cases, information is sought concerning the technical knowledges and abilities of the candidate, since there has been no written examination for this purpose. More commonly, however, an oral test is used to supplement a written examination.

Who conducts interviews?

The composition of oral boards varies among different jurisdictions. In nearly all, a representative of the personnel department serves as chairman. One of the members of the board may be a representative of the department in which the candidate would work. In some cases, "outside experts" are used, and, frequently, a businessman or some other representative of the general public is asked to serve. Labor and management or other special groups may be represented. The aim is to secure the services of experts in the appropriate field.

However the board is composed, it is a good idea (and not at all improper or unethical) to ascertain in advance of the interview who the members are and what groups they represent. When you are introduced to them, you will have some idea of their backgrounds and interests, and at least you will not stutter and stammer over their names.

What should be done before the interview?

While knowledge about the board members is useful and takes some of the surprise element out of the interview, there is other preparation which is more substantive. It *is* possible to prepare for an oral interview – in several ways:

1) Keep a copy of your application and review it carefully before the interview

This may be the only document before the oral board, and the starting point of the interview. Know what education and experience you have listed there, and the sequence and dates of all of it. Sometimes the board will ask you to review the highlights of your experience for them; you should not have to hem and haw doing it.

2) Study the class specification and the examination announcement

Usually, the oral board has one or both of these to guide them. The qualities, characteristics or knowledges required by the position sought are stated in these documents. They offer valuable clues as to the nature of the oral interview. For example, if the job involves supervisory responsibilities, the announcement will usually indicate that knowledge of modern supervisory methods and the qualifications of the candidate as a supervisor will be tested. If so, you can expect such questions, frequently in the form of a hypothetical situation which you are expected to solve. NEVER go into an oral without knowledge of the duties and responsibilities of the job you seek.

3) Think through each qualification required

Try to visualize the kind of questions you would ask if you were a board member. How well could you answer them? Try especially to appraise your own knowledge and background in each area, *measured against the job sought*, and identify any areas in which you are weak. Be critical and realistic – do not flatter yourself.

4) Do some general reading in areas in which you feel you may be weak

For example, if the job involves supervision and your past experience has NOT, some general reading in supervisory methods and practices, particularly in the field of human relations, might be useful. Do NOT study agency procedures or detailed manuals. The oral board will be testing your understanding and capacity, not your memory.

5) Get a good night's sleep and watch your general health and mental attitude

You will want a clear head at the interview. Take care of a cold or any other minor ailment, and of course, no hangovers.

What should be done on the day of the interview?

Now comes the day of the interview itself. Give yourself plenty of time to get there. Plan to arrive somewhat ahead of the scheduled time, particularly if your appointment is in the fore part of the day. If a previous candidate fails to appear, the board might be ready for you a bit early. By early afternoon an oral board is almost invariably behind schedule if there are many candidates, and you may have to wait. Take along a book or magazine to read, or your application to review, but leave any extraneous material in the waiting room when you go in for your interview. In any event, relax and compose yourself.

The matter of dress is important. The board is forming impressions about you – from your experience, your manners, your attitude, and your appearance. Give your personal appearance careful attention. Dress your best, but not your flashiest. Choose conservative, appropriate clothing, and be sure it is immaculate. This is a business interview, and your appearance should indicate that you regard it as such. Besides, being well groomed and properly dressed will help boost your confidence.

Sooner or later, someone will call your name and escort you into the interview room. *This is it.* From here on you are on your own. It is too late for any more preparation. But remember, you asked for this opportunity to prove your fitness, and you are here because your request was granted.

What happens when you go in?

The usual sequence of events will be as follows: The clerk (who is often the board stenographer) will introduce you to the chairman of the oral board, who will introduce you to the other members of the board. Acknowledge the introductions before you sit down. Do not be surprised if you find a microphone facing you or a stenotypist sitting by. Oral interviews are usually recorded in the event of an appeal or other review.

Usually the chairman of the board will open the interview by reviewing the highlights of your education and work experience from your application – primarily for the benefit of the other members of the board, as well as to get the material into the record. Do not interrupt or comment unless there is an error or significant misinterpretation; if that is the case, do not hesitate. But do not quibble about insignificant matters. Also, he will usually ask you some question about your education, experience or your present job – partly to get you to start talking and to establish the interviewing "rapport." He may start the actual questioning, or turn it over to one of the other members. Frequently, each member undertakes the questioning on a particular area, one in which he is perhaps most competent, so you can expect each member to participate in the examination. Because time is limited, you may also expect some rather abrupt switches in the direction the questioning takes, so do not be upset by it. Normally, a board member will not pursue a single line of questioning unless he discovers a particular strength or weakness.

After each member has participated, the chairman will usually ask whether any member has any further questions, then will ask you if you have anything you wish to add. Unless you are expecting this question, it may floor you. Worse, it may start you off on an extended, extemporaneous speech. The board is not usually seeking more information. The question is principally to offer you a last opportunity to present further qualifications or to indicate that you have nothing to add. So, if you feel that a significant qualification or characteristic has been overlooked, it is proper to point it out in a sentence or so. Do not compliment the board on the thoroughness of their examination – they have been sketchy, and you know it. If you wish, merely say, "No thank you, I have nothing further to add." This is a point where you can "talk yourself out" of a good impression or fail to present an important bit of information. Remember, *you close the interview yourself.*

The chairman will then say, "That is all, Mr. _____, thank you." Do not be startled; the interview is over, and quicker than you think. Thank him, gather your belongings and take your leave. Save your sigh of relief for the other side of the door.

How to put your best foot forward

Throughout this entire process, you may feel that the board individually and collectively is trying to pierce your defenses, seek out your hidden weaknesses and embarrass and confuse you. Actually, this is not true. They are obliged to make an appraisal of your qualifications for the job you are seeking, and they want to see you in your best light. Remember, they must interview all candidates and a non-cooperative candidate may become a failure in spite of their best efforts to bring out his qualifications. Here are 15 suggestions that will help you:

1) Be natural – Keep your attitude confident, not cocky

If you are not confident that you can do the job, do not expect the board to be. Do not apologize for your weaknesses, try to bring out your strong points. The board is interested in a positive, not negative, presentation. Cockiness will antagonize any board member and make him wonder if you are covering up a weakness by a false show of strength.

2) Get comfortable, but don't lounge or sprawl

Sit erectly but not stiffly. A careless posture may lead the board to conclude that you are careless in other things, or at least that you are not impressed by the importance of the occasion. Either conclusion is natural, even if incorrect. Do not fuss with your clothing, a pencil or an ashtray. Your hands may occasionally be useful to emphasize a point; do not let them become a point of distraction.

3) Do not wisecrack or make small talk

This is a serious situation, and your attitude should show that you consider it as such. Further, the time of the board is limited – they do not want to waste it, and neither should you.

4) Do not exaggerate your experience or abilities

In the first place, from information in the application or other interviews and sources, the board may know more about you than you think. Secondly, you probably will not get away with it. An experienced board is rather adept at spotting such a situation, so do not take the chance.

5) If you know a board member, do not make a point of it, yet do not hide it

Certainly you are not fooling him, and probably not the other members of the board. Do not try to take advantage of your acquaintanceship – it will probably do you little good.

6) Do not dominate the interview

Let the board do that. They will give you the clues – do not assume that you have to do all the talking. Realize that the board has a number of questions to ask you, and do not try to take up all the interview time by showing off your extensive knowledge of the answer to the first one.

7) Be attentive

You only have 20 minutes or so, and you should keep your attention at its sharpest throughout. When a member is addressing a problem or question to you, give him your undivided attention. Address your reply principally to him, but do not exclude the other board members.

8) Do not interrupt

A board member may be stating a problem for you to analyze. He will ask you a question when the time comes. Let him state the problem, and wait for the question.

9) Make sure you understand the question

Do not try to answer until you are sure what the question is. If it is not clear, restate it in your own words or ask the board member to clarify it for you. However, do not haggle about minor elements.

10) Reply promptly but not hastily

A common entry on oral board rating sheets is "candidate responded readily," or "candidate hesitated in replies." Respond as promptly and quickly as you can, but do not jump to a hasty, ill-considered answer.

11) Do not be peremptory in your answers

A brief answer is proper – but do not fire your answer back. That is a losing game from your point of view. The board member can probably ask questions much faster than you can answer them.

12) Do not try to create the answer you think the board member wants

He is interested in what kind of mind you have and how it works – not in playing games. Furthermore, he can usually spot this practice and will actually grade you down on it.

13) Do not switch sides in your reply merely to agree with a board member

Frequently, a member will take a contrary position merely to draw you out and to see if you are willing and able to defend your point of view. Do not start a debate, yet do not surrender a good position. If a position is worth taking, it is worth defending.

14) Do not be afraid to admit an error in judgment if you are shown to be wrong

The board knows that you are forced to reply without any opportunity for careful consideration. Your answer may be demonstrably wrong. If so, admit it and get on with the interview.

15) Do not dwell at length on your present job

The opening question may relate to your present assignment. Answer the question but do not go into an extended discussion. You are being examined for a *new* job, not your present one. As a matter of fact, try to phrase ALL your answers in terms of the job for which you are being examined.

Basis of Rating

Probably you will forget most of these "do's" and "don'ts" when you walk into the oral interview room. Even remembering them all will not ensure you a passing grade. Perhaps you did not have the qualifications in the first place. But remembering them will help you to put your best foot forward, without treading on the toes of the board members.

Rumor and popular opinion to the contrary notwithstanding, an oral board wants you to make the best appearance possible. They know you are under pressure – but they also want to see how you respond to it as a guide to what your reaction would be under the pressures of the job you seek. They will be influenced by the degree of poise you display, the personal traits you show and the manner in which you respond.

ABOUT THIS BOOK

This book contains tests divided into Examination Sections. Go through each test, answering every question in the margin. We have also attached a sample answer sheet at the back of the book that can be removed and used. At the end of each test look at the answer key and check your answers. On the ones you got wrong, look at the right answer choice and learn. Do not fill in the answers first. Do not memorize the questions and answers, but understand the answer and principles involved. On your test, the questions will likely be different from the samples. Questions are changed and new ones added. If you understand these past questions you should have success with any changes that arise. Tests may consist of several types of questions. We have additional books on each subject should more study be advisable or necessary for you. Finally, the more you study, the better prepared you will be. This book is intended to be the last thing you study before you walk into the examination room. Prior study of relevant texts is also recommended. NLC publishes some of these in our Fundamental Series. Knowledge and good sense are important factors in passing your exam. Good luck also helps. So now study this Passbook, absorb the material contained within and take that knowledge into the examination. Then do your best to pass that exam.

EXAMINATION SECTION

EXAMINATION SECTION
TEST 1

DIRECTIONS: Each question or incomplete statement is followed by several suggested answers or completions. Select the one that BEST answers the question or completes the statement. *PRINT THE LETTER OF THE CORRECT ANSWER IN THE SPACE AT THE RIGHT.*

1. The officer who investigates accidents is always required to make a complete and accurate report.
   Of the following, the BEST reason for this procedure is to

   A. protect the operating agency against possible false claims
   B. provide a file of incidents which can be used as basic material for an accident prevention campaign
   C. provide the management with concrete evidence of violations of the rules by employees
   D. indicate what repairs need to be made

   1.____

2. It is suggested that an officer keep all persons away from the area of an accident until an investigation has been completed.
   This suggested procedure is

   A. *good;* witnesses will be more likely to agree on a single story
   B. *bad;* such action blocks traffic flow and causes congestion
   C. *good;* objects of possible use as evidence will be protected from damage or loss
   D. *bad;* the flow of normal pedestrian traffic provides an opportunity for an investigator to determine the cause of the accident

   2.____

3. A man having business with your agency is arguing with you and accuses you of being prejudiced against him. Although you explain to him that this is not so, he demands to see your supervisor.
   Of the following, the BEST course of action for you to take is to

   A. continue arguing with him until you have worn him out or convinced him
   B. take him to your supervisor
   C. ignore him and walk away from him to another part of the office
   D. escort him out of the office

   3.____

4. An officer receives instructions from his supervisor which he does not fully understand.
   For the officer to ask for a further explanation would be

   A. *good;* chiefly because his supervisor will be impressed with his interest in his work
   B. *poor;* chiefly because the time of the supervisor will be needlessly wasted
   C. *good;* chiefly because proper performance depends on full understanding of the work to be done
   D. *poor;* chiefly because officers should be able to think for themselves

   4.____

5. A person is making a complaint to an officer which seems unreasonable and of little importance.
   Of the following, the BEST action for the officer to take is to

   5.____

A. criticize the person making the complaint for taking up his valuable time
B. laugh over the matter to show that the complaint is minor and silly
C. tell the person that anyone responsible for his grievance will be prosecuted
D. listen to the person making the complaint and tell him that the matter will be investigated

6. A member of the department shall not indulge in intoxicating liquor while in uniform. A member of the department is not required to wear a uniform, and a uniformed member while out of uniform shall not indulge in intoxicants to an extent unfitting him for duty.
Of the following, the MOST correct interpretation of this rule is that a

A. member, off duty, not in uniform, may drink intoxicating liquor
B. member, not on duty, but in uniform, may drink intoxicating liquor
C. member, on duty, in uniform, may drink intoxicants
D. uniformed member, in civilian clothes, may not drink intoxicants

7. You have a suggestion for an important change which you believe will improve a certain procedure in your agency. Of the following, the next course of action for you to take is to

A. try it out yourself
B. submit the suggestion to your immediate supervisor
C. write a letter to the head of your agency asking for his approval
D. wait until you are asked for suggestions before submitting this one

8. An officer shall study maps and literature concerning his assigned area and the streets and points of interest nearby.
Of the following, the BEST reason for this rule is that

A. the officer will be better able to give correct information to persons desiring it
B. the officer will be better able to drive a vehicle in the area
C. the officer will not lose interest in his work
D. supervisors will not need to train the officers in this subject

9. In asking a witness to a crime to identify a suspect, it is a common practice to place the suspect with a group of persons and ask the witness to pick out the person in question.
Of the following, the BEST reason for this practice is that it will

A. make the identification more reliable than if the witness were shown the suspect alone
B. protect the witness against reprisals
C. make sure that the witness is telling the truth
D. help select other participants in the crime at the same time

10. It is most important for all officers to obey the "Rules and Regulations" of their agency.
Of the following, the BEST reason for this statement is that

A. supervisors will not need to train their new officers
B. officers will never have to use their own judgment
C. uniform procedures will be followed
D. officers will not need to ask their supervisors for assistance

Questions 11-13.

DIRECTIONS: Answer questions 11 to 13 SOLELY on the basis of the following paragraph.

All members of the police force must recognize that the people, through their representatives, hire and pay the police and that, as in any other employment, there must exist a proper employer-employee relationship. The police officer must understand that the essence of a correct police attitude is a willingness to serve, but at the same time, he should distinguish between service and servility, and between courtesy and softness. He must be firm but also courteous, avoiding even an appearance of rudeness. He should develop a position that is friendly and unbiased, pleasant and sympathetic, in his relations with the general public, but firm and impersonal on occasions calling for regulation and control. A police officer should understand that his primary purpose is to prevent violations, not to arrest people. He should recognize the line of demarcation between a police function and passing judgment which is a court function. On the other side, a public that cooperates with the police, that supports them in their efforts and that observes laws and regulations, may be said to have a desirable attitude.

11. In accordance with this paragraph, the PROPER attitude for a police officer to take is to 11._____

    A. be pleasant and sympathetic at all times
    B. be friendly, firm, and impartial
    C. be stern and severe in meting out justice to all
    D. avoid being rude, except in those cases where the public is uncooperative

12. Assume that an officer is assigned by his superior officer to a busy traffic intersection and is warned to be on the lookout for motorists who skip the light or who are speeding. According to this paragraph, it would be proper for the officer in this assignment to 12._____

    A. give a summons to every motorist whose ear was crossing when the light changed
    B. hide behind a truck and wait for drivers who violate traffic laws
    C. select at random motorists who seem to be impatient and lecture them sternly on traffic safety
    D. stand on post in order to deter violations and give offenders a summons or a warning as required

13. According to this paragraph, a police officer must realize that the primary purpose of police work is to 13._____

    A. provide proper police service in a courteous manner
    B. decide whether those who violate the law should be punished
    C. arrest those who violate laws
    D. establish a proper employer-employee relationship

Questions 14-15.

DIRECTIONS: Answer questions 14 and 15 SOLELY on the basis of the following paragraph.

If a motor vehicle fails to pass inspection, the owner will be given a rejection notice by the inspection station. Repairs must be made within ten days after this notice is issued. It is not necessary to have the required adjustment or repairs made at the station where the inspection occurred. The vehicle may be taken to any other garage. Re-inspection after repairs may be made at any official inspection station, not necessarily the same station which made the initial inspection. The registration of any motor vehicle for which an inspection sticker has not been obtained as required, or which is not repaired and inspected within ten days after inspection indicates defects, is subject to suspension. A vehicle cannot be used on public highways while its registration is under suspension.

14. According to the above paragraph, the owner of a car which does NOT pass inspection must

    A. have repairs made at the same station which rejected his car
    B. take the car to another station and have it re-inspected
    C. have repairs made anywhere and then have the car re-inspected
    D. not use the car on a public highway until the necessary repairs have been made

15. According to the above paragraph, the one of the following which may be cause for suspension of the registration of a vehicle is that

    A. an inspection sticker was issued before the rejection notice had been in force for ten days
    B. it was not re-inspected by the station that rejected it originally
    C. it was not re-inspected either by the station that rejected it originally or by the garage which made the repairs
    D. it has not had defective parts repaired within ten days after inspection

Questions 16-20.

DIRECTIONS: Answer questions 16 to 20 SOLELY on the basis of the following paragraph.

If we are to study crime in its widest social setting, we will find a variety of conduct which, although criminal in the legal sense, is not offensive to the moral conscience of a considerable number of persons. Traffic violations, for example, do not brand the offender as guilty of moral offense. In fact, the recipient of a traffic ticket is usually simply the subject of some good-natured joking by his friends. Although there may be indignation among certain groups of citizens against gambling and liquor law violations, these activities are often tolerated, if not openly supported, by the more numerous residents of the community. Indeed, certain social and service clubs regularly conduct gambling games and lotteries for the purpose of raising funds. Some communities regard violations involving the sale of liquor with little concern in order to profit from increased license fees and taxes paid by dealers. The thousand and one forms of political graft and corruption which infest our urban centers only occasionally arouse public condemnation and official action.

16. According to the paragraph, all types of illegal conduct are

    A. condemned by all elements of the community
    B. considered a moral offense, although some are tolerated by a few citizens
    C. violations of the law, but some are acceptable to certain elements of the community
    D. found in a social setting which is not punishable by law

17. According to the paragraph, traffic violations are generally considered by society as

    A. crimes requiring the maximum penalty set by the law
    B. more serious than violations of the liquor laws

C. offenses against the morals of the community
D. relatively minor offenses requiring minimum punishment

18. According to the paragraph, a lottery conducted for the purpose of raising funds for a church   18._____

    A. is considered a serious violation of law
    B. may be tolerated by a community which has laws against gambling
    C. may be conducted under special laws demanded by the more numerous residents of a community
    D. arouses indignation in most communities

19. On the basis of the paragraph, the MOST likely reaction in the community to a police raid on a gambling casino would be   19._____

    A. more an attitude of indifference than interest in the raid
    B. general approval of the raid
    C. condemnation of the raid by most people
    D. demand for further action since this raid is not sufficient to end gambling activities

20. The one of the following which BEST describes the central thought of this paragraph and would be MOST suitable as a title for it is   20._____

    A. CRIME AND THE POLICE
    B. PUBLIC CONDEMNATION OF GRAFT AND CORRUPTION
    C. GAMBLING IS NOT ALWAYS A VICIOUS BUSINESS
    D. PUBLIC ATTITUDE TOWARD LAW VIOLATIONS

Questions 21-23.

DIRECTIONS: Answer questions 21 to 23 SOLELY on the basis of the following paragraph.

The law enforcement agency is one of the most important agencies in the field of juvenile delinquency prevention. This is so not because of the social work connected with this problem, however, for this is not a police matter, but because the officers are usually the first to come in contact with the delinquent. The manner of arrest and detention makes a deep impression upon him and affects his life-long attitude toward society and the law. The juvenile court is perhaps the most important agency in this work. Contrary to the general opinion, however, it is not primarily concerned with putting children into correctional schools. The main purpose of the juvenile court is to save the child and to develop his emotional make-up in order that he can grow up to be a decent and well-balanced citizen. The system of probation is the means whereby the court seeks to accomplish these goals.

21. According to this paragraph, police work is an important part of a program to prevent juvenile delinquency because   21._____

    A. social work is no longer considered important in juvenile delinquency prevention
    B. police officers are the first to have contact with the delinquent
    C. police officers jail the offender in order to be able to change his attitude toward society and the law
    D. it is the first step in placing the delinquent in jail

22. According to this paragraph, the CHIEF purpose of the juvenile court is to

    A. punish the child for his offense
    B. select a suitable correctional school for the delinquent
    C. use available means to help the delinquent become a better person
    D. provide psychiatric care for the delinquent

23. According to this paragraph, the juvenile court directs the development of delinquents under its care CHIEFLY by

    A. placing the child under probation
    B. sending the child to a correctional school
    C. keeping the delinquent in prison
    D. returning the child to his home

Questions 24-27.

DIRECTIONS: Answer questions 24 to 27 SOLELY on the basis of the following paragraph.

When a vehicle has been disabled in the tunnel, the officer on patrol in this zone shall press the EMERGENCY TRUCK light button. In the fast lane, red lights will go on throughout the tunnel; in the slow lane, amber lights will go on throughout the tunnel. The yellow zone light will go on at each signal control station throughout the tunnel and will flash the number of the zone in which the stoppage has occurred. A red flashing pilot light will appear only at the signal control station at which the EMERGENCY TRUCK button was pressed. The emergency garage will receive an audible and visual signal indicating the signal control station at which the EMERGENCY TRUCK button was pressed. The garage officer shall acknowledge receipt of the signal by pressing the acknowledgment button. This will cause the pilot light at the operated signal control station in the tunnel to cease flashing and to remain steady. It is an answer to the officer at the operated signal control station that the emergency truck is responding to the call.

24. According to this paragraph, when the EMERGENCY TRUCK light button is pressed,

    A. amber lights will go on in every lane throughout the tunnel
    B. emergency signal lights will go on only in the lane in which the disabled vehicle happens to be
    C. red lights will go on in the fast lane throughout the tunnel
    D. pilot lights at all signal control stations will turn amber

25. According to this paragraph, the number of the zone in which the stoppage has occurred is flashed

    A. immediately after all the lights in the tunnel turn red
    B. by the yellow zone light at each signal control station
    C. by the emergency truck at the point of stoppage
    D. by the emergency garage

26. According to this paragraph, an officer near the disabled vehicle will know that the emergency tow truck is coming when

    A. the pilot light at the operated signal control station appears and flashes red
    B. an audible signal is heard in the tunnel

C. the zone light at the operated signal control station turns red
D. the pilot light at the operated signal control station becomes steady

27. Under the system described in the paragraph, it would be CORRECT to come to the conclusion that 27.____

    A. officers at all signal control stations are expected to acknowledge that they have received the stoppage signal
    B. officers at all signal control stations will know where the stoppage has occurred
    C. all traffic in both lanes of that side of the tunnel in which the stoppage has occurred must stop until the emergency truck has arrived
    D. there are two emergency garages, each able to respond to stoppages in traffic going in one particular direction

Questions 28-30.

DIRECTIONS: Answer questions 28 to 30 SOLELY on the basis of the following paragraphs.

In cases of accident, it is most important for an officer to obtain the name, age, residence, occupation, and a full description of the person injured, names and addresses of witnesses. He shall also obtain a statement of the attendant circumstances. He shall carefully note contributory conditions, if any, such as broken pavement, excavation, tights not burning, snow and ice on the roadway, etc. He shall enter all facts in his memorandum book and on Form 17 or Form 18 and promptly transmit the original of the form to his superior officer and the duplicate to headquarters.

An officer shall render reasonable assistance to sick or injured persons. If the circumstances appear to require the services of a physician, he shall summon a physician by telephoning the superior officer on duty and notifying him of the apparent nature of the illness or accident and the location where the physician will be required. He may summon other officers to assist if circumstances warrant.

In case of an accident or where a person is sick on city property, an officer shall obtain the information necessary to fill out card Form 18 and record this in his memorandum book and promptly telephone the facts to his superior officer. He shall deliver the original card at the expiration of his tour to his superior officer and transmit the duplicate to headquarters.

28. According to this quotation, the MOST important consideration in any report on a case of accident or injury is to 28.____

    A. obtain all the facts
    B. telephone his superior officer at once
    C. obtain a statement of the attendant circumstances
    D. determine ownership of the property on which the accident occurred

29. According to this quotation, in the case of an accident on city property, the officer should always 29.____

    A. summon a physician before filling out any forms or making any entries in his memorandum book
    B. give his superior officer on duty a prompt report by telephone

C. immediately bring the original of Form 18 to his superior officer on duty
D. call at least one other officer to the scene to witness conditions

30. If the procedures stated in this quotation were followed for all accidents in the city, an impartial survey of accidents occurring during any period of time in this city may be MOST easily made by

   A. asking a typical officer to show you his memorandum book
   B. having a superior officer investigate whether contributory conditions mentioned by witnesses actually exist
   C. checking all the records of all superior officers
   D. checking the duplicate card files at headquarters

Questions 31-55.

DIRECTIONS: In each of questions 31 to 55, select the lettered word or phrase which means MOST NEARLY the same as the first word in the row.

31. RENDEZVOUS
   A. parade   B. neighborhood
   C. meeting place   D. wander about

32. EMINENT
   A. noted   B. rich   C. rounded   D. nearby

33. CAUSTIC
   A. cheap   B. sweet   C. evil   D. sharp

34. BARTER
   A. annoy   B. trade   C. argue   D. cheat

35. APTITUDE
   A. friendliness   B. talent
   C. conceit   D. generosity

36. PROTRUDE
   A. project   B. defend   C. choke   D. boast

37. FORTITUDE
   A. disposition   B. restlessness
   C. courage   D. poverty

38. PRELUDE
   A. introduction   B. meaning
   C. prayer   D. secret

39. SECLUSION
   A. primitive   B. influence
   C. imagination D. privacy

40. RECTIFY
    A. correct   B. construct   C. divide   D. scold

41. TRAVERSE
    A. rotate   B. compose   C. train   D. cross

42. ALLEGE
    A. raise   B. convict   C. declare   D. chase

43. MENIAL
    A. pleasant   B. unselfish
    C. humble   D. stupid

44. DEPLETE
    A. exhaust   B. gather   C. repay   D. close

45. ERADICATE
    A. construct   B. advise   C. destroy   D. exclaim

46. CAPITULATE
    A. cover   B. surrender   C. receive   D. execute

47. RESTRAIN
    A. restore   B. drive   C. review   D. limit

48. AMALGAMATE
    A. join   B. force   C. correct   D. clash

49. DEJECTED
    A. beaten   B. speechless
    C. weak   D. low-spirited

50. DETAIN
    A. hide   B. accuse   C. hold   D. mislead

KEY (CORRECT ANSWERS)

1. A	11. B	21. B	31. C	41. D
2. C	12. D	22. C	32. A	42. C
3. B	13. A	23. A	33. D	43. C
4. C	14. C	24. C	34. B	44. A
5. D	15. D	25. B	35. B	45. C
6. A	16. C	26. D	36. A	46. B
7. B	17. D	27. B	37. C	47. D
8. A	18. B	28. A	38. A	48. A
9. A	19. A	29. B	39. D	49. D
10. C	20. D	30. D	40. A	50. C

TEST 2

DIRECTIONS: Each question or incomplete statement is followed by several suggested answers or completions. Select the one that BEST answers the question or completes the statement. *PRINT THE LETTER OF THE CORRECT ANSWER IN THE SPACE AT THE RIGHT.*

1. AMPLE

    A. necessary   B. plentiful   C. protected   D. tasty

    1._____

2. EXPEDITE

    A. sue   B. omit   C. hasten   D. verify

    2._____

3. FRAGMENT

    A. simple tool   B. broken part
    C. basic outline   D. weakness

    3._____

4. ADVERSARY

    A. thief   B. partner   C. loser   D. foe

    4._____

5. ACHIEVE

    A. accomplish   B. begin   C. develop   D. urge

    5._____

Questions 6-10.

DIRECTIONS: Answer Questions 6 to 10 on the basis of the information given in the table on the following page. The numbers which have been omitted from the table can be calculated from the other numbers which are given.

NUMBER OF DWELLING UNITS CONSTRUCTED

Year	Private one-family houses	In private apt. houses	In public housing	Total dwelling units
1996	4,500	500	600	5,600
1997	9,200	5,300	2,800	17,300
1998	8,900	12,800	6,800	28,500
1999	12,100	15,500	7,100	34,700
2000	?	12,200	14,100	39,200
2001	10,200	26,000	8,600	44,800
2002	10,300	17,900	7,400	35,600
2003	11,800	18,900	7,700	38,400
2004	12,700	22,100	8,400	43,200
2005	13,300	24,300	8,100	45,700
TOTALS	105,900	?	?	?

6. According to this table, the average number of public housing units constructed yearly during the period 1996 through 2005 was

    A. 7,160   B. 6,180   C. 7,610   D. 6,810

    6._____

7. Of the following, the two years in which the number of private one-family homes constructed was GREATEST for the two years together is

   A. 1998 and 1999   B. 1997 and 2003
   C. 1998 and 2004   D. 2001 and 2002

8. For the entire period of 1996 through 2005, the total of all private one-family houses constructed exceeded the total of all public housing units constructed by

   A. 34,300   B. 45,700   C. 50,000   D. 83,900

9. Of the total number of private apartment house dwelling units constructed in the ten years given in the table, the percentage which was constructed in 2002 was MOST NEARLY

   A. 5%   B. 11%   C. 16%   D. 21%

10. Considering dwelling units of all types, the average number constructed annually in the period from 2001 through 2005 was GREATER than the average number constructed annually in the period from 1996 through 2000 by

    A. 16,480   B. 33,320   C. 79,300   D. 82,400

11. A car speeds through the toll entrance of a 2 1/4 mile long bridge without paying the toll and reaches the other end of the bridge 1 minute and 30 seconds later. The car was traveling MOST NEARLY at a rate of _____ miles per hour.

    A. 60   B. 70   C. 80   D. 90

12. During one week, 21,500 vehicles passed through the toll booths of a certain bridge. Of these, 550 were buses, 2,230 were trucks, and the rest were passenger cars. The toll charges were $3.50 for a passenger car, $7 for a truck and $14 for a bus. The total income for the week was

    A. $80,850   B. $88,830   C. $102,550   D. $109,550

13. A bullet fired from a revolver travels 100 feet the first second, and each succeeding second it travels a distance 10% less than during the immediately preceding second. The number of feet the bullet will have traveled at the end of the fourth second is MOST NEARLY

    A. 272   B. 320   C. 344   D. 360

14. An officer receives a uniform allowance of $500 a year in a lump sum. Of this amount, he spends $180 for a winter jacket and 40% of the remainder for two pairs of trousers. The officer now wishes to buy a winter overcoat which costs $240.
    The percentage of the purchase price of the overcoat by which he will be short is

    A. 20%   B. 25%   C. 48%   D. 60%

15. It has been suggested that small light cars can be used for certain kinds of police work. These light vehicles can run 30 miles per gallon of gasoline as contrasted with standard cars which run only 15 miles per gallon. Assume gasoline costs the city $3.75 per gallon. During 9,000 miles of travel, use of the small light car in preference to the standard car would result in a saving in gasoline costs of MOST NEARLY

    A. $1,125   B. $1,500   C. $1,875   D. $2,250

16. Out of a total of 34,750 felony complaints in 2006, 14,200 involved burglary. In 2005, there was a total of 32,300 felony complaints of which 12,800 were burglary.
Of the increase in felonies from 2005 to 2006, the increase in burglaries comprised APPROXIMATELY

    A. 27%   B. 37%   C. 47%   D. 57%

17. A certain city department has two offices which issue permits, one office handling twice as many applicants as the other. The smaller office grants permits to 40% of its applicants. The larger office handling twice as many applicants grants permits to 60% of its applicants.
If there were 900 applicants at both offices together on a given day, the total number of permits granted by both offices would be MOST NEARLY

    A. 420   B. 450   C. 480   D. 510

18. If a co-worker is not breathing after receiving an electric shock but is no longer in contact with the electricity, it is MOST important for you to

    A. avoid moving him
    B. wrap the victim in a blanket
    C. start artificial respiration promptly
    D. force him to take hot liquids

19. Employees using supplies from one of the first-aid kits available throughout the building are required to submit an immediate report of the occurrence.
Logical reasoning shows that the MOST important reason for this report is so that the

    A. supplies used will be sure to be replaced
    B. first-aid kit can be properly sealed again
    C. employee will be credited for his action
    D. record of first-aid supplies will be up-to-date

20. The BEST IMMEDIATE first-aid treatment for a scraped knee is to

    A. apply plain vaseline   B. wash it with soap and water
    C. apply heat   D. use a knee splint

21. Artificial respiration after a severe electrical shock is ALWAYS necessary when the shock results in

    A. unconsciousness   B. stoppage of breathing
    C. bleeding   D. a burn

22. The authority gives some of its maintenance employees instruction in first aid.
The MOST likely reason for doing this is to

    A. eliminate the need for calling a doctor in case of accident
    B. provide temporary emergency treatment in case of accident
    C. lower the cost of accidents to the authority
    D. reduce the number of accidents

23. The BEST IMMEDIATE first aid if a chemical solution splashes into the eyes is to

    A. protect the eyes from the light by bandaging
    B. rub the eyes dry with a towel

C. cause tears to flow by staring at a bright light
D. flush the eyes with large quantities of clean water

24. If you had to telephone for an ambulance because of an accident, the MOST important information for you to give the person who answered the telephone would be the

   A. exact time of the accident
   B. cause of the accident
   C. place where the ambulance is needed
   D. names and addresses of those injured

25. If a person has a deep puncture wound in his finger caused by a sharp nail, the BEST IMMEDIATE first aid procedure would be to

   A. encourage bleeding by exerting pressure around the injured area
   B. stop all bleeding
   C. prevent air from reaching the wound
   D. probe the wound for steel particles

26. In addition to cases of submersion, artificial respiration is a recommended first aid procedure for

   A. sunstroke   B. electrical shock   C. chemical poisoning   D. apoplexy

27. Assume that you are called on to render first aid to a man injured in an accident. You find he is bleeding profusely, is unconscious, and has a broken arm. There is a strong odor of alcohol about him.
The FIRST thing for which you should treat him is the

   A. bleeding   B. unconsciousness   C. broken arm   D. alcoholism

28. In applying first aid for removal of a foreign body in the eye, an important precaution to be observed is NOT to

   A. attempt to wash out the foreign body
   B. bring the upper eyelid down over the lower
   C. rub the eye
   D. touch or attempt to remove a speck on the lower lid

29. The one of the following symptoms which is LEAST likely to indicate that a person involved in an accident requires first aid for shock is that

   A. he has fainted twice
   B. his face is red and flushed
   C. his skin is wet with sweat
   D. his pulse is rapid

30. When giving first aid to a person suffering from shock as a result of an auto accident, it is MOST important to

   A. massage him in order to aid blood circulation
   B. have him sip whiskey
   C. prop him up in a sitting position
   D. cover the person and keep him warm

Questions 31-34.

DIRECTIONS: Answer questions 31 to 34 SOLELY on the basis of the following paragraph.

Assume that you are an officer assigned to one large office which issues and receives applications for various permits and licenses. The office consists of one section where the necessary forms are issued; another section where fees are paid to a cashier; and desks where applicants are interviewed and their forms reviewed and completed. There is also a section containing tables and chairs where persons may sit and fill out their applications before being interviewed or paying the fees. your duties consist of answering simple questions, directing the public to the correct section of the office, and maintaining order.

31. A man who speaks English poorly asks you for assistance in obtaining and filling out an application for a permit. You should

    A. send him to an interviewer who can assist him
    B. try to determine what permit he wants and fill out the form for him
    C. refer the man to the office supervisor
    D. ask another applicant to help this person

32. The office becomes noisy and crowded, with people milling around waiting for service at the various sections.
    Of the following, the BEST action for you to take is to

    A. stand in a prominent place and in a loud voice request the people to be quiet
    B. direct all the people not being served to wait at the unoccupied tables until you call them
    C. line up the people in front of each section and keep the lines in good order
    D. tell the people to form a single line outside the office and let in a few at a time

33. A man who has just been denied a permit becomes angry and shouts that if he "knew the right people" he too could get a permit. His behavior is disturbing the office.
    Of the following, the BEST action for you to take is to

    A. order the man to leave at once since his business is done
    B. tell the man to be quiet and file another application
    C. suggest to the supervisor that a pamphlet be prepared explaining the requirements for permits in simple language
    D. ask an interviewer to explain the requirements for his permit to the person and his right of appeal

34. Just before the close of business, a man rushes in and insists on being interviewed for a permit because his present one expires that night.
    Of the following, the BEST action for you to take is to

    A. tell the man that the office is closed
    B. tell the man that there will be no penalty if he returns early the next morning
    C. inquire if an interviewer is still available to take care of him and send him to that desk
    D. tell the cashier to collect the fee and tell the man to return the next morning for an interview

35. Fingerprints are often taken of applicants for licenses. Of the following, the MOST valid reason for this procedure is that

   A. the license of someone who commits a crime can be more readily revoked
   B. applicants can be checked for possible criminal records
   C. it helps to make sure that the proper license fee is paid
   D. a complete employment record of the applicant is obtained

36. Assume that an officer is on patrol at 2 A.M. He notices that the night light inside one of the stores in a public building is out. The store is locked.
Of the following, the FIRST action for him to take at this time is to

   A. continue on his patrol since the light probably burned out
   B. enter the store by any means possible so he can check it
   C. report the matter to his superior
   D. shine his flashlight through the window to look for anything unusual

37. In questioning a man suspected of having committed a theft, the BEST procedure for an officer to follow is to

   A. induce the man to express his feelings about the police, the courts, and his home environment
   B. threaten him with beatings when he refuses to answer your questions
   C. make any promises necessary to get him to confess
   D. remain calm and objective

38. As an officer, you are on duty in one of the offices of a large public building. A woman who has just finished her business with this office comes to you and reports that her son who was with her is missing.
The one of the following which is the BEST action for you to take FIRST is to

   A. tell the mother that the child is probably all right and ask her to go to the local police station for help in finding the boy
   B. suggest that the mother wait in the office until the child turns up
   C. check nearby offices in an attempt to locate the child
   D. telephone the local police station and ask if any reports fitting the description of the child have been received

39. An officer assigned to patrol inside a public building at night has observed two men standing outside the doorway. Of the following, the MOST appropriate action for the officer to take FIRST is to

   A. approach the two men and ask them why they are standing there
   B. hide and wait for the two men to take some action
   C. phone the local police station and ask for help since these men may be planning criminal action
   D. check all the entrance doors of the building to make sure that they are locked

40. It is standard practice for special officers to inspect the restrooms in public buildings. This is done at regular intervals while on patrol.
Of the following, the BEST reason for this practice is to

   A. inspect sanitary conditions
   B. discourage loiterers and potential criminals

C. check the ventilation
D. determine if all the equipment and plumbing is working properly

41. While on duty in the evening as an officer assigned to a public building, you receive a report that a card game is going on in one of the offices. Gambling is forbidden on government property.
Of the following, the BEST course of action for you to take is to

   A. go to the office and order the card players to leave
   B. ignore the complaint since this is probably just harmless social card playing
   C. report the matter to the building manager the next day
   D. go to the office and, if warranted, issue an appropriate warning

42. It has been suggested that special officers establish good working relationships with the local police officers of the police department on duty in the neighborhood.
Of the following, the MOST valid reason for this practice is that

   A. a spirit of good feeling and high morale will be created among members of the police department
   B. local police officers will probably cooperate more readily with the special officer
   C. local police officers can take over the building patrol duties of the special officer in case he is absent
   D. special officers have an even stronger obligation than ordinary citizens to cooperate with the police

43. It has been proposed that an officer assigned to a public building at night remain at one location in the building, instead of walking on patrol through the building.
This proposal is

   A. *bad;* chiefly because the officer would probably sit instead of stand at the proper location
   B. *good;* chiefly because the officer could do a better job of watching the entire building from one point
   C. *bad;* chiefly because anyone seeking to enter the building for illegal purposes might be able to do so at a point other than where the special officer is on duty
   D. *good;* chiefly because his supervisors would know exactly where to find him

44. In a busy office, an officer has been assigned the duty of making sure that the public is served in the order of their arrival at the office and that some employee is always taking care of a person desiring help.
Of the following, the BEST method for the officer to follow is to

   A. line up the persons in the waiting room
   B. give a numbered ticket to each person waiting and call out the numbers, in order, when an employee becomes available
   C. loudly announce "next" when an employee is available to serve someone
   D. seat one person next to each employee's desk and let the others wait for the first vacant seat

45. Two men have broken into and entered a building at night. The officer on duty at this building sees them, chases them out, and then observes them in the adjoining building.
Of the following, the BEST course of action for the officer to take is to

    A. notify the local police station and be ready to aid the police
    B. enter the adjoining building to find the men
    C. notify the manager of his own building
    D. continue on duty since these men have left the building for which he is responsible

46. While an officer is on duty in a crowded waiting room, he finds a woman's purse on the floor.
Of the following, the FIRST course of action for him to take is to

    A. hold it up in the air, ask who owns it, and give it to whoever claims it
    B. keep the purse until someone claims it
    C. immediately deliver the purse to the "lost and found" desk
    D. ask the lady who is nearest to him if she lost a purse

47. Special officers often have the power of arrest.
Of the following, the BEST reason for this practice is to

    A. have the officer always arrest any person who refuses to obey his orders
    B. aid in maintaining order in places where he is assigned
    C. promote good public relations
    D. aid in preventing illegal use of public buildings by tenants or employees

48. An officer has told a mother that he found her son writing on the walls of the building with chalk. The mother tells the officer that he should be more concerned with "crooks" than with children's minor pranks.
Of the following, the BEST answer for the officer to make to this woman is that

    A. children should be taught good conduct by their parents
    B. damage to public property means higher taxes
    C. serious criminals often begin their careers with minor violations
    D. it is his duty to enforce all rules and regulations

49. A man asks you, a special officer, where to get a certain kind of license not issued in your office. You don't know where such licenses are issued.
Of the following, the BEST procedure for you to follow is to

    A. refer him to the manager of the office
    B. get the information if you can and give it to the man
    C. tell the man to inquire at any police station house
    D. tell the man that you just do not know

50. Special officers are not permitted to ask private citizens to buy tickets for dances or other such social functions, not even when such functions are operated by charitable organizations. Of the following, the BEST reason for this rule is that

    A. private citizens are under no obligation to buy any such tickets
    B. not all groups are allowed equal opportunity in the sale of their tickets
    C. private citizens might complain to officials
    D. private citizens might feel they would not get proper service unless they bought such tickets

KEY (CORRECT ANSWERS)

1. B	11. D	21. B	31. A	41. D
2. C	12. B	22. B	32. C	42. B
3. B	13. C	23. D	33. D	43. C
4. D	14. A	24. C	34. C	44. B
5. A	15. A	25. A	35. B	45. A
6. A	16. D	26. B	36. D	46. C
7. C	17. C	27. A	37. D	47. B
8. A	18. C	28. C	38. C	48. D
9. B	19. A	29. B	39. D	49. B
10. A	20. B	30. D	40. B	50. D

SOLUTIONS TO ARITHMETIC PROBLEMS

11. $2\frac{1}{4}$ miles are completed in 1 1/2 minutes (1 minute and 30 seconds)

    $$\therefore 2\frac{1}{4} \div 1\frac{1}{2} = \text{rate per minute}$$

    $$= \frac{9}{4} \div 1\frac{1}{2}$$

    $$= \frac{9}{4} \div \frac{3}{2}$$

    $$= \frac{9}{4} \times \frac{2}{3}$$

    $$= \frac{3}{2} \text{ miles per minute}$$

    $\therefore \frac{3}{2} \times 60$ (minutes in an hour) = rate per hour = 90 miles per hour

    (Ans. D)

12. 550 + 2230 = 2780; 21,500 - 2780 = 18,720 passengers

550 buses at $14.00	=	$ 7,700
2230 trucks at $7.00	=	15,610
18720 passengers at $3.50	=	65,520
		$88,830

    (Ans. B)

13. Given: speed = 100 feet the first second

100 - 10 (10% of 100)	=	90 feet - the second second
90 - 9 (10% of 90)	=	81 feet - the third second
81 - 8.1 (10% of 81)	=	72.9 feet - the fourth second
		343.9 (total at end of the fourth second)

    (Ans. C)

14. Given: 500 = uniform allowance

    $500 - 180 = $320 (amount left after buying winter jacket)
    $320 x 40% = $128 (amount spent for two pairs of trousers)
    $320 - 128 = $192 (amount now left)

    Since the winter overcoat costs $240, he is now short $48 ($240 - 192) or 20% of the purchase price of the overcoat. (48/240 = $\frac{1}{5}$ = 20%)

(Ans. A)

15. Light care: 9000(miles)÷30(miles per gallon)×3.75(per gallon)

$$= \frac{9000}{30} \times 3.75$$
$$= 300 \times 3.75$$
$$= \$1,125 \text{ (total gasoline cost)}$$

Standard cars: 9000 (miles) ÷ 15 (miles per gallon) x 3.75

$$= \frac{9000}{15} \times 3.75$$
$$= 600 \times 3.75$$
$$= \$2,250 \text{ (total gasoline cost)}$$

∴ use of light car would result in a saving in gasoline costs of $1,125 ($2,250 - $1,125).

(Ans. A)

16.
2006:	14,200	(burglary)
2005:	12,800	(burglary)
	1,400	(increase in burglaries)

2006:	34,750	(felony)
2005:	32,300	(felony)
	2,450	(increase in felonies

$$\therefore 1400 \div 2450 = \frac{1400}{2450} = .57$$

WORK

```
         .57
2450 )1400.0
      1225.0
       175.00
       171.50
```

(Ans. D)

17. Given: smaller office: grants permits to 40% of 1/3 of the total number of applicants (900)

larger office: grants permits to 60% of 2/3 of the total number of applicants (900)

Solving: smaller office: $.40 \times \frac{1}{3} \times 900 = 120$ permits

larger office: $.60 \times \frac{2}{3} \times 900 = \underline{360}$ permits
$\phantom{larger office: .60 \times \frac{2}{3} \times 900 = }480$ permits (total)

(Ans. C)

EXAMINATION SECTION
TEST 1

DIRECTIONS: Each question or incomplete statement is followed by several suggested answers or completions. Select the one that BEST answers the question or completes the statement. *PRINT THE LETTER OF THE CORRECT ANSWER IN THE SPACE AT THE RIGHT.*

1. Of the following, the MOST important single factor in any building security program is

    A. a fool-proof employee identification system
    B. an effective control of entrances and exits
    C. bright illumination of all outside areas
    D. clearly marking public and non-public areas

2. There is general agreement that the BEST criterion of what is a good physical security system in a large public building is

    A. the number of uniformed officers needed to patrol sensitive areas
    B. how successfully the system prevents rather than detects violations
    C. the number of persons caught in the act of committing criminal offenses
    D. how successfully the system succeeds in maintaining good public relations

3. Which one of the following statements most correctly expresses the CHIEF reason why women were originally made eligible for appointment to the position of officer?

    A. Certain tasks in security protection can be performed best by assigning women.
    B. More women than men are available to fill many vacancies in this position.
    C. The government wants more women in law enforcement because of their better attendance records.
    D. Women can no longer be barred from any government jobs because of sex.

4. The MOST BASIC purpose of patrol by officers is to

    A. eliminate as much as possible the opportunity for successful misconduct
    B. investigate criminal complaints and accident cases
    C. give prompt assistance to employees and citizens in distress or requesting their help
    D. take persons into custody who commit criminal offenses against persons and property

5. The highest quality of patrol service is MOST generally obtained by

    A. frequently changing the post assignments of each officer
    B. assigning officers to posts of equal size
    C. assigning problem officers to the least desirable posts
    D. assigning the same officers to the same posts

6. The one of the following requirements which is MOST essential to the successful performance of patrol duty by individual officers is their

    A. ability to communicate effectively with higher-level officers
    B. prompt signalling according to a prescribed schedule to insure post coverages at all times

C. knowledge of post conditions and post hazards
D. willingness to cover large areas during periods of critical manpower shortages

7. Officers on patrol are constantly warned to be on the alert for suspicious persons, actions, and circumstances.
   With this in mind, a senior officer should emphasize the need for them to

   A. be cautious and suspicious when dealing officially with any civilian regardless of the latter's overt actions or the circumstances surrounding his dealings with the police
   B. keep looking for the unusual persons, actions, and circumstances on their posts and pay less attention to the usual
   C. take aggressive police action immediately against any unusual person or condition detected on their posts, regardless of any other circumstances
   D. become thoroughly familiar with the usual on their posts so as to be better able to detect the unusual

8. Of primary importance in the safeguarding of property from theft is a good central lock and key issuance and control system.
   Which one of the following recommendations about maintaining such a control system would be LEAST acceptable?

   A. In selecting locks to be used for the various gates, building, and storage areas, consideration should be given to the amount of security desired.
   B. Master keys should have no markings that will identify them as such and the list of holders of these keys should be frequently reviewed to determine the continuing necessity for the individuals having them.
   C. Whenever keys for outside doors or gates or for other doors which permit access to important buildings and areas are misplaced, the locks should be immediately changed or replaced pending an investigation.
   D. Whenever an employee fails to return a borrowed key at the time specified, a prompt investigation should be made by the security force.

9. In a crowded building, a fire develops in the basement, and smoke enters the crowded rooms on the first floor. Of the following, the BEST action for an officer to take after an alarm is turned in is to

   A. call out a warning that the building is on fire and that everyone should evacuate because of the immediate danger
   B. call all of the officers together for an emergency meeting and discuss a plan of action
   C. immediately call for assistance from the local police station to help in evacuating the crowd
   D. tell everyone that there is a fire in the building next door and that they should move out onto the streets through available exits

10. Which of the following is in a key position to carry out successfully a safety program of an agency? The

    A. building engineer   B. bureau chiefs
    C. immediate supervisors   D. public relations director

11. It is GENERALLY considered that a daily roll call inspection, which checks to see that the officers and their equipment are in good order, is

    A. *desirable,* chiefly because it informs the superior officer what men will have to purchase new uniforms within a month
    B. *desirable,* chiefly because the public forms their impressions of the organization from the appearance of the officers
    C. *undesirable,* chiefly because this kind of daily inspection unnecessarily delays officers in getting to their assigned patrol posts
    D. *undesirable,* chiefly because roll call inspection usually misses individuals reporting to work late

12. A supervising officer in giving instructions to a group of officers on the principles of accident investigation remarked, "A conclusion that appears reasonable will often be changed by exploring a factor of apparently little importance".
    Which one of the following precautions does this statement emphasize as MOST important in any accident investigation?

    A. Every accident clue should be fully investigated.
    B. Accidents should not be too promptly investigated.
    C. Only specially trained officers should investigate accidents.
    D. Conclusions about accident causes are highly unreliable.

13. On a rainy day, a senior officer found that 9 of his 50 officers reported to work. What percentage of his officers was ABSENT?

    A. 18%   B. 80%   C. 82%   D. 90%

14. Officer A and Officer B work at the same post on the same days, but their hours are different. Officer A comes to work at 9:00 A.M. and leaves at 5:00 P.M., with a lunch period between 12:15 P.M. and 1:15 P.M. Officer B comes to work at 10:50 A.M. and works until 6:50 P.M., and he takes an hour for lunch between 3:00 P.M. and 4:00 P.M. What is the total amount of time between 9:00 A.M. and 6:50 P.M. that only ONE officer will be on duty?

    A. 4 hours
    B. 4 hours and 40 minutes
    C. 5 hours
    D. 5 hours and 40 minutes

15. An officer's log recorded the following attendance of 30 officers:

    | Monday | 20 | present; | 10 | absent |
    | Tuesday | 28 | present; | 2 | absent |
    | Wednesday | 30 | present; | 0 | absent |
    | Thursday | 21 | present; | 9 | absent |
    | Friday | 16 | present; | 14 | absent |
    | Saturday | 11 | present; | 19 | absent |
    | Sunday | 14 | present; | 16 | absent |

    On the average, how many men were present on the weekdays (Monday - Friday)?

    A. 21   B. 23   C. 25   D. 27

16. An angry woman is being questioned by an officer when she begins shouting abuses at him.
    The BEST of the following procedures for the officer to follow is to

    A. leave the room until she has cooled off
    B. politely ignore anything she says
    C. place her under arrest by handcuffing her to a fixed object
    D. warn her that he will have to use force to restrain her making remarks

17. Of the following, which is NOT a recommended practice for an officer placing a woman offender under arrest?

    A. Assume that the offender is an innocent and virtuous person and treat her accordingly.
    B. Protect himself from attack by the woman.
    C. Refrain from using excessive physical force on the offender.
    D. Make the public aware that he is not abusing the woman.

Questions 18-21.

DIRECTIONS: Questions 18 through 21 are to be answered SOLELY on the basis of the following passage.

Specific measures for prevention of pilferage will be based on careful analysis of the conditions at each agency. The most practical and effective method to control casual pilferage is the establishment of psychological deterrents.

One of the most common means of discouraging casual pilferage is to search individuals leaving the agency at unannounced times and places. These spot searches may occasionally detect attempts at theft but greater value is realized by bringing to the attention of individuals the fact that they may be apprehended if they do attempt the illegal removal of property.

An aggressive security education program is an effective means of convincing employees that they have much more to lose than they do to gain by engaging in acts of theft. It is important for all employees to realize that pilferage is morally wrong no matter how insignificant the value of the item which is taken. In establishing any deterrent to casual pilferage, security officers must not lose sight of the fact that most employees are honest and disapprove of thievery. Mutual respect between security personnel and other employees of the agency must be maintained if the facility is to be protected from other more dangerous forms of human hazards. Any security measure which infringes on the human rights or dignity of others will jeopardize, rather than enhance, the overall protection of the agency.

18. The $100,000 yearly inventory of an agency revealed that $50 worth of goods had been stolen; the only individuals with access to the stolen materials were the employees. Of the following measures, which would the author of the preceding paragraph MOST likely recommend to a security officer?

    A. Conduct an intensive investigation of all employees to find the culprit.
    B. Make a record of the theft, but take no investigative or disciplinary action against any employee.
    C. Place a tight security check on all future movements of personnel.
    D. Remove the remainder of the material to an area with much greater security.

19. What does the passage imply is the percentage of employees whom a security officer should expect to be honest?

    A. No employee can be expected to be honest all of the time
    B. Just 50%
    C. Less than 50%
    D. More than 50%

20. According to the passage, the security officer would use which of the following methods to minimize theft in buildings with many exits when his staff is very small?

    A. Conduct an inventory of all material and place a guard near that which is most likely to be pilfered.
    B. Inform employees of the consequences of legal prosecution for pilfering.
    C. Close off the unimportant exits and have all his men concentrate on a few exits.
    D. Place a guard at each exit and conduct a casual search of individuals leaving the premises.

21. Of the following, the title BEST suited for this passage is:

    A. Control Measures for Casual Pilfering
    B. Detecting the Potential Pilferer
    C. Financial losses Resulting from Pilfering
    D. The Use of Moral Persuasion in Physical Security

22. Of the following first aid procedures, which will cause the GREATEST harm in treating a fracture?

    A. Control hemorrhages by applying direct pressure
    B. Keep the broken portion from moving about
    C. Reset a protruding bone by pressing it back into place
    D. Treat the suffering person for shock

23. During a snowstorm, a man comes to you complaining of frostbitten hands. PROPER first aid treatment in this case is to

    A. place the hands under hot running water
    B. place the hands in lukewarm water
    C. call a hospital and wait for medical aid
    D. rub the hands in melting snow

24. While on duty, an officer sees a woman apparently in a state of shock. Of the following, which one is NOT a symptom of shock?

    A. Eyes lacking luster
    B. A cold, moist forehead
    C. A shallow, irregular breathing
    D. A strong, throbbing pulse

25. You notice a man entering your building who begins coughing violently, has shortness of breath, and complains of severe chest pains.
    These symptoms are GENERALLY indicative of

    A. a heart attack
    B. a stroke
    C. internal bleeding
    D. an epileptic seizure

26. When an officer is required to record the rolled fingerprint impressions of a prisoner on the standard fingerprint form, the technique recommended by the F.B.I, as MOST likely to result in obtaining clear impressions is to roll

   A. all fingers away from the center of the prisoner's body
   B. all fingers toward the center of the prisoner's body
   C. the thumbs away from and the other fingers toward the center of the prisoner's body
   D. the thumbs toward and the other fingers away from the center of the prisoner's body

27. The principle which underlies the operation and use of a lie detector machine is that

   A. a person who is not telling the truth will be able to give a consistent story
   B. a guilty mind will unconsciously associate ideas in a very indicative manner
   C. the presence of emotional stress in a person will result in certain abnormal physical reactions
   D. many individuals are not afraid to lie

Questions 28-32.

DIRECTIONS: Questions 28 through 32 are based SOLELY on the following diagram and the paragraph preceding this group of questions. The paragraph will be divided into two statements. Statement one (1) consists of information given to the senior officer by an agency director; *this information will detail the specific security objectives the senior officer has to meet.* Statement two (2) gives the resources available to the senior officer.

NOTE: The questions are correctly answered only when all of the agency's objectives have been met and when the officer has used all his resources efficiently (i.e., to their maximum effectiveness) in meeting these objectives. All X's in the diagram indicate possible locations of officers' posts. Each X has a corresponding number which is to be used when referring to that location.

7 (#1)

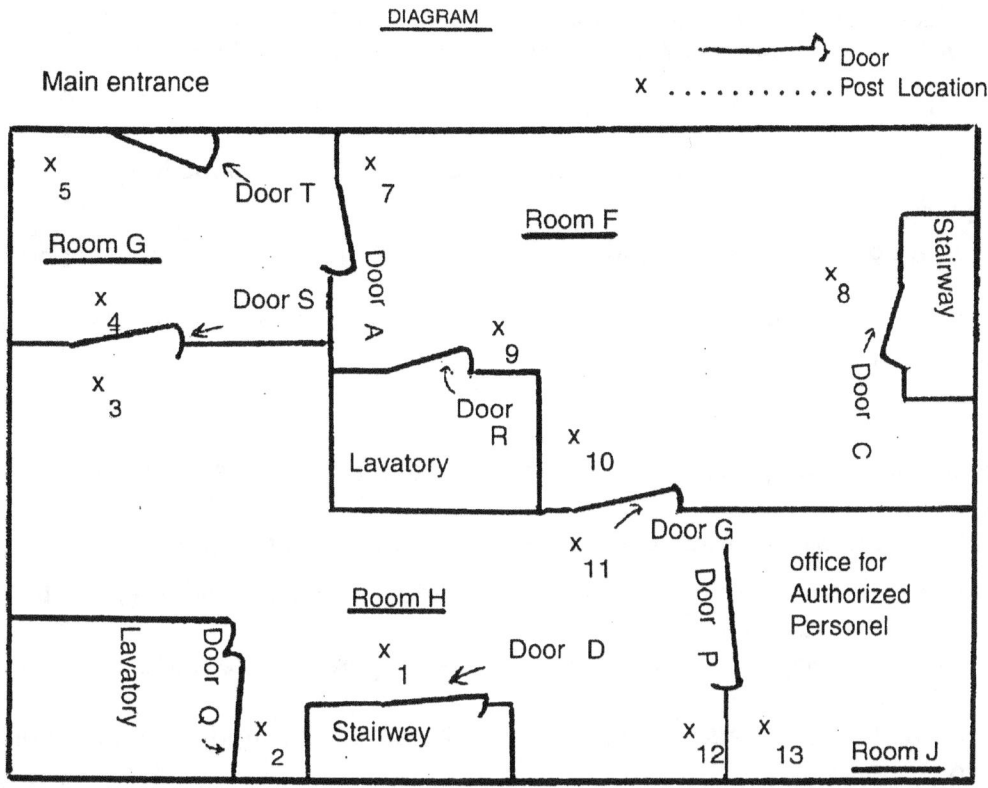

DIAGRAM

PARAGRAPH

PARAGRAPH

STATEMENT 1: Room G will be the public intake room from which persons will be directed to Room F or Room H; under no circumstances are they to enter the wrong room, and they are not to move from Room F to Room H or vice-versa. A minimum of two officers must be in each room frequented by the public at all times, and they are to keep unauthorized individuals from going to the second floor or into restricted areas. All usable entrances or exits must be covered.

STATEMENT 2: The senior officer can lock any door except the main entrance and stairway doors. He has a staff of five officers to carry out these operations.

NOTE: The senior officer is available for guard duty. Room J is an active office.

28. According to the instructions, how many officers should be assigned inside the office for authorized personnel (Room J)?   28. ____

    A. 0   B. 1   C. 2   D. 3

29. In order to keep the public from moving between Room F and Room H, which door(s) can be locked without interfering with normal office operations? Door   29. ____

    A. G   B. P   C. R and Q   D. S

30. When placing officers in Room H, the only way the senior officer can satisfy the agency's objectives and his manpower limitations is by placing men at locations

    A. 1 and 3 B. 1 and 12 C. 3 and 11 D. 11 and 12

31. In accordance with the instructions, the LEAST effective locations to place officers in Room F are locations

    A. 7 and 9 B. 7 and 10 C. 8 and 9 D. 9 and 10

32. In which room is it MOST difficult for each of the officers to see all the movements of the public? Room

    A. G B. F C. H D. J

33. According to its own provisions, the Penal Law of the State has a number of general purposes.
    It would be LEAST accurate to state that one of these general purposes is to

    A. give fair warning of the nature of the conduct forbidden and the penalties authorized upon conviction
    B. define the act or omission and accompanying mental state which constitute each offense
    C. regulate the procedure which governs the arrest, trial and punishment of convicted offenders
    D. insure the public safety by preventing the commission of offenses through the deterrent influence of the sentences authorized upon conviction

34. Officers must be well-informed about the meaning of certain terms in connection with their enforcement duties. Which one of the following statements about such terms would be MOST accurate according to the Penal Law of the State? A(n)

    A. offense is always a crime
    B. offense is always a violation
    C. violation is never a crime
    D. felony is never an offense

35. According to the Penal Law of the State, the one of the following elements which must ALWAYS be present in order to justify the arrest of a person for criminal assault is

    A. the infliction of an actual physical injury
    B. an intent to cause an injury
    C. a threat to inflict a physical injury
    D. the use of some kind of weapon

36. A recent law of the State defines who are police officers and who are peace officers. The official title of this law is: The

    A. Criminal Code of Procedure
    B. Law of Criminal Procedure
    C. Criminal Procedure Law
    D. Code of Criminal Procedure

37. If you are required to appear in court to testify as the complainant in a criminal action, it would be MOST important for you to

    A. confine your answers to the questions asked when you are testifying
    B. help the prosecutor even if some exaggeration in your testimony may be necessary
    C. be as fair as possible to the defendant even if some details have to be omitted from your testimony
    D. avoid contradicting other witnesses testifying against the defendant

38. A senior officer is asked by the television news media to explain to the public what happened on his post during an important incident.
    When speaking with departmental permission in front of the tape recorders and cameras, the senior officer can give the MOST favorable impression of himself and his department by

    A. refusing to answer any questions but remaining calm in front of the cameras
    B. giving a detailed report of the wrong decisions made by his agency for handling the particular incident
    C. presenting the appropriate factual information in a competent way
    D. telling what should have been done during the incident and how such incidents will be handled in the future

39. Of the following suggested guidelines for officers, the one which is LEAST likely to be effective in promoting good manners and courtesy in their daily contacts with the public is:

    A. Treat inquiries by telephone in the same manner as those made in person
    B. Never look into the face of the person to whom you are speaking
    C. Never give misinformation in answer to any inquiry on a matter on which you are uncertain of the facts
    D. Show respect and consideration in both trivial and important contacts with the public

40. Assume you are an officer who has had a record of submitting late weekly reports and that you are given an order by your supervisor which is addressed to all line officers. The order states that weekly reports will be replaced by twice-weekly reports.
    The MOST logical conclusion for you to make, of the following, is:

    A. Fully detailed information was missing from your past reports
    B. Most officers have submitted late reports
    C. The supervisor needs more timely information
    D. The supervisor is attempting to punish you for your past late reports

41. A young man with long hair and "mod" clothing makes a complaint to an officer about the rudeness of another officer.
    If the senior officer is not on the premises, the officer receiving the complaint should

    A. consult with the officer who is being accused to see if the youth's story is true
    B. refer the young man to central headquarters
    C. record the complaint made against his fellow officer and ask the youth to wait until he can locate the senior officer
    D. search for the senior officer and bring him back to the site of the complainant

42. During a demonstration, which area should ALWAYS be kept clear of demonstrators?　42.___

    A. Water fountains　　　　　　　　B. Seating areas
    C. Doorways　　　　　　　　　　　D. Restrooms

43. During demonstrations, an officer's MOST important duty is to　43.___

    A. aid the agency's employees to perform their duties
    B. promptly arrest those who might cause incidents
    C. promptly disperse the crowds of demonstrators
    D. keep the demonstrators from disrupting order

44. Of the following, what is the FIRST action a senior officer should take if a demonstration develops in his area without advance warning?　44.___

    A. Call for additional assistance from the police department
    B. Find the leaders of the demonstrators and discuss their demands
    C. See if the demonstrators intend to break the law
    D. Inform his superiors of the event taking place

45. If a senior officer is informed in the morning that a demonstration will take place during the afternoon at his assigned location, he should assemble his officers to discuss the nature and aspects of this demonstration. Of the following, the subject which it is LEAST important to discuss during this meeting is　45.___

    A. making a good impression if an officer is called before the television cameras for a personal interview
    B. the known facts and causes of the demonstration
    C. the attitude and expected behavior of the demonstrators
    D. the individual responsibilities of the officers during the demonstration

46. A male officer has probable reason to believe that a group of women occupying the ladies' toilet are using illicit drugs.
    The BEST action, of the following, for the officer to take is to　46.___

    A. call for assistance and, with the aid of such assistance, enter the toilet and escort the occupants outside
    B. ignore the situation but recommend that the ladies' toilet be closed temporarily
    C. immediately rush into the ladies' toilet and search the occupants therein
    D. knock on the door of the ladies' toilet and ask their permission to enter so that he will not be accused of trying to molest them

47. Assume that you know that a group of demonstrators will not cooperate with your request to throw handbills in a waste basket instead of on the sidewalk. You ask one of the leaders of the group, who agrees with you, to speak to the demonstrators and ask for their cooperation in this matter.
    Your request of the group leader is　47.___

    A. *desirable,* chiefly because an officer needs civilians to control the public since the officer is usually unfriendly to the views of public groups
    B. *undesirable,* chiefly because an officer should never request a civilian to perform his duties
    C. *desirable,* chiefly because the appeal of an acknowledged leader helps in gaining group cooperation

D. *undesirable,* chiefly because an institutional leader is motivated to maneuver a situation to gain his own personal advantage

48. A vague letter received from a female employee in the agency accuses an officer of improper conduct.
The initial investigative interview by the senior officer assigned to check the accusation should GENERALLY be with the

   A. accused officer
   B. female employee
   C. highest superior about disciplinary action against the officer
   D. immediate supervisor of the female employee

Questions 49-50.

DIRECTIONS: Questions 49 and 50 are to be answered SOLELY on the basis of the information in the following paragraph.

The personal conduct of each member of the Department is the primary factor in promoting desirable police-community relations. Tact, patience, and courtesy shall be strictly observed under all circumstances. A favorable public attitude toward the police must be earned; it is influenced by the personal conduct and attitude of each member of the force, by his personal integrity and courteous manner, by his respect for due process of law, by his devotion to the principles of justice, fairness, and impartiality.

49. According to the preceding paragraph, what is the BEST action an officer can take in dealing with people in a neighborhood?

   A. Assist neighborhood residents by doing favors for them.
   B. Give special attention to the community leaders in order to be able to control them effectively.
   C. Behave in an appropriate manner and give all community members the same just treatment.
   D. Prepare a plan detailing what he, the officer, wants to do for the community and submit it for approval.

50. As used in the paragraph, the word *impartiality* means *most nearly*

   A. observant
   B. unbiased
   C. righteousness
   D. honesty

KEY (CORRECT ANSWERS)

1. B	11. B	21. A	31. D	41. C
2. B	12. A	22. C	32. C	42. C
3. A	13. C	23. B	33. C	43. D
4. A	14. D	24. D	34. C	44. D
5. D	15. B	25. A	35. A	45. A
6. C	16. B	26. D	36. C	46. A
7. D	17. A	27. C	37. A	47. C
8. C	18. B	28. A	38. C	48. B
9. D	19. D	29. A	39. B	49. C
10. C	20. B	30. B	40. C	50. B

TEST 2

DIRECTIONS: Each question or incomplete statement is followed by several suggested answers or completions. Select the one that BEST answers the question or completes the statement. *PRINT THE LETTER OF THE CORRECT ANSWER IN THE SPACE AT THE RIGHT.*

Questions 1-5.

DIRECTIONS: Questions 1 through 5 consist of short paragraphs. Each paragraph contains one word which is INCORRECTLY used because it is NOT in keeping with the meaning of the paragraph. Find the word in each paragraph which is INCORRECTLY used, and then select as the answer the suggested word which should be substituted for the incorrectly used word.

SAMPLE QUESTION

In determining who is to do the work in your unit, you will have to decide just who does what from day to day. One of your lowest responsibilities is to assign work so that everybody gets a fair share and that everyone can do his part well.
    A. new   B. old   C. important   D. performance

EXPLANATION

The word which is NOT in keeping with the meaning of the paragraph is "lowest". This is the INCORRECTLY used word. The suggested word "important" would be in keeping with the meaning of the paragraph and should be substituted for "lowest". Therefore, the CORRECT answer is Choice C.

1. If really good practice in the elimination of preventable injuries is to be achieved and held in any establishment, top management must refuse full and definite responsibility and must apply a good share of its attention to the task.

    A. accept   B. avoidable   C. duties   D. problem

2. Recording the human face for identification is by no means the only service performed by the camera in the field of investigation. When the trial of any issue takes place, a word picture is sought to be distorted to the court of incidents, occurrences, or events which are in dispute.

    A. appeals   B. description
    C. portrayed   D. deranged

3. In the collection of physical evidence, it cannot be emphasized too strongly that a haphazard systematic search at the scene of the crime is vital. Nothing must be overlooked. Often the only leads in a case will come from the results of this search.

    A. important   B. investigation
    C. proof   D. thorough

4. If an investigator has reason to suspect that the witness is mentally stable or a habitual drunkard, he should leave no stone unturned in his investigation to determine if the witness was under the influence of liquor or drugs, or was mentally unbalanced either at the time of the occurrence to which he testified or at the time of the trial.

    A. accused   B. clue   C. deranged   D. question

5. The use of records is a valuable step in crime investigation and is the main reason every department should maintain accurate reports. Crimes are not committed through the use of departmental records alone but from the use of all records, of almost every type, wherever they may be found and whenever they give any incidental information regarding the criminal.

    A. accidental   B. necessary   C. reported   D. solved

Questions 6-8.

DIRECTIONS: Questions 6 through 8 are to be answered SOLELY on the basis of the following passage.

The mass media are an integral part of the daily life of virtually every American. Among these media, the youngest, television, is the most persuasive. Ninety-five percent of American homes have at least one television set, and on the average that set is in use for about 40 hours each week. The central place of television in American life makes this medium the focal point of a growing national concern over the effects of media portrayals of violence on the values, attitudes, and behavior of an ever increasing audience.

In our concern about violence and its causes, it is easy to make television a scapegoat. But we emphasise the fact that there is no simple answer to the problem of violence -- no single explanation of its causes, and no single prescription for its control. It should be remembered that America also experienced high levels of crime and violence in periods before the advent of television.

The problem of balance, taste, and artistic merit in entertaining programs on television are complex. We cannot countenance government censorship of television. Nor would we seek to impose arbitrary limitations on programming which might jeopardize television's ability to deal in dramatic presentations with controversial social issues. Nonetheless, we are deeply troubled by television's constant portrayal of violence, not in any genuine attempt to focus artistic expression on the human condition, but rather in pandering to a public preoccupation with violence that television itself has helped to generate.

6. According to the passage, television uses violence MAINLY

    A. to highlight the reality of everyday existence
    B. to satisfy the audience's hunger for destructive action
    C. to shape the values and attitudes of the public
    D. when it films documentaries concerning human conflict

7. Which one of the following statements is BEST supported by this passage?

    A. Early American history reveals a crime pattern which is not related to television.
    B. Programs should give presentations of social issues and never portray violent acts.
    C. Television has proven that entertainment programs can easily make the balance between taste and artistic merit a simple matter.
    D. Values and behavior should be regulated by governmental censorship.

8. Of the following, which word has the same meaning as countenance as it is used in the above passage?

    A. approve   B. exhibit   C. oppose   D. reject

Questions 9-12.

DIRECTIONS: Questions 9 through 12 are to be answered SOLELY on the basis of the following graph relating to the burglary rate in the city, 2003 to 2008, inclusive.

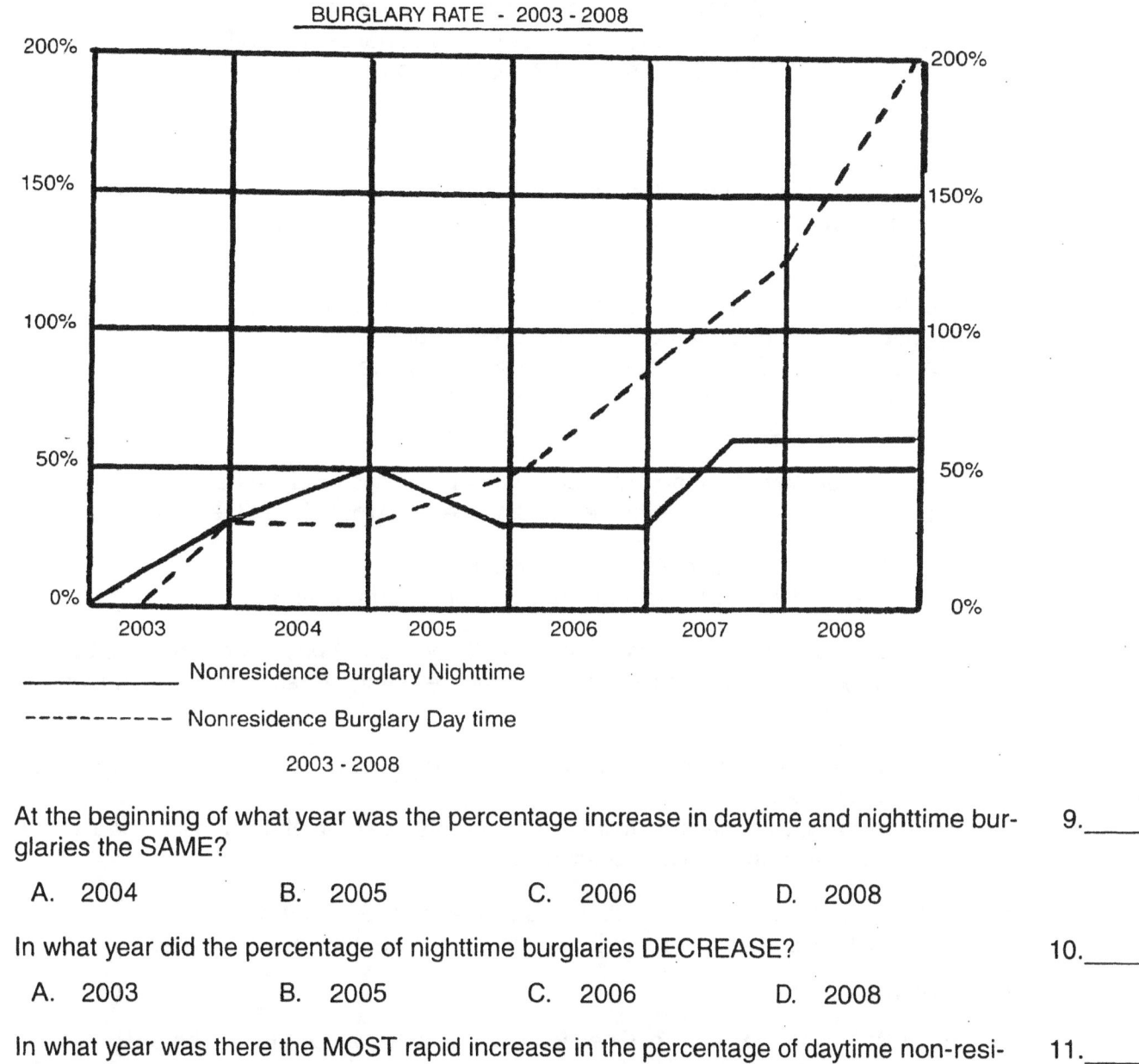

9. At the beginning of what year was the percentage increase in daytime and nighttime burglaries the SAME?

  A. 2004 B. 2005 C. 2006 D. 2008

10. In what year did the percentage of nighttime burglaries DECREASE?

  A. 2003 B. 2005 C. 2006 D. 2008

11. In what year was there the MOST rapid increase in the percentage of daytime non-residence burglaries?

  A. 2004 B. 2006 C. 2007 D. 2008

12. At the end of 2007, the actual number of nighttime burglaries committed

  A. was about 20%
  B. was 40%
  C. was 400
  D. cannot be determined from the information given

Questions 13-17.

DIRECTIONS: Questions 13 through 17 consist of two sentences numbered 1 and 2 taken from police officers' reports. Some of these sentences are correct according to ordinary formal English usage. Other sentences are incorrect because they contain errors in English usage or punctuation. Consider a sentence correct if it contains no errors in English usage or punctuation even if there may be other ways of writing the sentence correctly. Mark your answer to each question in the space at the right as follows:
- A. If only sentence 1 is correct, but not sentence 2
- B. If only sentence 2 is correct, but not sentence 1
- C. If sentences 1 and 2 are both correct
- D. If sentences 1 and 2 are both incorrect

SAMPLE QUESTION
1. The woman claimed that the purse was her's.
2. Everyone of the new officers was assigned to a patrol post.

EXPLANATION

Sentence 1 is INCORRECT because of an error in punctuation. The possessive words, "ours, yours, hers, theirs," do not have the apostrophe (').

Sentence 2 is CORRECT because the subject of the sentence is "Everyone" which is singular and requires the singular verb "was assigned".

Since only sentence 2 is correct, but not sentence 1, the CORRECT answer is B.

13. 1. Either the patrolman or his sergeant are always ready to help the public.
     2. The sergeant asked the patrolman when he would finish the report.

14. 1. The injured man could not hardly talk.
     2. Every officer had ought to hand in their reports on time.

15. 1. Approaching the victim of the assault, two large bruises were noticed by me.
     2. The prisoner was arrested for assault, resisting arrest, and use of a deadly weapon.

16. 1. A copy of the orders, which had been prepared by the captain, was given to each patrolman.
     2. It's always necessary to inform an arrested person of his constitutional rights before asking him any questions.

17. 1. To prevent further bleeding, I applied a tourniquet tothe wound.
     2. John Rano a senior officer was on duty at the time of the accident.

Questions 18-25.

DIRECTIONS: Answer each of Questions 18 through 25 SOLELY on the basis of the statement preceding the questions.

18. The criminal is one whose habits have been erroneously developed or, we should say, developed in anti-social patterns, and therefore the task of dealing with him is not one of punishment, but of treatment.
The basic principle expressed in this statement is BEST illustrated by the

   A. emphasis upon rehabilitation in penal institutions
   B. prevalence of capital punishment for murder
   C. practice of imposing heavy fines for minor violations
   D. legal provision for trial by jury in criminal cases

19. The writ of habeas corpus is one of the great guarantees of personal liberty. Of the following, the BEST justification for this statement is that the writ of habeas corpus is frequently used to

    A. compel the appearance in court of witnesses who are outside the state
    B. obtain the production of books and records at a criminal trial
    C. secure the release of a person improperly held in custody
    D. prevent the use of deception in obtaining testimony of reluctant witnesses

20. Fifteen persons suffered effects of carbon dioxide asphyxiation shortly before noon recently in a seventh-floor pressing shop. The accident occurred in a closed room where six steam presses were in operation. Four men and one woman were overcome.
    Of the following, the MOST probable reason for the fact that so many people were affected simultaneously is that

    A. women evidently show more resistance to the effects of carbon dioxide than men
    B. carbon dioxide is an odorless and colorless gas
    C. carbon dioxide is lighter than air
    D. carbon dioxide works more quickly at higher altitudes

21. Lay the patient on his stomach, one arm extended directly overhead, the other arm bent at the elbow, and with the face turned outward and resting on hand or forearm.
    To the officer who is skilled at administering first aid, these instructions should IMMEDIATELY suggest

    A. application of artificial respiration
    B. treatment for third degree burns of the arm
    C. setting a dislocated shoulder
    D. control of capillary bleeding in the stomach

22. The soda and acid fire extinguisher is the hand extinguisher most commonly used by officers. The main body of the cylinder is filled with a mixture of water and bicarbonate of soda. In a separate interior compartment, at the top, is a small bottle of sulphuric acid. When the extinguisher is inverted, the acid spills into the solution below and starts a chemical reaction. The carbon dioxide thereby generated forces the solution from the extinguisher.
    The officer who understands the operation of this fire extinguisher should know that it is LEAST likely to operate properly

    A. in basements or cellars
    B. in extremely cold weather
    C. when the reaction is of a chemical nature
    D. when the bicarbonate of soda is in solution

23. Suppose that, at a training lecture, you are told that many of the men in our penal institutions today are second and third offenders.
    Of the following, the MOST valid inference you can make SOLELY on the basis of this statement is that

    A. second offenders are not easily apprehended
    B. patterns of human behavior are not easily changed
    C. modern laws are not sufficiently flexible
    D. laws do not breed crimes

24. In all societies of our level of culture, acts are committed which arouse censure severe enough to take the form of punishment by the government. Such acts are crimes, not because of their inherent nature, but because of their ability to arouse resentment and to stimulate repressive measures.
Of the following, the MOST valid inference which can be drawn from this statement is that

   A. society unjustly punishes acts which are inherently criminal
   B. many acts are not crimes but are punished by society because such acts threaten the lives of innocent people
   C. only modern society has a level of culture
   D. societies sometimes disagree as to what acts are crimes

25. Crime cannot be measured directly. Its amount must be inferred from the frequency of some occurrence connected with it; for example, crimes brought to the attention of the police, persons arrested, prosecutions, convictions, and other dispositions, such as probation or commitment. Each of these may be used as an index of the amount of crime.
SOLELY on the basis of the foregoing statement, it is MOST correct to state that

   A. the incidence of crime cannot be estimated with any accuracy
   B. the number of commitments is usually greater than the number of probationary sentences
   C. the amount of crime is ordinarily directly correlated with the number of persons arrested
   D. a joint consideration of crimes brought to the attention of the police and the number of prosecutions undertaken gives little indication of the amount of crime in a locality

KEY (CORRECT ANSWERS)

1. B
2. A
3. D
4. C
5. D

6. B
7. A
8. A
9. A
10. B

11. D
12. D
13. D
14. D
15. B

16. C
17. A
18. A
19. C
20. B

21. A
22. B
23. B
24. D
25. C

EXAMINATION SECTION
TEST 1

DIRECTIONS: Each question or incomplete statement is followed by several suggested answers or completions. Select the one that BEST answers the question or completes the statement. *PRINT THE LETTER OF THE CORRECT ANSWER IN THE SPACE AT THE RIGHT.*

Questions 1-4.

DIRECTIONS: Questions 1 through 4 are based on the picture entitled *Contents of a Woman's Handbag.* Assume that all of the contents are shown in the picture.

<u>CONTENTS OF A WOMAN'S HANDBAG</u>

1. Where does Gladys Constantine live?

    A. Chalmers Street in Manhattan
    B. Summer Street in Manhattan
    C. Summer Street in Brooklyn
    D. Chalmers Street in Brooklyn

2. How many keys were in the handbag?

    A. 2   B. 3   C. 4   D. 5

3. How much money was in the handbag? _____ dollar(s).

    A. Exactly five
    B. More than five
    C. Exactly ten
    D. Less than one

4. The sales slip found in the handbag shows the purchase of which of the following?

    A. The handbag
    B. Lipstick
    C. Tissues
    D. Prescription medicine

Questions 5-8.

DIRECTIONS: Questions 5 through 8 are based on the floor plan below.

FLOOR PLAN

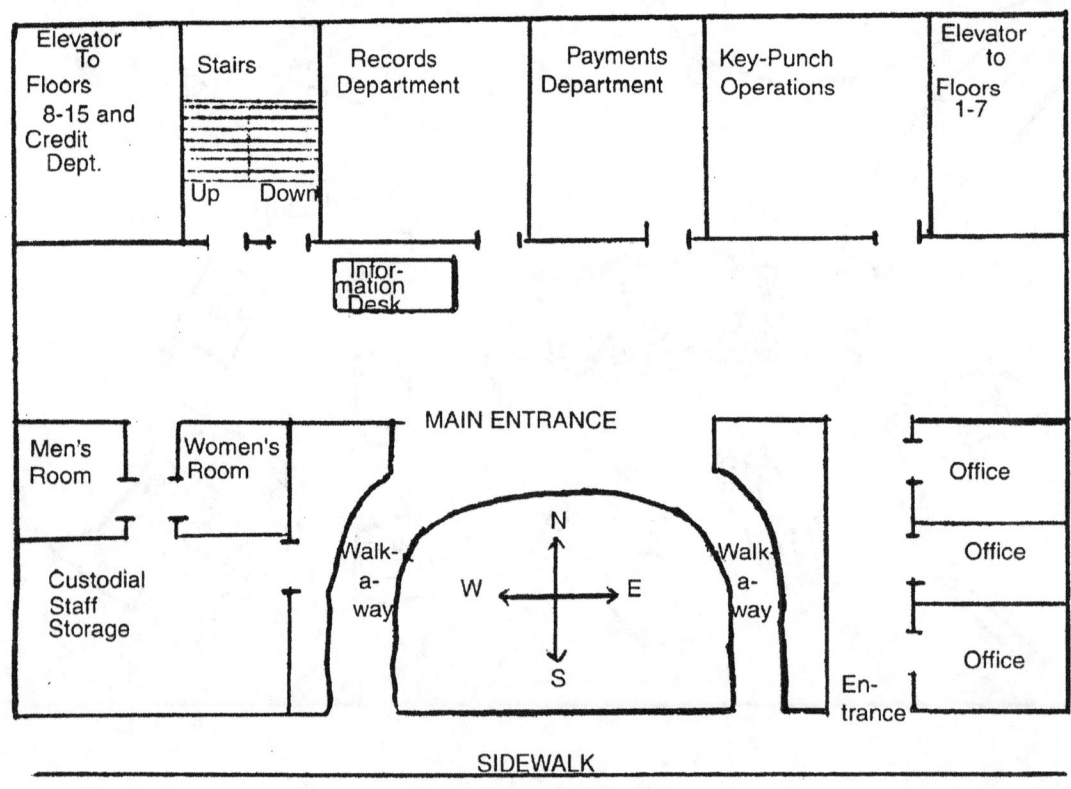

5. A special officer (security officer) on duty at the main entrance must be aware of other outside entrances to his area of the building. These unguarded entrances are usually kept locked, but they are important in case of fire or other emergency.
Besides the main entrance, how many OTHER entrances shown on the floor plan directly face Forty-ninth Street?
_____ other entrances.

   A. No   B. One   C. Two   D. Three

6. A person who arrives at the main entrance and asks to be directed to the Credit Department SHOULD be told to

   A. take the elevator on the left
   B. take the elevator on the right
   C. go to a different entrance
   D. go up the stairs on the left

7. On the east side of the entrance can be found

   A. a storage room   B. offices
   C. toilets   D. stairs

8. The space DIRECTLY BEHIND the Information Desk in the floor plan is occupied by

   A. up and down stairs   B. key punch operations
   C. toilets   D. the records department

Questions 9-12.

DIRECTIONS: Answer Questions 9 to 12 on the basis of the information given in the passage below.

The public often believes that the main job of a uniformed officer is to enforce laws by simply arresting people. In reality, however, many of the situations that an officer deals with do not call for the use of his arrest power. In the first place, an officer spends much of his time preventing crimes from happening, by spotting potential violations or suspicious behavior and taking action to prevent illegal acts. In the second place, many of the situations in which officers are called on for assistance involve elements like personal arguments, husband-wife quarrels, noisy juveniles, or mentally disturbed persons. The majority of these problems do not result in arrests and convictions, and often they do not even involve illegal behavior. In the third place, even in situations where there seems to be good reason to make an arrest, an officer may have to exercise very good judgment. There are times when making an arrest too soon could touch off a riot, or could result in the detention of a minor offender while major offenders escaped, or could cut short the gathering of necessary on-the-scene evidence.

9. The above passage IMPLIES that most citizens

   A. will start to riot if they see an arrest being made
   B. appreciate the work that law enforcement officers do
   C. do not realize that making arrests is only a small part of law enforcement
   D. never call for assistance unless they are involved in a personal argument or a husband-wife quarrel

10. According to the passage, one way in which law enforcement officers can prevent crimes from happening is by

   A. arresting suspicious characters
   B. letting minor offenders go free
   C. taking action on potential violations
   D. refusing to get involved in husband-wife fights

11. According to the passage, which of the following statements is NOT true of situations involving mentally disturbed persons?

   A. It is a waste of time to call on law enforcement officers for assistance in such situations.
   B. Such situations may not involve illegal behavior
   C. Such situations often do not result in arrests.
   D. Citizens often turn to law enforcement officers for help in such situations.

12. The last sentence in the passage mentions *detention of minor offenders.*
    Of the following, which BEST explains the meaning of the word *detention* as used here?

   A. Sentencing someone
   B. Indicting someone
   C. Calling someone before a grand jury
   D. Arresting someone

Questions 13-28.

   DIRECTIONS: In answering Questions 13 through 28, assume that *you* means a special officer (security officer) on duty. Your basic responsibilities are safeguarding people and property and maintaining order in the area to which you are assigned. You are in uniform, and you are not armed. You keep in touch with your supervisory station either by telephone or by a two-way radio (walkie-talkie).

13. It is a general rule that if the security alarm goes off showing that someone has made an unlawful entrance into a building, no officer responsible for security shall proceed to investigate alone. Each officer must be accompanied by at least one other officer.
    Of the following, which is the MOST probable reason for this rule?

   A. It is dangerous for an officer to investigate such a situation alone.
   B. The intruder might try to bribe an officer to let him go.
   C. One officer may be inexperienced and needs an experienced partner.
   D. Two officers are better than one officer in writing a report of the investigation.

14. You are on weekend duty on the main floor of a public building. The building is closed to the public on weekends, but some employees are sometimes asked to work weekends. You have been instructed to use cautious good judgment in opening the door for such persons.
    Of the following, which one MOST clearly shows the poorest judgment?

A. Admitting an employee who is personally known to you without asking to see any identification except the permit slip signed by the employee's supervisor
B. Refusing to admit someone whom you do not recognize but who claims left his identification at home
C. Admitting to the building only those who can give a detailed description of their weekend work duties
D. Leaving the entrance door locked for a while to make regulation security checks of other areas in the building with the result that no one can either enter or leave during these periods

15. You are on duty at a public building. An office employee tells you that she left her purse in her desk when she went out to lunch, and she has just discovered that it is gone. She has been back from lunch for half an hour and has not left her desk during this period. What should you do FIRST?

    A. Warn all security personnel to stop any suspicious-looking person who is seen with a purse
    B. Ask for a description of the purse
    C. Call the Lost and Found and ask if a purse has been turned in
    D. Obtain statements from any employees who were in the office during the lunch hour

16. You are patrolling your assigned area in a public building. You hear a sudden crash and the sound of running footsteps. You investigate and find that someone has forced open a locked entrance to the building. What is the FIRST thing you should do?

    A. Close the door and try to fix the lock so that no one else can get in
    B. Use your two-way radio to report the emergency and summon help
    C. Chase after the person whose running footsteps you heard
    D. Go immediately to your base office and make out a brief written report

17. You and another special officer (security officer) are on duty in the main waiting area at a welfare center. A caseworker calls both of you over and whispers that one of the clients, Richard Roe, may be carrying a gun. Of the following, what is the BEST action for both of you to take?

    A. You should approach the man, one on each side, and one of you should say loudly and clearly, "Richard Roe, you are under arrest."
    B. Both of you should ask the man to go with you to a private room, and then find out if he is carrying a gun
    C. Both of you should grab him, handcuff him, and take him to the nearest precinct station house
    D. Both of you should watch him carefully but not do anything unless he actually pulls a gun

18. You are on duty at a welfare center. You are told that a caseworker is being threatened by a man with a knife. You go immediately to the scene, and you find the caseworker lying on the floor with blood spurting from a wound in his arm. You do not know who the attacker is. What should you do FIRST?

    A. Ask the caseworker for a description of the attacker so that you can set out in pursuit and try to catch him
    B. Take down the names and addresses of any witnesses to the incident

C. Give first aid to the caseworker, if you can, and immediately call for an ambulance
D. Search the people standing around in the room for the knife

19. As a special officer (security officer), you have been patrolling a special section of a hospital building for a week. Smoking is not allowed in this section because the oxygen tanks in use here could easily explode. However, you have observed that some employees sneak into the linen-supply room in this section in order to smoke without anybody seeing them.
Of the following, which is the BEST way for you to deal with this situation?

    A. Whenever you catch anyone smoking, call his supervisor immediately
    B. Request the Building Superintendent to put a padlock on the door of the linen-supply room
    C. Ignore the smoking because you do not want to get a reputation for interfering in the private affairs of other employees
    D. Report the situation to your supervisor and follow his instructions

19._____

20. You are on duty at a hospital. You have been assigned to guard the main door, and you are responsible for remaining at your post until relieved. On one of the wards for which you are not responsible, there is a patient who was wounded in a street fight. This patient is under arrest for killing another man in this fight, and he is supposed to be under round-the-clock police guard. A nurse tells you that one of the police officers assigned to guard the patient has suddenly taken ill and has to periodically leave his post to go to the washroom. The nurse is worried because she thinks the patient might try to escape.
Of the following, which is the BEST action for you to take?

    A. Tell the nurse to call you whenever the police officer leaves his post so that you can keep an eye on the patient while the officer is gone
    B. Assume that the police officer probably knows his job, and that there is no reason for you to worry
    C. Alert your supervisor to the nurse's report
    D. Warn the police officer that the nurse has been talking about him

20._____

21. You are on night duty at a hospital where you are responsible for patrolling a large section of the main building. Your supervisor tells you that there have been several nighttime thefts from a supply room in your section and asks you to be especially alert for suspicious activity near this supply room.
Of the following, which is the MOST reasonable way to carry out your supervisor's direction?

    A. Check the supply room regularly at half-hour intervals
    B. Make frequent checks of the supply room at irregular intervals
    C. Station yourself by the door of the supply room and stay at this post all night
    D. Find a hidden spot from which you can watch the supply room and stay there all night

21._____

22. You are on duty at a vehicle entrance to a hospital. Parking space on the hospital grounds is strictly limited, and no one is ever allowed to park there unless they have an official parking permit. You have just stopped a driver who does not have a parking permit, but he explains that
he is a doctor and he has a patient in the hospital. What should you do?

22._____

A. Let him park since he has explained that he is a doctor
   B. Ask in a friendly way, *"Can I check your identification?"*
   C. Call the Information Desk to make sure there is such a patient in the hospital
   D. Tell the driver politely but firmly that he will have to park somewhere else

23. You are on duty at a public building. A man was just mugged on a stairway. The mugger took the man's wallet and started to run down the stairs but tripped and fell. Now the mugger is lying unconscious at the bottom of the stairs and bleeding from the mouth.
The FIRST thing you should do is to

   A. search him to see if he is carrying any other stolen property
   B. pick him up and carry him away from the stairs
   C. try and revive him for questioning
   D. put in a call for an ambulance and police assistance

24. After someone breaks into an employee's locker at a public building, you interview the employee to determine what is missing from the locker. The employee becomes hysterical and asks why you are *wasting time with all these questions* instead of going after the thief.
The MOST reasonable thing for you to do is

   A. tell the employee that it is very important to have an accurate description of the missing articles
   B. quietly tell the employee to calm down and stop interfering with your work
   C. explain to the employee that you are only doing what you were told to do and that you don't make the rules
   D. assure the employee that there are a lot of people working on the case and that someone else is probably arresting the thief right now

25. You are on duty at a public building. An employee reports that a man has just held her up and taken her money. The employee says that the man was about 25 years old, with short blond hair and a pale complexion and was wearing blue jeans.
Of the following additional facts, which one would probably be MOST valuable to officers searching the building for the suspect?

   A. The man was wearing dark glasses.
   B. He had on a green jacket.
   C. He was about 5 feet 8 inches tall.
   D. His hands and fingernails were very dirty.

26. When the fire alarm goes off, it is your job as a special officer (security officer) to see that all employees leave the building quickly by the correct exits. A fire alarm has just sounded, and you are checking the offices on one of the floors. A supervisor in one office tells you, *"This is probably just another fire drill. I've sent my office staff out, but I don't want to stop my own work."*
What should you do?

   A. Insist politely but firmly that the supervisor must obey the fire rules.
   B. Tell the supervisor that it is all right this time but that the rules must be followed in the future.
   C. Tell the supervisor that he is under arrest.
   D. Allow the supervisor to do as he sees fit since he is in charge of his own office.

27. You are on duty on the main floor of a public building. You have been informed that a briefcase has just been stolen from an office on the tenth floor. You see a man getting off the elevator with a briefcase that matches the description of the one that was stolen. What is the FIRST action you should take?

    A. Arrest the man and take him to the nearest public station
    B. Stop the man and say politely that you want to take a look at the briefcase
    C. Take the briefcase from the man and tell him that he cannot have it back unless he can prove that it is his
    D. Do not stop the man but note down his description and the exact time he got off the elevator

28. You are on duty at a welfare center. You have been told that two clients are arguing with a caseworker and making loud threats. You go to the scene, but the caseworker tells you that everything is now under control. The two clients, who are both mean-looking characters, are still there but seem to be acting normally.
What SHOULD you do?

    A. Apologize for having made a mistake and go away.
    B. Arrest the two men for having caused a disturbance.
    C. Insist on standing by until the interview is over, then escort the two men from the building.
    D. Leave the immediate scene but watch for any further developments.

29. You are on duty at a welfare center. A client comes up to you and says that two men just threatened him with a knife and made him give them his money. The client has alcohol on his breath and he is shabbily dressed. He points out the two men he says took the money.
Of the following, which is the BEST action to take?

    A. Arrest the two men on the client's complaint.
    B. Ignore the client's complaint since he doesn't look as if he could have had any money.
    C. Suggest to the client that he may be imagining things.
    D. Investigate and find out what happened.

Questions 30-35.

DIRECTIONS: Answer Questions 30 through 35 on the basis of the information given in the passage below. Assume that all questions refer to the same state described in the passage.

The courts and the police consider an "offense" as any conduct that is punishable by a fine or imprisonment. Such offenses include many kinds of acts - from behavior that is merely annoying, like throwing a noisy party that keeps everyone awake, all the way up to violent acts like murder. The law classifies offenses according to the penalties that are provided for them. In one state, minor offenses are called "violations." A violation is punishable by a fine of not more than $250 or imprisonment of not more than. 15 days, or both. The annoying behavior mentioned above is an example of a violation. More serious offenses are classified as "crimes." Crimes are classified by the kind of penalty that is provided. A "misdemeanor" is a crime that is punishable by a fine of not more than $1,000 or by imprisonment of not more than one year, or both. Examples of misdemeanors include stealing something with a value of $100 or less, turning in a false alarm, or illegally possessing less than 1/8 of an ounce of a dangerous drug. A "felony" is a criminal offense punishable by imprisonment of more than one year. Murder is clearly a felony.

30. According to the above passage, any act that is punishable by imprisonment or by a fine is called a(n)

    A. offense   B. violation   C. crime   D. felony

31. According to the above passage, which of the following is classified as a crime?

    A. Offense punishable by 15 days imprisonment
    B. Minor offense
    C. Violation
    D. Misdemeanor

32. According to the above passage, if a person guilty of burglary can receive a prison sentence of 7 years or more, burglary would be classified as a

    A. violation   B. misdemeanor
    C. felony   D. violent act

33. According to the above passage, two offenses that would BOTH be classified as misdemeanors are

    A. making unreasonable noise and stealing a $90 bicycle
    B. stealing a $75 radio and possessing 1/16 of an ounce of heroin
    C. holding up a bank and possessing 1/4 of a pound of marijuana
    D. falsely reporting a fire and illegally double-parking

34. The above passage says that offenses are classified according to the penalties provided for them.
    On the basis of clues in the passage, who probably decides what the maximum penalties should be for the different kinds of offenses?

    A. The State lawmakers   B. The City police
    C. The Mayor   D. Officials in Washington, B.C.

35. Of the following, which BEST describes the subject matter of the passage?

    A. How society deals with criminals
    B. How offenses are classified
    C. Three types of criminal behavior
    D. The police approach to offenders

10 (#1)

KEY (CORRECT ANSWERS)

1.	C		16.	B
2.	C		17.	B
3.	B		18.	C
4.	D		19.	D
5.	B		20.	C
6.	A		21.	B
7.	B		22.	D
8.	D		23.	D
9.	C		24.	A
10.	C		25.	C
11.	A		26.	A
12.	D		27.	B
13.	A		28.	D
14.	C		29.	D
15.	B		30.	A

31. D
32. C
33. B
34. A
35. B

TEST 2

DIRECTIONS: Each question or incomplete statement is followed by several suggested answers or completions. Select the one that BEST answers the question or completes the statement. *PRINT THE LETTER OF THE CORRECT ANSWER IN THE SPACE AT THE RIGHT.*

Questions 1-5.

DIRECTIONS: Questions 1 through 5 are based on the drawing below showing a view of a waiting area in a public building.

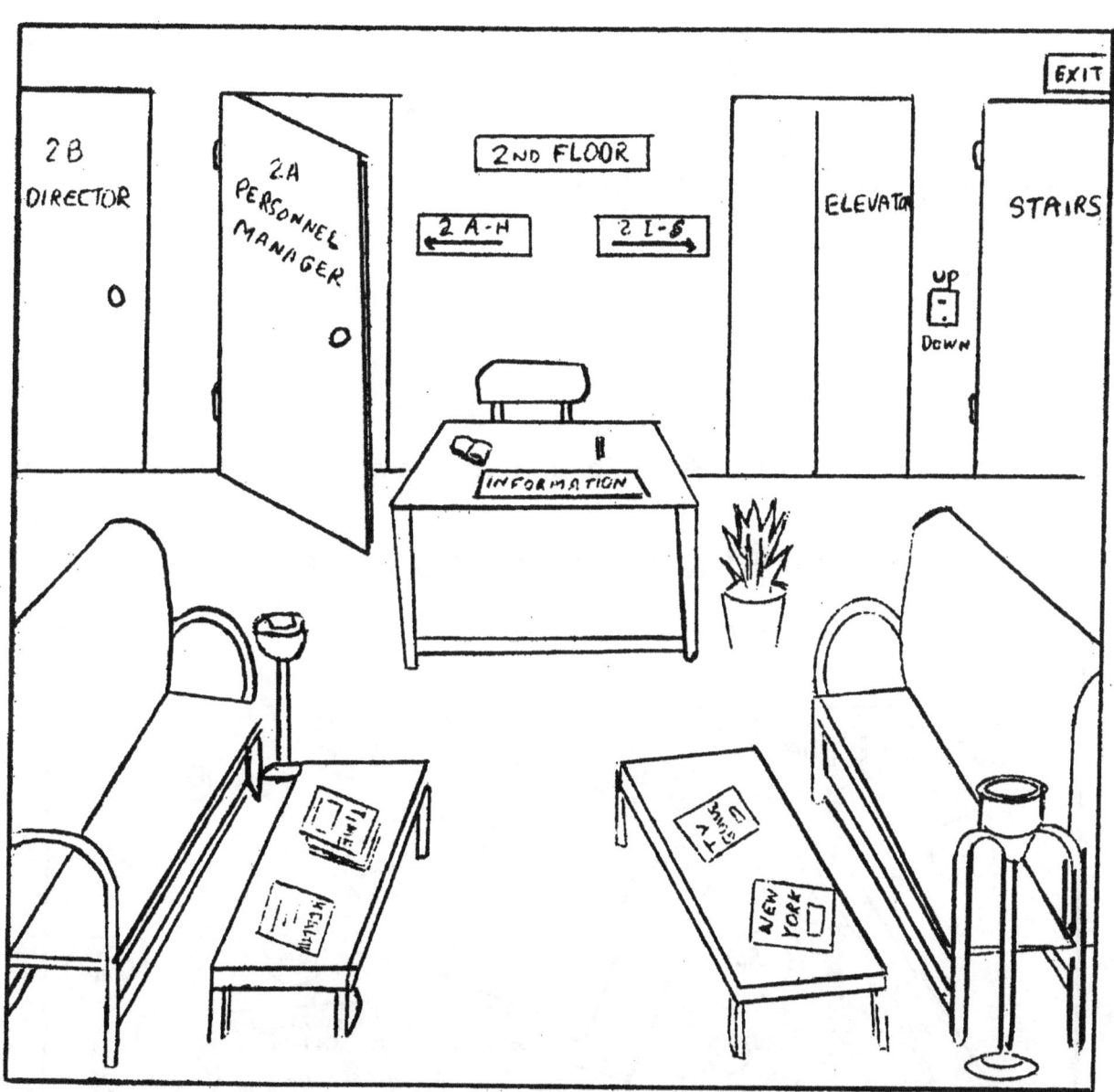

1. A desk is shown in the drawing. Which of the following is on the desk? A(n) 1.____

    A. plant   B. telephone
    C. In-Out file   D. *Information* sign

2. On which floor is the waiting area?

   A. Basement B. Main floor
   C. Second floor D. Third floor

3. The door IMMEDIATELY TO THE RIGHT of the desk is a(n)

   A. door to the Personnel Office
   B. elevator door
   C. door to another corridor
   D. door to the stairs

4. Among the magazines on the tables in the waiting area are

   A. TIME and NEWSWEEK
   B. READER'S DIGEST and T.V. GUIDE
   C. NEW YORK and READER'S DIGEST
   D. TIME and T.V. GUIDE

5. One door is partly open. This is the door to

   A. the Director's office
   B. the Personnel Manager's office
   C. the stairs
   D. an unmarked office

Questions 6-9.

DIRECTIONS: Questions 6 through 9 are based on the drawing below showing the contents of a male suspect's pockets.

CONTENTS OF A MALE SUSPECT'S POCKETS

6. The suspect had a slip in his pockets showing an appointment at an out-patient clinic on   6._____

   A. February 9, 2013   B. September 2, 2013
   C. February 19, 2013   D. September 12, 2013

7. The MP3 player that was found on the suspect was made by   7._____

   A. RCA   B. GE   C. Sony   D. Zenith

8. The coins found in the suspect's pockets have a TOTAL value of   8._____

   A. 56¢   B. 77¢   C. $1.05   D. $1.26

9. All except one of the following were found in the suspect's pockets.   9._____
   Which was NOT found? A

   A. ticket stub   B. comb
   C. subway fare   D. pen

Questions 10-18

DIRECTIONS: In answering Questions 10 through 18, assume that *you* means a special officer (security officer) on duty. Your basic responsibilities are safeguarding people and property and maintaining order in the area to which you are assigned. You are in uniform, and you are not armed. You keep in touch with your supervisory station either by telephone or by a two-way radio (a walkie-talkie).

10. You are on duty at a center run by the Department of Social Services. Two teenaged   10._____
    boys are on their way out of the center. As they go past you, they look at you and laugh, and one makes a remark to you in Spanish. You do not understand Spanish, but you suspect it was a nasty remark.
    What SHOULD you do?

    A. Give the boys a lecture about showing respect for a uniform.
    B. Tell the boys that they had better stay away from the center from now on.
    C. Call for an interpreter and insist that the boy repeat the remark to the interpreter.
    D. Let the boys go on their way since they have done nothing requiring your intervention.

11. You are on duty at a shelter run by the Department of Social Services. You know that   11._____
    many of the shelter clients have drinking problems, drug problems, or mental health problems. You get a call for assistance from a caseworker who says a fight has broken out. When you arrive on the scene, you see that about a dozen clients are engaged in a free-for-all and that two or three of them have pulled knives.
    The BEST course of action is to

    A. call for additional assistance and order all bystanders away from the area
    B. jump into the center of the fighting group and try to separate the fighters
    C. pick up a heavy object and start swinging at anybody who has a knife
    D. try to find out what clients started the fight and place them under arrest

12. You have been assigned to duty at a children's shelter run by the Department of Social Services. The children range in age from 6 to 15, and many of them are at the shelter because they have no homes to go to.
    Of the following, which is the BEST attitude for you to take in dealing with these youngsters?

    A. Assume that they admire and respect anyone in uniform and that they will not usually give you much trouble
    B. Assume that they fear and distrust anyone in uniform and that they are going to give you a hard time unless you act tough
    C. Expect that many of them are going to become juvenile delinquents because of their bad backgrounds and that you should be suspicious of everything they do
    D. Expect that many of them may be emotionally upset and that you should be alert for unusual behavior

13. You are on duty outside the emergency room of a hospital. You notice that an old man has been sitting on a bench outside the room for a long time. He arrived alone, and he has not spoken to anyone at all.
    What SHOULD you do?

    A. Pay no attention to him since he is not bothering anyone.
    B. Tell him to leave since he does not seem to have any business there.
    C. Ask him if you can help him in any way.
    D. Do not speak to him, but keep an eye on him.

14. You are patrolling a section of a public building. An elderly woman carrying a heavy shopping bag asks you if you would watch the shopping bag for her while she keeps an appointment in the building.
    What SHOULD you do?

    A. Watch the shopping bag for her since her appointment probably will not take long.
    B. Refuse her request, explaining that your duties keep you on the move.
    C. Agree to her request just to be polite, but then continue your patrol after the woman is out of sight.
    D. Find a bystander who will agree to watch the shopping bag for her.

15. You are on duty at a public building. It is nearly 6:00 P.M., and most employees have left for the day.
    You see two well-dressed men carrying an office calculating machine out of the building. You SHOULD

    A. stop them and ask for an explanation
    B. follow them to see where they are going
    C. order them to put down the machine and leave the building immediately
    D. take no action since they do not look like burglars

16. You are on duty patrolling a public building. You have just tripped on the stairs and turned your ankle. The ankle hurts and is starting to swell.
    What is the BEST thing to do?

A. Take a taxi to a hospital emergency room, and from there have a hospital employee call your supervisor to explain the situation.
B. First try soaking your foot in cold water for half an hour, then go off duty if you really cannot walk at all.
C. Report the situation to your supervisor, explaining that you need prompt medical attention for your ankle.
D. Find a place where you can sit until you are due to go off duty, then have a doctor look at your ankle.

17. One of your duties as a special officer (security officer) on night patrol in a public building is to check the washrooms to see that the taps are turned off and that there are no plumbing leaks.
Of the following possible reasons for this inspection, which is probably the MOST important reason?

   A. If the floor gets wet, someone might slip and fall the next morning.
   B. A running water tap might be a sign that there is an intruder in the building.
   C. A washroom flood could leak through the ceilings and walls below and cause a lot of damage.
   D. Leaks must be reported quickly so that repairs can be scheduled as soon as possible.

17.____

18. You are on duty at a public building. A department supervisor tells you that someone has left a suspicious-looking package in the hallway on his floor. You investigate, and you hear ticking in the parcel. You think it could be a bomb.
The FIRST thing you should do is to

   A. rapidly question employees on this floor to get a description of the person who left the package
   B. write down the description of the package and the name of the department supervisor
   C. notify your security headquarters that there may be a bomb in the building and that all personnel should be evacuated
   D. pick up the package carefully and remove it from the building as quickly as you can

18.____

Questions 19-22.

DIRECTIONS: Answer Questions 19 through 22 on the basis of the Fact Situation and the Report of Arrest form below. Questions 19 through 22 ask how the report form should be filled in based on the information given in the Fact Situation.

FACT SITUATION

Jesse Stein is a special officer (security officer) who is assigned to a welfare center at 435 East Smythe Street, Brooklyn. He was on duty there Thursday morning, February 1. At 10:30 A.M., a client named Jo Ann Jones, 40 years old, arrived with her ten-year-old son, Peter. Another client, Mary Alice Wiell, 45 years old, immediately began to insult Mrs. Jones. When Mrs. Jones told her to "go away," Mrs. Wiell pulled out a long knife. The special officer (security officer) intervened and requested Mrs. Wiell to drop the knife. She would not, and he had to use necessary force to disarm her. He arrested her on charges of disorderly conduct, harassment, and possession of a dangerous weapon. Mrs. Wiell lives at 118 Heally Street,

Brooklyn, Apartment 4F, and she is unemployed. The reason for her aggressive behavior is not known.

```
REPORT OF ARREST
01) _____      (08) _____
    (Prisoner's surname) (first) (initial)        (Precinct)
(02) _____      (09) _____
     (Address)                                   (Date of arrest)
                                                 (Month, Day)
(03) _____ (04) _____ (05) _____       (10) _____
    (Date of birth)  (Age)   (Sex)                (Time of arrest)
(06) _____ (07) _____         (11) _____
    (Occupation)    (Where employed)              (Place of arrest)

(12) _____
     (Specific offenses)

(13) _____      (14) _____
     (Arresting Officer)                         (Officer's No.)
```

19. What entry should be made in Blank 01?

    A. Jo Ann Jones B. Jones, Jo Ann
    C. Mary Wiell   D. Wiell, Mary A.

20. Which of the following should be entered in Blank 04?

    A. 40 B. 40's C. 45 D. Middle-aged

21. Which of the following should be entered in Blank 09?

    A. Wednesday, February 1, 10:30 A.M.
    B. February 1
    C. Thursday morning, February 2
    D. Morning, February 4

22. Of the following, which would be the BEST entry to make in Blank 11?

    A. Really Street Welfare Center
    B. Brooklyn
    C. 435 E. Smythe St., Brooklyn
    D. 118 Heally St., Apt. 4F

Questions 23-27.

DIRECTIONS: Answer Questions 23 through 27 on the basis of the information given in the Report of Loss or Theft that appears below.

```
| REPORT OF LOSS OR THEFT              Date: 12/4     Time: 9:15 a.m. |
| Complaint made by: Richard Aldridge          ☐ Owner                |
|                    306 S. Walter St.          ☒ Other - explain:    |
|                                               Head of Accty. Dept.  |
```

Type of property: Computer   Value: $550.00
Description: Dell
Location: 768 N Margin Ave., Accounting Dept., 3rd Floor
Time: Overnight 12/3 - 12/4
Circumstances: Mr. Aldridge reports he arrived at work 8:45 A.M., found office door open and machine missing. Nothing else reported missing. I investigated and found signs of forced entry: door lock was broken.   Signature of Reporting Officer: B.L. Ramirez

Notify:
☐ Building & Grounds Office, 768 N. Margin Ave.
☐ Lost Property Office, 110 Brand Ave.
☒ Security Office, 703 N. Wide Street

23. The person who made this complaint is

    A. a secretary   B. a security officer
    C. Richard Aldridge   D. B.L. Ramirez

24. The report concerns a computer that has been

    A. lost   B. damaged   C. stolen   D. sold

25. The person who took the computer probably entered the office through

    A. a door   B. a window   C. the roof   D. the basement

26. When did the head of the Accounting Department first notice that the computer was missing?

    A. December 4 at 9:15 A.M.   B. December 4 at 8:45 A.M.
    C. The night of December 3   D. The night of December 4

27. The event described in the report took place at

    A. 306 South Walter Street   B. 768 North Margin Avenue
    C. 110 Brand Avenue   D. 703 North Wide Street

Questions 28-33.

DIRECTIONS: Answer Questions 28 through 33 on the basis of the instructions, the code, and the sample question given below.

Assume that a special officer (security officer) at a certain location is equipped with a two-way radio to keep him in constant touch with his security headquarters. Radio messages and replies are given in code form, as follows:

Radio Code for Situation	J	P	M	F	B
Radio Code for Action to be Taken	o	r	a	z	q
Radio Response for Action Being Taken	1	2	3	4	5

Assume that each of the above capital letters is the radio code for a particular type of situation, that the small letter below each capital letter is the radio code for the action a special officer (security officer) is directed to take, and that the number directly below each small letter is the radio response a special officer (security officer) should make to indicate what action was actually taken.

In each of the following Questions 28 through 33, the code letter for the action directed (Column 2) and the code number for the action taken (Column 3) should correspond to the capital letters in Column 1.

If only Column 2 is different from Column 1, mark your answer A.

If only Column 3 is different from Column 1, mark your answer B.

If both Column 2 and Column 3 are different from Column 1, mark your answer C.

If both Columns 2 and 3 are the same as Column 1, mark your answer D.

SAMPLE QUESTION

Column I	Column 2	Column 3
JPFMB	orzaq	12453

The code letters in Column 2 are correct, but the numbers 53 in Column 3 should be 35. Therefore, the answer is B.

	Column 1	Column 2	Column 3	
28.	PBFJM	rqzoa	25413	28.___
29.	MPFBJ	zrqao	32541	29.___
30.	JBFPM	oqzra	15432	30.___
31.	BJPMF	qaroz	51234	31.___
32.	PJFMB	rozaq	21435	32.___
33.	FJBMP	zoqra	41532	33.___

9 (#2)

Questions 34-40.

DIRECTIONS: Questions 34 through 40 are based on the instructions given below. Study the instructions and the sample question; then answer Questions 34 through 40 on the basis of this information

INSTRUCTIONS:

In each of the following Questions 34 through 40, the 3-line name and address in Column 1 is the master-list entry, and the 3-line entry in Column 2 is the information to be checked against the master list.

If there is one line that does not match, mark your answer A.

If there are two lines that do not match, mark your answer B.

If all three lines do not match, mark your answer C.

If the lines all match exactly, mark your answer D.

SAMPLE QUESTION:

Column 1
Mark L. Field
11-09 Prince Park Blvd.
Bronx, N.Y. 11402

Column 2
Mark L. Field
11-99 Prince Park
Bronx, N.Y. 11401

The first lines in each column match exactly. The second lines do not match, since 11-09 does not match 11-99 and Blvd. does not match Way. The third lines do not match either, since 11402 does not match 11401. Therefore, there are two lines that do not match and the correct answer is B.

	Column 1	Column 2	
34.	Jerome A. Jackson 1243 14th Avenue New York, N.Y. 10023	Jerome A. Johnson 1234 14th Avenue New York, N.Y. 10023	34.____
35.	Sophie Strachtheim 33-28 Connecticut Ave. Far Rockaway, N.Y. 11697	Sophie Strachtheim 33-28 Connecticut Ave. Far Rockaway, N.Y. 11697	35.____
36.	Elisabeth N.T. Gorrell 256 Exchange St. New York, N.Y. 10013	Elizabeth N.T. Gorrell 256 Exchange St. New York, N.Y. 10013	36.____
37.	Maria J. Gonzalez 7516 E. Sheepshead Rd. Brooklyn, N.Y. 11240	Maria J. Gonzalez 7516 N. Shepshead Rd. Brooklyn, N.Y. 11240	37.____
38.	Leslie B. Brautenweiler 21 57A Seller Terr. Flushing, N.Y. 11367	Leslie B. Brautenwieler 21-75A Seiler Terr. Flushing, N.J. 11367	38.____

39. Rigoberto J. Peredes
    157 Twin Towers, #18F
    Tottenville, S.I., N.Y.

    Rigoberto J. Peredes
    157 Twin Towers, #18F
    Tottenville, S.I., N.Y.

    39._____

40. Pietro F. Albino
    P.O. Box 7548
    Floral Park, N.Y. 11005

    Pietro F. Albina
    P.O. Box 7458
    Floral Park, N.Y. 11005

    40._____

KEY (CORRECT ANSWERS)

1. D	11. A	21. B	31. A
2. C	12. D	22. C	32. D
3. B	13. C	23. C	33. A
4. D	14. B	24. C	34. B
5. B	15. A	25. A	35. D
6. A	16. C	26. B	36. A
7. C	17. C	27. B	37. A
8. D	18. C	28. D	38. C
9. D	19. D	29. C	39. D
10. D	20. C	30. B	40. B

EXAMINATION SECTION
TEST 1

DIRECTIONS: Each question or incomplete statement is followed by several suggested answers or completions. Select the one that BEST answers the question or completes the statement. *PRINT THE LETTER OF THE CORRECT ANSWER IN THE SPACE AT THE RIGHT.*

Questions 1-9.

DIRECTIONS: Questions 1 through 9 are to be answered SOLELY on the basis of the following information and the DIRECTORY OF SERVICES.

    Officer Johnson has just been assigned to the North End Service Facility and is now on his post in the main lobby. The facility is open to the public from 9 A.M. to 5 P.M. each Monday through Friday, except on Thursdays when it is open from 9 A.M. to 7 P.M. The facility is closed on holidays.

    Officer Johnson must ensure an orderly flow of visitors through the lobby of the facility. To accomplish this, Officer Johnson gives directions and provides routine information to clients and other members of the public who enter and leave the facility through the lobby.

    In order to give directions and provide routine information to visitors, such as information concerning the location of services, Officer Johnson consults the Directory of Services shown below. Officer Johnson must ensure that clients are directed to the correct room for service and are sent to that room only during the hours that the particular service is available. When clients ask for the location of more than one service, they should be directed to go first to the service that will close soonest.

NORTH END SERVICE FACILITY
DIRECTORY OF SERVICES

Room	Type of Service	Days Available	Hours Open
101	Facility Receptionist	Monday, Tuesday, Wednesday, Friday Thursday	9 AM- 5 PM 9 AM- 7 PM
103	Photo Identification Cards	Monday, Wednesday, Friday	9 AM-12 Noon
104	Lost and Stolen Identification Cards	Wednesday, Thursday	9 AM-5 PM
105	Applications for Welfare/Food Stamps	Wednesday, Friday	1 PM-5 PM
107	Recertification for Welfare/Food Stamps	Monday, Thursday	10 AM- 12 Noon
108	Medicaid Applications	Tuesday, Wednesday	2 PM-5 PM
109	Medicaid Complaints	Tuesday, Wednesday	10 AM-2 PM
110, 111	Social Worker	Monday, Wednesday Tuesday, Friday Thursday	9 AM-12 Noon 1 PM-5 PM 9 AM- 5 PM
114	Hearing Room (By appointment only)	Monday, Thursday	9 AM-5 PM

DIRECTORY OF SERVICES
(CONT'D)

Room	Type of Service	Days Available	Hours Open
115	Hearing Information	Monday, Tuesday, Wednesday, Thursday, Friday	9 AM-1 PM
206, 207	Nutrition Aid	Monday, Wednesday, Friday	10 AM-2 PM
		Tuesday, Thursday	9 AM-12 Noon
215	Health Clinic	Monday, Tuesday, Wednesday, Friday	9 AM-5 PM
		Thursday	9 AM-7 PM
220	Facility Administrative Office	Monday, Tuesday, Wednesday, Thursday, Friday	9 AM-5 PM

1. It is Tuesday morning and Ms. Loretta Rogers, a client of the North End Service Facility, asks Officer Johnson where she should go in order to apply for Medicaid. Officer Johnson tells Ms. Rogers to go to Room _____ at _____.

    A. 108; 1:00 P.M.
    B. 109; 11:00 A.M.
    C. 108; 2:00 P.M.
    D. 109; 2:00 P.M.

2. On Friday at 11:00 A.M., Mrs. Ruth Ramos, a new client at the North End Service Facility, tells Officer Johnson that she wants to obtain a photo identification card and see a social worker.
   Officer Johnson should direct Mrs. Ramos to first go to Room

    A. 103
    B. 104
    C. 110
    D. 220

3. On Friday at 10:30 A.M., a client at the North End Service Facility who is directed by Officer Johnson to go to Room 206 will be able to receive service regarding

    A. Recertification for Welfare/Food Stamps
    B. Hearing Information
    C. Medicaid Applications
    D. Nutrition Aid

4. At 9:00 A.M. on Monday, a client at the North End Service Facility who is directed by Officer Johnson to Room 101 for service will find

    A. Nutrition Aid
    B. Facility Receptionist
    C. Health Clinic
    D. Hearing Information

5. On Tuesday at 12:30 P.M., Mr. Paul Brown tells Officer Johnson that he lost his identification card and wants to obtain a new one as soon as possible.
   Officer Johnson should direct Mr. Brown to go to Room 104

    A. immediately
    B. at 1:00 P.M. that day
    C. at 9:00 A.M. on Wednesday
    D. at 2:00 P.M. on Friday

6. A client at the North End Service Facility explains to Officer Johnson that he wants to make an appointment with a Social Worker.
   The client should be directed to go to Room

   A. 104 B. 110 C. 115 D. 215

7. Ms. Alice Lee is a client at the North End Service Facility who has a 10:00 A.M. appointment on Thursday in the Hearing Room and does not know where to go.
   Officer Johnson should direct Ms. Lee to go to Room

   A. 101 B. 110 C. 112 D. 114

8. Officer Johnson is asked by a visitor which services are available on Thursdays between 5:00 P.M. and 7:00 P.M. Officer Johnson should inform the visitor that an available service during that time is

   A. Health Clinic
   B. Medicaid Complaints
   C. Nutrition Aid
   D. Social Worker

9. Mr. Jack Klein, a visitor to the North End Service Facility, asks Officer Johnson when and where he can file a complaint concerning Medicaid.
   Officer Johnson should inform Mr. Klein that he may go to Room

   A. 108 on Tuesday or Wednesday between 2:00 P.M. and 5:00 P.M.
   B. 109 on Tuesday or Wednesday between 10:00 A.M. and 2:00 P.M.
   C. 115 on Monday or Tuesday between 10:00 A.M. and 12:00 Noon
   D. 215 on Thursday between 9:00 A.M. and 7:00 P.M.

Questions 10-12.

DIRECTIONS: Questions 10 through 12 are to be answered SOLELY on the basis of the following information.

Security Officers should act in accordance with guidelines included in a manual provided to security staff. Assume that the following guidelines apply to Officers when in contact with visitors or clients in a facility:

1. Try to see things from the visitor's or client's point of view.
2. Ignore insulting comments.
3. Maintain a calm and patient manner.
4. Speak quietly, courteously, and tactfully.

10. Officer Renee Williams is patrolling the lobby area of her facility when she hears a client angrily yelling at the receptionist. She goes to investigate the situation and finds out from the receptionist that the client is one hour late for his appointment with a social worker who now has other appointments. The client demands to be seen by the social worker immediately. Officer Williams angrily tells the client that it is his own fault that he missed his appointment and he should stop bothering the receptionist and go home.
    In this situation, Officer Williams' behavior towards the client is

    A. *proper,* chiefly because it is the client's fault that he missed his appointment
    B. *improper,* chiefly because security officers should stay calm and speak courteously when dealing with clients
    C. *proper,* chiefly because the client had yelled at the receptionist
    D. *improper,* chiefly because the security officer should have ignored the whole incident

11. During his tour, Officer Montgomery is passing through his facility's waiting room on the way to the cafeteria for a break. As Officer Montgomery passes by a visitor, the visitor mutters an insulting remark about the Officer's appearance. Officer Montgomery ignores the visitor and the remark and proceeds on his way to the cafeteria.
Officer Montgomery's action in this situation is

    A. *correct,* chiefly because it is not necessary for Officer Montgomery to respond to visitors while on a break
    B. *incorrect,* chiefly because Officer Montgomery should have ejected the visitor from the facility
    C. *correct,* chiefly because special officers should ignore insults
    D. *incorrect,* chiefly because visitors should not be allowed to ridicule authority figures such as special officers

12. While patrolling the facility parking lot, Officer Klausner sees an unoccupied car parked in front of a fire hydrant. Officer Klausner writes out a summons for a parking violation and places it on the windshield of the car. As the Officer begins to walk away, the owner of the car spots the summons on the windshield and runs over to the car. The car owner is furious at getting the summons, confronts the Officer, and curses him loudly.
In this situation, Officer Klausner should

    A. curse back at the car owner just as loudly
    B. push him out of the way and resume patrol
    C. calmly explain to him the nature of the violation
    D. return all the insults but in a calm tone

Question 13.

DIRECTIONS: Question 13 is to be answered SOLELY on the basis of the following information.

Special Officers are permitted to give only general information about social services. They shall not provide advice concerning specific procedures.

13. Special Officer Lynn King is on post near the Medicaid Office in the Manhattan Income Maintenance Center. While Officer King is on post, a client approaches her and asks which forms must be filled out in order to apply for Medicaid benefits. Officer King tells the client that she cannot help him and directs the client to the Medicaid Office.
In this situation, Officer King's response to the client's question is

    A. *correct,* chiefly because Officer King's duties do not include providing any information to clients
    B. *incorrect,* chiefly because Officer King should have provided as much specific information as possible to the client
    C. *correct,* chiefly because Officer King may not advise clients on social services procedures
    D. *incorrect,* chiefly because Officer King should know which forms are used in the facility

Question 14.

DIRECTIONS: Question 14 is to be answered SOLELY on the basis of the following information.

Security Officers must request that visitors and clients show identification and inspect that identification before allowing them to enter restricted areas in the facility.

14. Security Officer Crane is assigned to a fixed post outside Commissioner Maxwell's office, which is a restricted area. A visitor approaches Officer Crane's desk and states that he is Robert Maxwell and has an appointment with the Commissioner, who is his brother. Officer Crane checks the appointment book, verifies that Robert Maxwell has an appointment with the Commissioner, and allows the visitor to enter the office.
In this situation, Officer Crane's action in allowing the visitor admittance to the Commissioner's office is

   A. *correct,* chiefly because he verified that Robert Maxwell had an appointment with the Commissioner
   B. *incorrect,* chiefly because all visitors must show identification before entering restricted areas
   C. *correct,* chiefly because it would insult the Commissioner's brother if he was asked to show identification
   D. *incorrect,* chiefly because he should have called the Commissioner to verify that he has a brother

14.____

Question 15.

DIRECTIONS: Question 15 is to be answered SOLELY on the basis of the following information.

While on duty, a Special Officer must give his rank, name, and shield number to any person who requests it.

15. Special Officer Karen Mitchell is assigned to patrol an area in the North Bronx Service Facility. While on patrol, Officer Mitchell observes a visitor asking other clients in the lobby for money. Upon investigation, she determines that the visitor has no official business in the facility and asks the visitor to leave the premises. The individual says that he will leave but demands to know Officer Mitchell's name and shield number.
In response to the visitor's demand, Officer Mitchell should

   A. give the individual her name and shield number
   B. inform him that he can only obtain that information from her supervisor
   C. ignore his demand and resume her patrol
   D. tell the visitor that she will issue a summons to him if he keeps bothering her

15.____

Question 16.

DIRECTIONS: Question 16 is to be answered SOLELY on the basis of the following information.

A member of the Security Staff must follow guidelines for providing information to reporters concerning official facility business. Special Officers shall not be interviewed, nor make public speeches or statements pertaining to official business unless authorized. Security Staff must receive authorization from the Office of Public Affairs before speaking to reporters on any matters pertaining to official facility business.

16. You are a Special Officer in a Men's Shelter. A reporter approaches you as you are leaving the building. The reporter requests that you give an insider's view on conditions in the shelter. He assures you that you will remain anonymous.
You should tell the reporter that you

- A. must obtain permission from your immediate supervisor before giving any interviews
- B. will be more than happy to provide him with information concerning conditions in the shelter
- C. must receive authorization from the Office of Public Affairs before giving any interviews
- D. may not give him any information, but that your supervisor will be able to provide him with the requested information.

Questions 17-21.

DIRECTIONS: Questions 17 through 21 are to be answered SOLELY on the basis of the following information.

During their tours, Security Officers are required to transmit and receive information and commands over two-way portable radios from other security staff members. Officers use a numbered code to transmit information over the radio. For example, an officer who calls *10-13* into his radio communicates to other officers and supervisors that he is in need of assistance. Assume that the code numbers shown below along with their specified meanings are those used by Special Officers.

Code	Meaning
10-01	Call your command
10-02	Report to your command
10-03	Call Dispatcher
10-04	Acknowledgment
10-05	Repeat message
10-06	Stand-by
10-07	Verify
10-08	Respond to specified area and advise
10-10	Investigate
10-13	Officer needs help
10-20	Robbery in progress
10-21	Burglary in progress
10-22	Larceny in progress
10-24	Assault in progress
10-30	Robbery has occurred

10-31	Burglary has occurred
10-34	Assault has occurred
10-40	Unusual incident
10-41	Vehicle accident
10-42	Traffic or parking problem
10-43	Electrical problem
10-50	Dispute or noise
10-52	Disorderly person/group
10-60	Ambulance needed
10-61	Police Department assistance required
10-64	Fire alarm
10-70	Arrived at scene
10-71	Arrest
10-72	Unfounded
10-73	Condition corrected
10-74	Resuming normal duties

17. Officer Cramer is patrolling Parking Lot A when he receives a radio message from Sergeant Wong. Sergeant Wong directs Officer Cramer to respond to Parking Lot B to investigate a reported traffic problem. Upon arriving at Parking Lot B, Officer Cramer observes a vehicle blocking a loading dock so that a delivery truck cannot gain access to the dock. After notification is made to the owner of the vehicle, the vehicle is moved, allowing the delivery truck to gain access to the loading dock. Which of the following should Officer Cramer use to BEST report the events that occurred back to Sergeant Wong?

    A. 10-72, 10-41, 10-73
    B. 10-70, 10-42, 10-73
    C. 10-70, 10-41, 10-74
    D. 10-72, 10-42, 10-74

18. Officer Garret receives a message of *10-24, 10-10* on his radio from his supervisor, Sergeant Gomez. Officer Garret responds to the scene and later sends Sergeant Gomez the following message in response: *10-70, 10-72, 10-74*. Which of the following events are reported by use of those codes?
    Sergeant Gomez ordered Officer Garret to investigate an assault

    A. in progress. Officer Garret arrived at the scene, discovered that the report was unfounded, and resumed normal duties.
    B. that had occurred. Officer Garret arrived at the scene, made an arrest, and then resumed normal duties.
    C. that had occurred. Officer Garret arrived at the scene and discovered that the report was unfounded and resumed normal duties.
    D. in progress. Officer Garret arrived at the scene, made an arrest, and then resumed normal duties.

19. Officer Torres is patrolling the grounds of his facility when he receives a radio message from Sergeant Washington. In response to the radio message, Officer Torres goes to the facility's parking lot and issues a summons to a vehicle blocking an ambulance entrance. The radio message that Officer Torres received from Sergeant Washington is 10-10,

   A. 10-21 B. 10-40 C. 10-42 D. 10-43

20. Officer Oxford transmits the following codes by radio to Sergeant Joseph: *10-20, 10-13.* The response that Officer Oxford receives from Sergeant Joseph on her radio is *10-04.* Which one of the following events are reported by the use of those codes?
Officer Oxford informed Sergeant Joseph that

   A. a robbery was in progress and that she needs assistance, and Sergeant Joseph acknowledged her message
   B. an assault was in progress and that she wants him to respond to the area, and Sergeant Joseph acknowledged her message
   C. a burglary was in progress and that someone must investigate, and Sergeant Joseph responded that he is standing by
   D. a larceny was in progress and that she needs him to call a dispatcher. Sergeant Joseph reports this incident to his command.

21. While on patrol, Officer Robinson observes that the hall lights in Wing *B* are flickering on and off. Officer Robinson calls the Maintenance Office and a maintenance worker responds and corrects the problem.
The radio code that Officer Robinson should transmit to his supervisor to report this incident is

   A. 10-06, 10-08
   B. 10-40, 10-64
   C. 10-43, 10-73
   D. 10-61, 10-07

Question 22.

DIRECTIONS: Question 22 is to be answered SOLELY on the basis of the following information.

The two-way portable radios used by Security or Special Officers to communicate with other security staff members are to be used for official business only. In addition, when transmitting official business, transmission time (time spent transmitting information to other staff) should be kept to a minimum.

22. During his tour, Special Officer Banks calls Sergeant Gates in the patrolroom over the radio and asks if his wife, Alice Banks, had telephoned. Sergeant Gates tells Officer Banks that his wife has not called. Officer Banks then requests that Sergeant Gates notify him as soon as his wife calls because he is expecting an important message concerning his family.
In this situation, Officer Banks' use of his radio is

   A. *appropriate,* chiefly because his transmission time was not excessive
   B. *inappropriate,* chiefly because he should have made the transmission on his break
   C. *appropriate,* chiefly because his transmission concerned an important family matter
   D. *inappropriate,* chiefly because radios are to be used for official business only

Question 23.

DIRECTIONS: Question 23 is to be answered SOLELY on the basis of the following information.

Special Officers are responsible for monitoring and responding to radio messages, even if the officer is on meal break, performing clerical duties, or away from his post for other reasons. An officer shall answer radio messages directed to him during his tour.

23. Officer Lewis is chatting with friends in the cafeteria while on her scheduled meal break when she receives a radio message from Sergeant Baker. Sergeant Baker informs Officer Lewis that trouble has broken out at Location A and directs her to report to Location A immediately to assist the officers on the scene. Officer Lewis leaves the cafeteria immediately and reports to the scene.
Officer Lewis' action in response to Sergeant Baker's radio message is

　　A. *correct*, chiefly because Officer Lewis is responsible for responding to all radio messages
　　B. *incorrect*, chiefly because Officer Lewis is on meal break and therefore *off-duty*
　　C. *correct*, chiefly because Officer Lewis was not doing anything important during her meal break
　　D. *incorrect*, chiefly because the situation was not declared a *total emergency*

Question 24.

DIRECTIONS: Question 24 is to be answered SOLELY on the basis of the following information.

Special Officers must immediately report to their supervisor any incident or condition in the facility that may cause danger or inconvenience to the public.

24. Special Officer Scott is patrolling a small, crowded waiting room in his facility when two male clients start arguing with each other, shoving chairs around and frightening the other clients. Officer Scott intervenes in the argument, issues summonses for Disorderly Conduct to the individuals involved in the dispute, and escorts them off the premises. Officer Scott then records the incident in his memo book and resumes patrol.
In this situation, the FIRST action that Officer Scott should have taken when he observed the argument start between the two men is to

　　A. call for help from Special Officers on nearby posts to restrain the men who were fighting
　　B. report the incident to his supervisor immediately
　　C. attempt to separate the men who were fighting in order to stop the fight
　　D. evacuate the waiting room so that innocent bystanders would not be injured

Question 25.

DIRECTIONS: Question 25 is to be answered SOLELY on the basis of the following information.

An Officer on duty in a facility must remain on post until properly relieved. If not properly relieved as scheduled, he must notify his immediate supervisor by radio of this fact and follow the supervisor's instructions.

25. Officer Clough is working on an 8:00 A.M. to 4:00 P.M. tour. Officer Clough is to be relieved at 4:00 P.M. by Security Officer Crandall, who works the 4:00 P.M. to 12:00 Midnight shift. However, as of 4:15 P.M., Officer Crandall has not appeared to relieve Officer Clough, so Officer Clough leaves his post to find Officer Crandall. In this situation, Officer Clough's action is

    A. *correct,* chiefly because his tour was over and he wanted to go home
    B. *incorrect,* chiefly because he should have notified his supervisor of Officer Crandall's failure to relieve him
    C. *correct,* chiefly because Officer Clough is attempting to locate Officer Crandall so that the post will be covered
    D. *incorrect,* chiefly because Officer Clough should have left his post as soon as his tour ended rather than working any overtime

Questions 26-28.

DIRECTIONS: Questions 26 through 28 are to be answered SOLELY on the basis of the following information.

A summons is a written notice that a person is accused of violating a code or regulation. Special Officers have the authority to issue summonses to individuals for on-premises parking or traffic violations, or violations of the City Administrative Code. Summonses for violations of the Penal Law, such as for Disorderly Conduct, may also be issued.

The following is a list of types of summonses issued for violations and their descriptions:

Type of Summons	Description of Violation
Class A	Parking in fire lanes
Class A	Parking in space reserved for the handicapped
Class A	Vehicle blocking driveway
Class B	Disobeying stop sign
Class C	Disorderly Conduct
Class C	Harassment
Environmental Control Board	Smoking Violations
Environmental Control Board	Public Health Code

26. While on patrol, Special Officer Gladys Jones observes a parked car that is blocking a driveway.
She should issue a summons for a violation which is a

    A. Class A type
    B. Class B type
    C. Class C type
    D. Environmental Control Board

27. A man drives up to a facility, parks his car in a fire lane, and quickly runs inside the facility. An attempt to follow and locate the man is unsuccessful.
    Which one of the following is the type of summons that the Special Officer on duty should issue?

    A. Class A
    B. Class B
    C. Class C
    D. Environmental Control Board

28. While on patrol, Special Officer Mason observes a visitor smoking a cigarette in an area where smoking is prohibited. Officer Mason asks the visitor to stop smoking and shows him the *No Smoking* sign posted. The visitor refuses to comply.
    Officer Mason should issue which type of summons?

    A. Class A
    B. Class B
    C. Class C
    D. Environmental Control Board

Questions 29-31.

DIRECTIONS: Questions 29 through 31 are to be answered SOLELY on the basis of the following information and the Summons Form and Fact Pattern.

Special Officers must complete a summons form by filling in the appropriate information. A completed summons must include the name and address of the accused; license or other identification number; vehicle identification; the section number of the code, regulation, or law violated; a brief description of the violation; any scheduled fine; information about the time and place of occurrence; and the name, rank, and signature of the Special Officer issuing the summons.

The information listed on the Summons Form may or may not be correct.

SUMMONS FORM

LINE:	NOTICE OF VIOLATION No. 5 56784989		THE PEOPLE OF THE STATE OF NEW YORK VS.	
1		OPERATOR PRESENT NO (YES) REFUSED ID		
2	LAST NAME Tucker	FIRST NAME James		MIDDLE INITIAL T
3	STREET ADDRESS 205 E. 53rd Street			
4	CITY (AS SHOWN ON LICENSE) Brooklyn, NY 11234			
5	DRIVER LICENSE OR IDENTIFICATION NO. J-7156907834	STATE NY	CLASS 5	DATE EXPIRES 1/12/13
6	SEX M	DATE OF BIRTH 1/12/65		
7	LICENSE PLATE NO. CVR-632	STATE NY	DATE EXPIRES 8/12/12	OPERATOR OWN VEHICLE? (YES) NO
8	BODY TYPE Sedan	MAKE Dodge	COLOR Green	
	THE PERSON DESCRIBED ABOVE IS CHARGED AS FOLLOWS:			
9	ISSUE TIME 9:30 A.M.	DATE OF OFFENSE 2/5/12	TIME FIRST OBSERVED 9:28 A.M.	COUNTY Kings
10	PLACE OF OCCURRENCE 451 Clarkson Ave., Brooklyn, NY		PRECINCT 71st	
11	IN VIOLATION OF SECTION 81-B	CODE 40	LAW New York State Traffic Regulation	
12	DESCRIPTION OF VIOLATION Vehicle parked in front of a fire hydrant			
13	SCHEDULED FINE $10 $15 $20 $25 $30 ($40) Other $____			
14	RANK/NAME OF ISSUING OFFICER Special Officer Joseph Robbins		SIGNATURE OF ISSUING OFFICER Joseph Robbins	

FACT PATTERN

On February 5, 2012, at 9:28 A.M., Special Officer Joseph Robbins is patrolling the grounds of the Brooklyn Hills Income Maintenance Center, located at 451 Clarkson Ave., Brooklyn, NY, when he observes an unoccupied parked vehicle blocking a fire hydrant near the facility's entrance. As Officer Robbins begins to write up a summons for the violation, James Tucker, the owner of the vehicle, emerges from the facility and comes over. While getting in his car, he asks why he is getting a summons. Officer Robbins explains to Mr. Tucker that he is in violation of traffic regulations pertaining to access to fire hydrants and asks him for identification. Mr. Tucker gives Officer Robbins his driver's license, showing the following information:

Name:	Tucker, James T.
Address:	205 E. 53rd Street, Brooklyn, NY 11234
Date of Birth:	January 12, 1965
Driver's License:	J-7156907894
Driver License Expiration Date:	January 12, 2013
Class:	5

29. The *place of occurrence* of the violation described in the Fact Pattern is on line _____ of the Summons Form.

    A. 2   B. 3   C. 8   D. 10

30. Which one of the following lines on the Summons Form shows information that does NOT agree with information given in the Fact Pattern?

    A. 1   B. 2   C. 4   D. 5

31. Which of the following is the date on which the violation occurred?

    A. 1/12/12   B. 2/5/12   C. 8/12/12   D. 1/12/13

32. Following are two sentences which may or may not be written in correct English:
    I. Two clients assaulted the officer.
    II. The van is illegally parked.
    Which one of the following statements is CORRECT?

    A. Only Sentence I is written in correct English.
    B. Only Sentence II is written in correct English.
    C. Sentences I and II are both written in correct English.
    D. Neither Sentence I nor Sentence II is written in correct English.

33. Following are two sentences which may or may not be written in correct English:
    I. Security Officer Rollo escorted the visitor to the patrolroom.
    II. Two entry were made in the facility logbook.
    Which one of the following statements is CORRECT?

    A. Only Sentence I is written in correct English.
    B. Only Sentence II is written in correct English.
    C. Sentences I and II are both written in correct English.
    D. Neither Sentence I nor Sentence II is written in correct English.

34. Following are two sentences which may or may not be written in correct English:
    I. Officer McElroy putted out a small fire in the wastepaper basket.
    II. Special Officer Janssen told the visitor where he could obtained a pass.
    Which one of the following statements is CORRECT?

    A. Only Sentence I is written in correct English.
    B. Only Sentence II is written in correct English.
    C. Sentences I and II are both written in correct English.
    D. Neither Sentence I nor Sentence II are written in correct English.

35. Following are two sentences which may or may not be written in correct English:
    I. Security Officer Warren observed a broken window while he was on his post in Hallway C.
    II. The worker reported that two typewriters had been stoled from the office.
    Which one of the following statements is CORRECT?

    A. Only Sentence I is written in correct English.
    B. Only Sentence II is written in correct English.
    C. Sentences I and II are both written in correct English.
    D. Neither Sentence I nor Sentence II is written in correct English.

KEY (CORRECT ANSWERS)

1.	C	16.	C
2.	A	17.	B
3.	D	18.	A
4.	B	19.	C
5.	C	20.	A
6.	B	21.	C
7.	D	22.	D
8.	A	23.	A
9.	B	24.	B
10.	B	25.	B
11.	C	26.	A
12.	C	27.	A
13.	C	28.	D
14.	B	29.	D
15.	A	30.	D

31. B
32. C
33. A
34. D
35. A

TEST 2

DIRECTIONS: Each question or incomplete statement is followed by several suggested answers or completions. Select the one that BEST answers the question or completes the statement. *PRINT THE LETTER OF THE CORRECT ANSWER IN THE SPACE AT THE RIGHT.*

Questions 1-5.

DIRECTIONS: Questions 1 through 5 are to be answered SOLELY on the basis of the following information.

    Special Officers have the power to arrest members of the public who commit crimes in violation of the Penal Law. Assume that certain classes of crimes covered by various sections of the Penal Law are described below. Special Officers must be able to apply this information when making an arrest in order to accurately determine the type of crime that has been committed.

Crime	Class of Crime	Description of Crime	Section
Petit Larceny	A Misdemeanor	Stealing property worth up to $250	155.25
Grand Larceny 3rd Degree	E Felony	Stealing property worth more than $250	155.30
Grand Larceny 2nd Degree	D Felony	Stealing property worth more than $1,500	155.35
Grand Larceny 1st Degree	C Felony	Stealing property worth any amount of money while making a person fear injury or damage to property	155.40
Assault 3rd Degree	A Misdemeanor	Injuring a person	120.00
Assault 2nd Degree	D Felony	1. Seriously injuring a person; or 2. Injuring an officer of the law	120.05
Assault 1st Degree	C Felony	Seriously injuring a person using a deadly or dangerous weapon	120.10
Disorderly Conduct	Violation	1. Engages in fighting or threatening behavior; or 2. Makes unreasonable noise	240.20
Robbery 3rd Degree	D Felony	Stealing property by force	160.05
Robbery 2nd Degree	C Felony	1. Stealing property by force with the help of another person; or 2. Stealing property by force and injuring any person	160.10
Robbery 1st Degree	B Felony	Stealing property by force and seriously injuring the owner of property	160.15

77

1. Which one of the following crimes is considered to be Class A Misdemeanor?

   A. Grand Larceny - 3rd Degree
   B. Grand Larceny - 2nd Degree
   C. Assault - 3rd Degree
   D. Assault - 2nd Degree

2. Which one of the following crimes is considered to be Class B Felony?

   A. Robbery - 2nd Degree
   B. Robbery - 1st Degree
   C. Grand Larceny - 3rd Degree
   D. Grand Larceny - 2nd Degree

3. A worker at a facility reports that a typewriter worth $400 has been stolen from her office. Which one of the following is the type of crime that has been committed?

   A. Grand Larceny - 3rd Degree
   B. Grand Larceny - 2nd Degree
   C. Grand Larceny - 1st Degree
   D. Petit Larceny

4. A visitor at a facility begins yelling very loudly at a receptionist and shakes his fist at her. The visitor refuses to stop yelling when an officer tries to calm him down, and he shakes his fist at the officer. Which one of the following is the type of crime that occurred?

   A. Assault - 3rd Degree   B. Assault - 2nd Degree
   C. Assault - 1st Degree   D. Disorderly Conduct

5. An officer has apprehended and arrested a visitor who was attempting to leave the facility with a radio he had stolen from an office. The radio is worth $100.
   Under which one of the following sections of the Penal Law should the visitor be charged? Section

   A. 155.25   B. 155.30   C. 155.35   D. 155.40

Questions 6-12.

DIRECTIONS: Questions 6 through 12 are to be answered SOLELY on the basis of the Arrest Report Form and Incident Report shown on the following page. These reports were submitted by Special Officer John Clark, Shield #512, to his supervisor, Sergeant Joseph Lewis, Shield #818, of the North Bay Health Clinic

Special Officers are required to complete both an Arrest Report Form and an Incident Report whenever an unusual incident or an arrest occurs. The Arrest Report Form provides detailed information regarding the victim and the person arrested, along with a brief description of the incident.

The Incident Report provides a detailed description of the incident. Both reports include the following information: WHO was involved in the incident, including witnesses; WHAT happened and HOW it happened; WHERE and WHEN the incident occurred; and WHY the incident occurred.

ARREST REPORT FORM

ARREST INFORMATION (1)	TIME OF OCCURRENCE 11:15 A.M.	DATE OF OCCURRENCE February 1, 2012		DAY OF WEEK Monday
INFORMATION ABOUT VICTIM (2)	VICTIM'S NAME Darlene Kirk		ADDRESS 7855 Cruger St., Bronx, NY 10488	
(3)	SEX F	DATE OF BIRTH 9/3/75	RACE White	HOME TELEPHONE # 212-733-3462	SOCIAL SECURITY # 245-63-0772
INFORMATION ABOUT PERSON ARRESTED (4)	NAME OF PERSON ARRESTED Elsie Gardner		ADDRESS 2447 Southern Pkway, Bronx, NY 10467	
(5)	SEX F	DATE OF BIRTH 7/9/80	RACE White	HOME TELEPHONE # 212-513-7029	SOCIAL SECURITY # 244-08-0569
(6)	HEIGHT 5'5"	WEIGHT 135 lbs.	HAIR COLOR Brown	CLOTHING Black coat/red pants	
DESCRIPTION OF CRIME (7)	SECTION OF PENAL LAW 120.00		TYPE OF CRIME Assault - 3rd Degree	
(8)	TIME OF ARREST 11:35 A.M.	DATE OF ARREST 2/1/12	LOCATION OF ARREST 635 Bay Avenue Bronx, NY	
(9)	DESCRIPTION OF INCIDENT The defendant, Elsie Gardner, struck the victim after the victim requested that Ms. Gardner stop smoking in a "NO SMOKING" area. Two witnesses verified the victim's account of the incident.			
INFORMATION ABOUT ARRESTING OFFICER (10)	REPORTING OFFICER'S SIGNATURE John Clark		NAME PRINTED John Clark	
(11)	RANK Special Officer		SHIELD NUMBER 512	

INCIDENT REPORT

(1) At 11:15 A.M. on February 1, 2012, I was directed by Sergeant Mark Lewis via two-way radio to report to the Nutrition Clinic on the 4th Floor to investigate a disturbance. (2) Special Officer Anna Colon, Shield #433, was directed to assist me. (3) At 11:16 A.M., Officer Colon and I arrived at the Health Clinic and observed a patient, Elsie Gardner, repeatedly strike Health Clinic receptionist Darlene Kirk about the head and neck. (4) Officer Colon restrained Ms. Gardner while I placed handcuffs on her wrists. (5) Ms. Kirk complained that her neck felt sore. (6) After being examined by Dr. Stone, Ms. Kirk told us that Ms. Gardner entered the Health Clinic at approximately 11:10 A.M. and lit a cigarette in the waiting area. (7) At 11:20 A.M., Dr. Paul Stone examined Ms. Kirk. (8) Ms. Kirk explained to Ms. Gardner that smoking was not allowed in the Health Clinic and showed her the *NO SMOKING* signs posted on the walls. (9) Ms. Gardner ignored Ms. Kirk, and then grew very abusive and attacked her when Ms. Kirk insisted that she stop smoking. (10) Two witnesses, patients Edna Manning of 8937 4th Ave., Bronx, NY, and John Schultz of 357 149th Street, Bronx, NY, gave the same account of the incident as Ms. Kirk. (11) At 11:30 A.M., I read the prisoner her rights and placed her under arrest for violation of Penal Law Section 120.00 -Assault 3rd Degree. (12) At 11:35 A.M., I notified the 86th Precinct of Ms. Gardner's arrest and arranged for the transportation of the prisoner to the precinct. (13) At 11:40 A.M., Officer Colon escorted Ms. Gardner from the Nutrition Clinic to the patrolroom. (14) At 11:55 A.M., Police Officers Cranford, Shield #658, and Wargo, Shield #313, arrived at the facility to transport the prisoner to the precinct. (15) Officer Gray, Shield #936, assumed my post while I reported to the patrolroom to complete the necessary forms concerning the arrest.

6. At what time did Sergeant Lewis inform Officer John Clark of the disturbance in the Nutrition Clinic?
   _____ A.M.

   A. 11:00   B. 11:15   C. 11:16   D. 11:20

7. According to the Arrest Report and the Incident Report, how many witnesses gave the same account of the incident as Ms. Kirk?

   A. 1   B. 2   C. 3   D. 4

8. What information on the Arrest Report is NOT included in the Incident Report?

   A. Date of Occurrence
   B. Victim's address
   C. Section of the Penal Law violated
   D. Assault 3rd Degree

9. Which sentence in the Incident Report is out of order in terms of the sequence of events?

   A. 3   B. 6   C. 11   D. 12

10. According to the Incident Report, at 11:40 A.M. Ms. Gardner was

    A. escorted to the patrolroom
    B. transported to the 86th Precinct
    C. examined by Dr. Paul Stone
    D. giving an account of the incident to Special Officers Clark and Colon

11. According to the Incident Report, which one of the following officers relieved Officer Clark?
    Officer

    A. Colon   B. Cranford   C. Wargo   D. Gray

12. Which section of the Arrest Report contains information that does NOT agree with Sentence 11 of the Incident Report?
    Section

    A. 1   B. 7   C. 8   D. 9

Question 13.

DIRECTIONS: Question 13 is to be answered SOLELY on the basis of the following information.

A Security Officer must investigate any complaint or incident which occurs in the facility, whether he considers it is major or minor. The Officer must also interview the person(s) involved in the incident in order to complete the necessary forms and reports.

13. Ms. Peters, a clerical worker at the facility, complains to Officer Tynan that a pen set, which had been given to her as a gift, was missing from her desk. She tells Officer Tynan that she knows the pen set was on her desk the previous day because she was using it for her work. Officer Tynan informs Ms. Peters that there is nothing he can do since the pen set was personal property and not facility property.
In this situation, Officer Tynan's response to Ms. Peters is

13._____

   A. *correct*, chiefly because the pen set should not have been left out on a desk where it could be stolen
   B. *incorrect*, chiefly because a complaint of a loss of theft should be investigated and recorded
   C. *correct*, chiefly because Special Officers are only required to investigate a loss or theft of facility property
   D. *incorrect*, chiefly because Ms. Peters' work required use of the pen set

Question 14.

DIRECTIONS: Question 14 is to be answered SOLELY on the basis of the following information.

Assume that Security Officers are responsible for recording in a personal memobook all of their routine and non-routine activities and occurrences for each tour of duty. Before starting a tour of duty, a Security Officer must enter in his personal memobook the date, tour, and assigned post. An entry shall be made to record each absence from duty, such as a regular day off, sick leave, annual leave, or holiday. During each tour, a Security Officer shall enter a full and accurate record of duties performed, changes in post assignment, absences from post, and the reason for each absence, and all other patrol business.

14. Security Officer Ella Lewis is assigned to Gotham Center Facility, where she works Monday through Friday on a 9:00 A.M. to 5:00 P.M. tour. Officer Lewis' regular days off are Saturday and Sunday. Officer Lewis worked on Wednesday, November 25, 2012. She was absent on Thursday, November 26, 2012, for Thanksgiving Holiday, and on Friday, November 27, 2012, for annual leave.
According to the information given above, which of the following entries is the FIRST entry that Officer Lewis should record in her memobook when she returns to work on November 30, 2012?

14._____

   A. Saturday, 11/28/12 and Sunday, 11/29/12 - Regular days off
   B. Friday, 11/27/12 - Sick Leave
   C. Monday, 11/30/12 - On duty
   D. Thursday, 11/26/12 - Thanksgiving Holiday

Questions 15-16.

DIRECTIONS: Questions 15 and 16 are to be answered SOLELY on the basis of the following entries recorded by Security Officer Angela Russo in her memobook.

Date: January 8, 2012
Tour: 8:00 A.M. to 4:00 P.M.
Weather: Sunny and clear

7:30	Reported to *B* Command for Roll Call. Assigned to Post #2, *C* Building Emergency Room Corridor by Sergeant Robert Floyd. Break: 9:30 A.M. Meal: 1:30 P.M. Radio: #701
7:40	Arrived at Post #2 and relieved Special Officer Johnson, Shield #593.
7:45	On patrol - Post #2.
8:00	Post #2 - All secure at this time; conditions normal.
8:30	Fire Alarm Box 5-3-1 rings on 3rd Floor South in *C* Building. Upon arrival, Office Worker Molly Lewis reported that a waste-paper basket was on fire. Used fire extinguisher to put out fire.
8:50	Condition corrected; Incident Report prepared and submitted to Sergeant Floyd in *B* Command.
8:55	Resumed patrol of Post #2.
9:30	Relieved for break by Officer Tucker.
9:50	Resumed patrol of Post #2.
10:10	Disorderly person reported by Clinic Director Lila Jones on Ward C-32; Officer Bailey and myself responded. Clinic Director Jones informed officers that visitor Bradley Manna, male white, 19 years of age, 2 Park Place, Brooklyn, NY, is drunk and has been shouting insults to Clinic staff.
10:30	Condition corrected; Visitor Bradley Manna escorted off premises. *B* Command notified of incident.
10:40	Resumed patrol of Post #2.
11:40	Post #2 - All secure at this time.
12:40	Post #2 - All secure at this time.

15. The name of the Clinic Director who reported a disorderly person is

    A. Molly Lewis   B. Bradley Manna
    C. Lila Jones   D. Robert Floyd

16. Which of the following sets of officers responded to the report of a disorderly person on Ward C-32?
Officers

    A. Johnson and Bailey   B. Russo and Tucker
    C. Johnson and Tucker   D. Russo and Bailey

17. Security Officer Mace is completing an entry in her memo-book. The entry has the following five sentences:
    1. I observed the defendant removing a radio from a facility vehicle.
    2. I placed the defendant under arrest and escorted him to the patrolroom.
    3. I was patrolling the facility parking lot.
    4. I asked the defendant to show identification.
    5. I determined that the defendant was not authorized to remove the radio.

    The MOST logical order for these sentences to be entered in Officer Mace's memo-book is

    A. 1, 3, 2, 4, 5
    B. 2, 5, 4, 1, 3
    C. 3, 1, 4, 5, 2
    D. 4, 5, 2, 1, 3

18. Security Officer Riley is completing an entry in his memo-book. The entry has the following five sentences:
    1. Anna Jones admitted that she stole Mary Green's wallet.
    2. I approached the women and asked them who they were and why they were arguing.
    3. I arrested Anna Jones for stealing Mary Green's wallet.
    4. They identified themselves and Mary Green accused Anna Jones of stealing her wallet.
    5. I was in the lobby area when I observed two women arguing about a wallet.

    The MOST logical order for these sentences to be entered in Officer Riley's memobook is

    A. 2, 4, 1, 3, 5
    B. 3, 1, 4, 5, 2
    C. 4, 1, 5, 2, 3
    D. 5, 2, 4, 1, 3

19. Assume that Security Officer John Ryan is completing an entry in his memobook. The entry has the following five sentences:
    1. I then cleared the immediate area of visitors and staff.
    2. I noticed smoke coming from a broom closet outside Room A71.
    3. Sergeant Mueller arrived with other officers to assist in clearing the area.
    4. Upon investigation, I determined the smoke was due to burning material in the broom closet.
    5. I pulled the corridor fire alarm and notified Sergeant Mueller of the fire.

    The MOST logical order for these sentences to be entered in Officer Ryan's memo-book is

    A. 2, 3, 4, 5, 1
    B. 2, 4, 5, 1, 3
    C. 4, 1, 2, 3, 5
    D. 5, 3, 2, 1, 4

20. Security Officer Hernandez is completing an entry in his memobook. The entry has the following five sentences:
    1. I asked him to leave the premises immediately.
    2. A visitor complained that there was a strange man loitering in Clinic B hallway.
    3. I went to investigate and saw a man dressed in rags sitting on the floor of the hallway.
    4. As he walked out, he started yelling that he had no place to go.
    5. I asked to see identification, but he said that he did not have any.

    The MOST logical order for these sentences to be entered in Officer Hernandez's memobook is

| A. 2, 3, 5, 1, 4 | B. 3, 1, 2, 4, 5 |
| C. 4, 1, 5, 2, 3 | D. 3, 1, 5, 2, 4 |

21. Officer Hogan is completing an entry in his memobook. The entry has the following five sentences:
    1. When the fighting had stopped, I transmitted a message requesting medical assistance for Mr. Perkins.
    2. Special Officer Manning assisted me in stopping the fight.
    3. When I arrived at the scene, I saw a client, Adam Finley strike a facility employee, Peter Perkins.
    4. As I attempted to break up the fight, Special Officer Manning came on the scene.
    5. I received a radio message from Sergeant Valez to investigate a possible fight in progress in the waiting room.

    The MOST logical order for these sentences to be entered in Officer Hogan's memobook is

    | A. 2, 1, 4, 5, 3 | B. 3, 5, 2, 4, 1 |
    | C. 4, 5, 3, 1, 2 | D. 5, 3, 4, 2, 1 |

Questions 22-23.

DIRECTIONS: Questions 22 and 23 are to be answered SOLELY on the basis of the following information.

Assume that Security Officers may be assigned to the facility patrolroom and must follow the guidelines below in documenting all routine and non-routine activities and occurrences in the facility logbook.

At the beginning of each tour of duty, the Security Officer responsible for entering information in the logbook must transfer from the Roll Call Sheet to the logbook a list of all security staff personnel assigned to that tour. This list is to be entered in order of the rank of the security staff member. All other entries in the facility logbook shall be recorded in chronological order, in blue or black ink, and be neat and legible.

22. When recording the list of security staff personnel assigned to a tour, that entry shall be made in

    A. chronological order
    B. order of rank of security staff
    C. alphabetical order
    D. order of arrival at facility

23. A Security Officer has transmitted notification to the patrolroom that he has just issued a summons. The Security Officer responsible for documenting occurrences in the patrolroom logbook should record the information

    A. in red ink, immediately following the previous entry
    B. on a new page under the heading *Summonses Reported*
    C. in blue or black ink immediately following the previous entry
    D. on the last page of the logbook where it can be easily found

Question 24.

DIRECTIONS: Question 24 is to be answered SOLELY on the basis of the following information.

Assume that whenever a Security Officer is to begin a leave of absence, long-term sick leave, or other type of leave having an anticipated length of ten days or more, the officer shall surrender his or her security shield to his supervisor, who shall immediately forward it to Security Headquarters.

24. Two male clients were fighting in the waiting room of North End Hospital. Officer Gary Klott attempted to separate them and became involved in the altercation. Officer Klott sustained an injury to the right eye and was examined by a physician. The physician directed Officer Klott to stay home for a recovery period of 12 days. In this situation, Officer Klott should

    A. surrender his shield to his supervisor
    B. safeguard his shield in a safe place at home while he is recovering
    C. surrender his shield to the physician
    D. safeguard his shield with his uniform in his locker at the facility while he is recovering

24.____

Question 25.

DIRECTIONS: Question 25 is to be answered SOLELY on the basis of the following information.

Assume that Security Officers are required to follow certain procedures when on post at a restricted area of a facility. They must inspect the identification of employees and passes of visitors, as well as all bags and packages carried by individuals who wish to enter the restricted area.

25. Security Officer Stevens is assigned to a post at the Intensive Care Unit of Park View Hospital, a restricted area. Officer Stevens is responsible for inspecting identification and passes, as well as all bags and packages carried by individuals who want to enter the Unit. He sees Mr. Craig approach. He knows Mr. Craig's wife is a patient in the Unit. Officer Stevens has seen Mr. Craig visit his wife every day for the past four days. Mr. Craig brings a small duffel bag filled with magazines each time he comes. Today, Officer Stevens checks Mr. Craig's visitor's pass but lets Mr. Craig enter the Unit without checking his duffel bag. In this situation, Officer Stevens' action is

    A. *correct*, chiefly because he has checked to see that Mr. Craig has a visitor's pass
    B. *incorrect*, chiefly because all packages and bags must be inspected before anyone is allowed to enter a restricted area
    C. *correct*, chiefly because he is familiar with Mr. Craig and knows that he only carries magazines in his duffel bag
    D. *incorrect*, chiefly because Mr. Craig should not be allowed to carry a bag or package into a restricted area of the facility

25.____

Question 26.

DIRECTIONS: Question 26 is to be answered SOLELY on the basis of the following information.

Assume that Special Officers must safeguard evidence in cases involving firearms. Special Officers must mark recovered bullets for identification purposes. The Officer who recovers the bullet must mark his or her initials and the date of recovery of the bullet on the base or on the nose of the bullet.

26. On January 18, 2012, at 11:30 P.M., an unidentified person fired a shot at an unoccupied security patrol car in the facility parking lot. Officer Debra Johnson was assigned to investigate the matter. A fired bullet was recovered inside the patrol car by Officer Johnson at 1:00 A.M. on January 19, 2012.
Officer Johnson should mark *D.J. 1/19/12* on

    A. the base or the nose of the recovered bullet
    B. the side of the recovered bullet
    C. an envelope and place the recovered bullet inside
    D. the side of the patrol car from which the bullet was recovered

Question 27.

DIRECTIONS: Question 27 is to be answered SOLELY on the basis of the following information.

Patrolroom Observers are officers who are assigned to observe events when individuals, other than security staff, are present in the patrolroom. According to facility guidelines, a Patrolroom Observer must be called to the patrolroom to serve as a witness whenever any individual is brought to the patrolroom for any reason by a Special Officer.

27. Janet Childs, a client at Gotham Health Facility, was robbed in the facility's parking lot. Ms. Childs was not harmed as a result of the incident, but she was upset. Special Officer Grey escorted her to the patrol-room, where she remained until she felt better. While she was waiting in the patrolroom, Officer Grey did not call a Patrolman Observer to the patrolroom during the time that Ms. Childs was there.
In this situation, Officer Grey

    A. should not have taken Ms. Childs to the patrolroom without special authorization from his supervisor
    B. was not required to call a Patrolroom Observer to the patrolroom since Ms. Childs had not been placed under arrest
    C. should have called a Patrolroom Observer to be present while Ms. Childs was in the patrolroom
    D. should have escorted Ms. Childs to the patrolroom and left her in the care of the Special Officer assigned to the patrolroom

Question 28.

DIRECTIONS: Question 28 is to be answered SOLELY on the basis of the following information.

Special Officers escort individuals categorized as Emotionally Disturbed Persons to the hospital for observation or treatment when directed to do so. These individuals are transported to the hospital by Emergency Medical Service (EMS) ambulance. There must be one Special Officer present in the ambulance for each Emotionally Disturbed Person transferred to the hospital, along with an EMS Technician and the ambulance driver.

28. Special Officers Patrick Lawson and Grace Martin have been assigned to escort two individuals categorized as Emotionally Disturbed Persons from that facility to a nearby hospital. The EMS ambulance, with an EMS Technician and ambulance driver, has arrived at the facility to transport the individuals. Officer Lawson then suggests to Officer Martin that it is not necessary for him to go to the hospital since the EMS Technician will be with Officer Martin in the ambulance.
In this situation, Officer Lawson's suggestion is 28.____

   A. *correct*, since an EMS Technician will be present in the ambulance to accompany Officer Martin and the Emotionally Disturbed Persons to the hospital
   B. *incorrect*, since one Special Officer must be present in the ambulance for each Emotionally Disturbed Person transported to the hospital
   C. *correct*, since the Emotionally Disturbed Persons are unlikely to cause any disturbance inside the ambulance
   D. *incorrect*, since two EMS Technicians must be present in the ambulance when only one Special Officer is escorting two Emotionally Disturbed Persons to the hospital

Questions 29-32.

DIRECTIONS: Questions 29 through 32 are to be answered on the basis of the following information.

Assume that information concerning new or updated policies and procedures are sometimes provided to facility security staff in the form of a memorandum from Security Headquarters.

Question 29.

DIRECTIONS: Question 29 is to be answered SOLELY on the basis of the following memorandum.

TO: All Security Officers
FROM: Security Headquarters
SUBJECT: Smoking Regulations

At times, Security Officers have been observed smoking while on duty at their assigned posts. This is strictly prohibited. If Officers feel that they must smoke, they may smoke during breaks or lunch period in designated areas. Officers may not smoke while on official duty. If any Officer is observed smoking while on post or while performing official duties, appropriate disciplinary action will be taken.

29. According to the above memorandum, Security Officers may

   A. smoke while on duty, as long as they are out of view of the public
   B. not smoke while on duty except when assigned to a post in a designated smoking area
   C. smoke on breaks or during lunch period in designated areas
   D. not smoke at any time when dressed in official uniform

Question 30.

DIRECTIONS: Question 30 is to be answered SOLELY on the basis of the following memorandum.

TO: All Special Officers
FROM: Security Headquarters
SUBJECT: Safeguarding Shields and Identification Cards

Special Officers must ensure that their shields and identification cards are secure at all times. Should an officer become aware of the loss or theft of his shield or identification card, he shall immediately report such loss or theft to Security Headquarters.

30. According to the above memorandum, a Special Officer must

   A. report the loss or theft of his identification card to the nearest police precinct
   B. secure his shield in his locker at all times
   C. report the loss or theft of his shield or identification card to Security Headquarters immediately
   D. secure his identification card at Security Headquarters each night before leaving the facility

Question 31.

DIRECTIONS: Question 31 is to be answered SOLELY on the basis of the following memorandum.

TO: All Security Officers
FROM: Security Headquarters
SUBJECT: Fire in the Facility

Special Officers must report immediately to assist at the scene of a fire when directed to do so by a supervisor. Officers shall remain at the scene and ensure that only authorized personnel are in an area restricted by a fire emergency. Visitors and clients shall be directed to the nearest safe stairwell and out of the facility. Visitors and clients are not to use elevators to evacuate the area.

31. According to the above memorandum, a Security Officer should

   A. direct visitors and clients to the nearest elevator in case of fire
   B. report unauthorized personnel at a fire scene to the Fire Department
   C. escort visitors and clients down the nearest stairwell and out of the facility
   D. ensure that only authorized personnel are in an area restricted by a fire emergency

Question 32.

DIRECTIONS: Question 32 is to be answered SOLELY on the basis of the following memorandum.

TO: All Security Officers
FROM: Security Headquarters
SUBJECT: Reporting Unsafe Conditions

Security Officers shall report to their supervisors and appropriate facility staff any condition that could affect the safety or security of the facility. Conditions such as broken windows, unlocked doors and water leaks should be reported.

32. According to the above memorandum, a Security Officer shall   32._____

 A. make recommendations to his superiors concerning other facility staff members
 B. correct all unsafe conditions such as broken windows
 C. report a condition such as a water leak to his supervisor and appropriate facility staff
 D. make recommendations to facility staff concerning doors to be left unlocked

33. Following are two sentences that may or may not be written in correct English: 33._____
 I. Special Officer Cleveland was attempting to calm an emotionally disturbed visitor.
 II. The visitor did not stops crying and calling for his wife.
Which one of the following statements is CORRECT?

 A. Only Sentence I is written in correct English.
 B. Only Sentence II is written in correct English.
 C. Sentences I and II are both written in correct English.
 D. Neither Sentence I nor Sentence II is written in correct English.

34. Following are two sentences that may or may not be written in correct English: 34._____
 I. While on patrol, I observes a vagrant loitering near the drug dispensary.
 II. I escorted the vagrant out of the building and off the premises.
Which one of the following statements is CORRECT?

 A. Only Sentence I is written in correct English.
 B. Only Sentence II is written in correct English.
 C. Sentences I and II are both written in correct English.
 D. Neither Sentence I nor Sentence II is written in correct English.

35. Following are two sentences that may or may not be written in correct English: 35._____
 I. At 4:00 P.M., Sergeant Raymond told me to evacuate the waiting area immediately due to a bomb threat.
 II. Some of the clients did not want to leave the building.
Which one of the following statements is CORRECT?

 A. Only Sentence I is written in correct English.
 B. Only Sentence II is written in correct English.
 C. Sentences I and II are both written in correct English.
 D. Neither Sentence I nor Sentence II is written in correct English.

KEY (CORRECT ANSWERS)

1.	C	16.	D
2.	B	17.	C
3.	A	18.	D
4.	D	19.	B
5.	A	20.	A
6.	B	21.	D
7.	B	22.	B
8.	B	23.	C
9.	B	24.	A
10.	A	25.	B
11.	D	26.	A
12.	C	27.	C
13.	B	28.	B
14.	D	29.	C
15.	C	30.	C

31. D
32. C
33. A
34. B
35. C

READING COMPREHENSION
UNDERSTANDING AND INTERPRETING WRITTEN MATERIAL
EXAMINATION SECTION
TEST 1

Questions 1-10.

DIRECTIONS: Each question or incomplete statement is followed by several suggested answers or completions. Select the one that BEST answers the question or completes the statement. *PRINT THE LETTER OF THE CORRECT ANSWER IN THE SPACE AT THE RIGHT.*

1. Accident prevention is an activity which depends for success upon factual information, research, and analysis. Experience has proved that all accidents can be prevented through the correct application of basic accident prevention methods and techniques determined from factual cause data. Therefore, to achieve the maximum results from any safety and health program, a uniform system for the reporting of accidents and causes is established. The procedures required for a report, when properly carried out, will determine accurate cause factors and the most practical methods for applying preventive or remedial action. According to the above paragraphs, which of the following statements is MOST NEARLY correct?

    A. No matter how much effort is put forth, there are some accidents that cannot be prevented.
    B. Accident prevention is a research activity.
    C. Accident reporting systems are not related to accident prevention.
    D. The success of an accident prevention program depends on the correct use of a uniform accident reporting system.

1.____

Questions 2-7.

DIRECTIONS: Questions 2 through 7 are to be answered ONLY according to the information given in the following accident report.

DATE: February 2

TO:	Edward Moss, Superintendent Pacific Houses 2487 Shell Road Auburnsville, Illinois	SUBJECT:	Report of Accident to Philip Fay, Employee 1825 North 8th St. Auburnsville, Ill. Identification #374-24

    Philip Fay, an employee, came to my office at 10:15 A.M. yesterday and told me that he hurt his left elbow. When I asked him what happened, he told me that 15 minutes ago, while shoveling the snow from in front of Building #14 at 2280 Stone Ave., he slipped on some snow-covered ice and fell on his elbow. Joseph Sanchez and Arthur Campbell, who were working with him, saw what happened.

Mr. Fay complained of pain and could not bend his left arm. I called for an ambulance right away. A police patrol car from the 85th Precinct arrived 15 minutes later, and Patrolman Johnson, Shield #8743, said that an ambulance was on the way. At 10:45 A.M., an ambulance arrived from Auburn Hospital. Dr. Breen examined Mr. Fay and told me that he would have to go to the hospital for some x-ray pictures to determine how bad the injury was. The ambulance left with Mr. Fay at 11:00 A.M.

At 3:45 P.M., Mr. Fay called from the hospital and told me that his arm had been put in a cast in the emergency room of the hospital. He was told that he had fractured his left elbow and would have to stay out of work for about four weeks. He is to report back at the hospital in three weeks for another examination and to see if the cast can be taken off. His wife was at the hospital with him, and they were now going home.

Attached are the statements from the witnesses and our completed REPORT OF INJURY form.

William Fields
Foreman

2. Which one of the following did NOT see the accident?

   A. Campbell   B. Fay   C. Fields   D. Sanchez

3. The CORRECT date and time of accident is February

   A. 2, 10:00 A.M.
   B. 2, 10:15 A.M.
   C. 1, 10:00 A.M.
   D. 1, 10:15 A.M.

4. The ambulance came about _____ hour after _____.

   A. 1/4 ; the accident
   B. 1/4 ; it was called
   C. 1/2; the accident
   D. 1/2; it was called

5. It is not possible to tell whether Fay went to report the accident right away because the report does NOT say

   A. how long it takes to get from Building #14 to the foreman's office
   B. how long it takes to get from Stone Ave. to Shell Rd.
   C. whether Fay telephoned the foreman first
   D. whether the foreman was in his office as soon as Fay got there

6. From the facts in the report, Fay's action might be criticized because he

   A. did not give the foreman the complete story of what had happened
   B. did not take Campbell or Sanchez with him when he went to the foreman's office in case he should need help on the way
   C. did not remain at the accident site and send Sanchez and Campbell to bring the foreman
   D. telephoned from the hospital and by using his arm to do this he might have aggravated his condition

7. Assuming that the report gives the complete story of this incident, the action of the foreman may be criticized because he did NOT

    A. call an ambulance soon enough
    B. go to the hospital with the ambulance and stay with the injured man until he was discharged
    C. have the injured man sign a release of claim against the department
    D. make an on-the-spot investigation of the accident scene nor take corrective action

Questions 8-10.

DIRECTIONS: Questions 8 through 10 are to be answered ONLY according to the information given in the following passage.

A foreman has four maintainers and two helpers assigned to him. Listed below are the maintainers and helpers and their rate of speed in completing the assignments given to them. Assume all the foreman's men (maintainers and helpers) are of equal technical ability but some work faster than others while some are slower in completing their assignments. In all cases, no overtime is to be granted.

   Maintainer E - works at average rate of speed
   Maintainer F - works at twice the rate of speed as Maintainer E
   Maintainer G - works at the same rate of speed as Maintainer E
   Maintainer H - works at half the rate of speed as Maintainer E
   Helper J - works at same rate of speed as Maintainer G
   Helper K - works at same rate of speed as Maintainer H

8. A certain job must be done immediately, and Maintainer H and Helper J are the only men available.
   If Maintainer F, working alone, could normally complete this job in six days, the TOTAL time this foreman should allot to Maintainer H and Helper J to complete the same job is _____ days.

    A. 3   B. 4   C. 8   D. 12

9. While Maintainer E and Helper J are working on a job, Helper J reports that he will be out sick for at least a week. The job normally would have taken four more days to complete, and it must be completed within these four days.
   If Maintainer H and Helper K are the only two men available, this foreman should

    A. assign Helper K to replace Helper J
    B. assign Maintainer H to replace Helper J
    C. assign both Maintainer H and Helper K to replace Helper J
    D. inform his assistant supervisor that the job cannot be completed on time

10. This foreman has assigned all six of his men to a routine maintenance job. At the end of two days, the job is four-fifths completed; and instead of reassigning all his men the following day when they would finish early, the foreman cuts the gang so that the job will take one more full day to finish. The work gang on the last day should consist of Maintainer(s)

    A. F and H
    B. F and Helper J
    C. E and Helpers J and K
    D. G and H and Helper K

Questions 11-25.

DIRECTIONS: Each question consists of a statement. You are to indicate whether the statement is TRUE (T) or FALSE (F). *PRINT THE LETTER OF THE CORRECT ANSWER IN THE SPACE AT THE RIGHT.*

Questions 11-15.

DIRECTIONS: Questions 11 through 15 are to be answered ONLY according to the information given in the following paragraph.

USING LADDERS

All ladders must be checked each day for any defects before they are used. They should not be used if there are split rails or loose rungs or if they have become shaky. Two men should handle a stepladder which is over eight feet in height, one man if the ladder is smaller. One man must face the ladder and hold it with a firm grasp while the other is working on it. When you climb a ladder, always face it, grasp the siderails, and climb up one rung at a time. You should come down the same way.

11. A ladder which is new does not have to be inspected before it is used.   11.___

12. A ladder with a loose rung may be used if this rung is not stepped on.   12.___

13. A stepladder 6 feet long may be handled by one man.   13.___

14. If a 10-foot stepladder is used, one man must hold the ladder while the other works on it.   14.___

15. The siderails of a ladder do not have to be held when climbing down.   15.___

Questions 16-20.

DIRECTIONS: Questions 16 through 20 are to be answered ONLY according to the information given in the following paragraph.

TRAFFIC ACCIDENTS

Three auto accidents happened at the corner of Fifth Street and Seventh Avenue. The first, at 7:00 P.M. last night, knocked down a light pole when two cars collided. At 8:15 A.M. this morning, two other autos crashed head on. This afternoon, at 12:30 P.M., another pair of cars crashed. One of them jumped the curb, knocked over two traffic signs, and damaged three parked cars at the corner service station. No serious injury to the drivers was reported, but all the cars involved were severely damaged.

16. Nine cars were damaged in the three accidents.   16.___

17. The three accidents happened within a period of 14 hours.   17.___

18. A service station is located at the corner of Fifth Street and Seventh Avenue.   18.___

19. In the last accident, both cars jumped the curb and knocked over two light poles.   19.___

20. The drivers of the cars in the last accident were badly hurt.   20.___

Questions 21-25.

DIRECTIONS: Questions 21 through 25 are to be answered ONLY according to the information given in the following paragraph.

LIFTING

Improper lifting of heavy objects is a frequent cause of strains and ruptures. When a heavy object is to be lifted, an employee should stand close to the object and face it squarely. The feet are spread slightly apart, and one foot is a little ahead of the other. Then, bend the knees to bring the body down to the object and keep your back comfortably vertical. Raise the object slightly to see if you can lift it alone. If you can, get a firm grasp with both hands, balance the object, and raise it by straightening the legs, but still keeping the back erect. The raising motion is gradual, not swift. In this way you use the leg muscles which are the strongest muscles in the body. This method of lifting prevents strain to the back muscles which are weak and not built for lifting purposes.

21. Many ruptures are the result of not lifting heavy objects in the correct manner. 21.____

22. When an employee lifts a heavy package, he should keep his feet close together in order to balance the load. 22.____

23. When lifting a heavy object, the back should not be bent but kept upright. 23.____

24. It is best to lift heavy objects quickly in order to prevent strains and ruptures. 24.____

25. For purposes of lifting, the leg muscles are stronger than the arm muscles. 25.____

KEY (CORRECT ANSWERS)

1. D	11. F
2. C	12. F
3. C	13. T
4. D	14. T
5. A	15. F
6. B	16. T
7. D	17. F
8. C	18. T
9. C	19. F
10. B	20. F

21. T
22. F
23. T
24. F
25. T

TEST 2

DIRECTIONS: Each question or incomplete statement is followed by several suggested answers or completions. Select the one that BEST answers the question or completes the statement. *PRINT THE LETTER OF THE CORRECT ANSWER IN THE SPACE AT THE RIGHT.*

Questions 1-8.

DIRECTIONS: Questions 1 through 8, inclusive, are based on the ladder safety rules given below. Read these rules fully before answering these questions.

LADDER SAFETY RULES

When a ladder is placed on a slightly uneven supporting surface, use a flat piece of board or small wedge to even up the ladder feet. To secure the proper angle for resting a ladder, it should be placed so that the distance from the base of the ladder to the supporting wall is one-quarter the length of the ladder. To avoid overloading a ladder, only one person should work on a ladder at a time. Do not place a ladder in front of a door. When the top rung of a ladder rests against a pole, the ladder should be lashed securely. Clear loose stones or debris from the ground around the base of a ladder before climbing. While on a ladder, do not attempt to lean so that any part of the body, except arms or hands, extends more than 12 inches beyond the side rail. Always face the ladder when ascending or descending. When carrying ladders through buildings, watch for ceiling globes and lighting fixtures. Avoid the use of rolling ladders as scaffold supports.

1. A small wedge is used to

    A. even up the feet of a ladder resting on an uneven surface
    B. lock the wheels of a roller ladder
    C. secure the proper resting angle for a ladder
    D. secure a ladder against a pole

2. An 8-foot ladder resting against a wall should be so inclined that the distance between the base of the ladder and the wall is _____ feet.

    A. 2   B. 5   C. 7   D. 9

3. A ladder should be lashed securely when

    A. it is placed in front of a door
    B. loose stones are on the ground near the base of the ladder
    C. the top rung rests against a pole
    D. two people are working from the same ladder

4. Rolling ladders

    A. should be used for scaffold supports
    B. should not be used for scaffold supports
    C. are useful on uneven ground
    D. should be used against a pole

5. When carrying a ladder through a building, it is necessary to

   A. have two men to carry it
   B. carry the ladder vertically
   C. watch for ceiling globes
   D. face the ladder while carrying it

6. It is POOR practice to

   A. lash a ladder securely at any time
   B. clear debris from the base of a ladder before climbing
   C. even up the feet of a ladder resting on slightly uneven ground
   D. place a ladder in front of a door

7. A person on a ladder should NOT extend his head beyond the side rail by more than _____ inches.

   A. 12   B. 9   C. 7   D. 5

8. The MOST important reason for permitting only one person to work on a ladder at a time is that

   A. both could not face the ladder at one time
   B. the ladder will be overloaded
   C. time would be lost going up and down the ladder
   D. they would obstruct each other

Questions 9-13.

DIRECTIONS: Questions 9 through 13 concern an excerpt of written material which you are to read and study carefully. The excerpt is immediately followed by five statements which refer to it alone. You are required to judge whether each statement

   A. is entirely true
   B. is entirely false
   C. is partly true and partly false
   D. may or may not be true but cannot be answered on the basis of the facts as given in the excerpt

It is true that in 1987 there were more strikes than in any year, excepting 1986, since 1970. However, the number of workers involved was less in 1987 than in any year since 1981, and man-days of idleness due to strikes, the MOST accurate measure of industrial strife, were less in 1987 than in any year since 1980, again excepting 1986.

9. There were fewer workers involved in strikes in 1986 than in 1981.

10. There were more strikes in 1986 than in 1987.

11. There were more strikes in 1986 than in 1970.

12. There were fewer workers involved in strikes but more man-days of idleness in 1981 than 1987.

13. There were fewer man-days of idleness and fewer workers involved in strikes in 1986 than 1987.

Questions 14-16.

DIRECTIONS: Questions 14 through 16 are to be answered on the basis of the information given in the following passage.

Telephone service in a government agency should be adequate and complete with respect to information given or action taken. It must be remembered that telephone contacts should receive special consideration since the caller cannot see the operator. People like to feel that they are receiving personal attention and that their requests or criticisms are receiving individual rather than routine consideration. All this contributes to what has come to be known as Tone of Service. The aim is to use standards which are clearly very good or superior. The factors to be considered in determining what makes good Tone of Service are speech, courtesy, understanding, and explanations. A caller's impression of Tone of Service will affect the general attitude toward the agency and city services in general.

14. The above passage states that people who telephone a government agency like to feel that they are

    A. creating a positive image of themselves
    B. being given routine consideration
    C. receiving individual attention
    D. setting standards for telephone service

15. Which of the following is NOT mentioned in the above passage as a factor in determining good Tone of Service?

    A. Courtesy   B. Education
    C. Speech   D. Understanding

16. The above passage IMPLIES that failure to properly handle telephone calls is *most likely* to result in

    A. a poor impression of city agencies by the public
    B. a deterioration of courtesy toward operators
    C. an effort by operators to improve the Tone of Service
    D. special consideration by the public of operator difficulties

Questions 17-20.

DIRECTIONS: Questions 17 through 20 are to be answered ONLY according to the information given in the following passage.

ACCIDENT PREVENTION

Many accidents and injuries can be prevented if employees learn to be more careful. The wearing of shoes with thin or badly worn soles or open toes can easily lead to foot injuries from tacks, nails, and chair and desk legs. Loose or torn clothing should not be worn near moving machinery. This is especially true of neckties which can very easily become caught in the machine. You should not place objects so that they block or partly block hallways, corridors, or other passageways. Even when they are stored in the proper place, tools, supplies, and equipment should be carefully placed or piled so as not to fall, nor have anything stick out from a pile. Before cabinets, lockers or ladders are moved, the tops should be cleared of anything which might injure someone or fall off. If necessary, use a dolly to move these or other bulky objects.

Despite all efforts to avoid accidents and injuries, however, some will happen. If an employee is injured, no matter how small the injury, he should report it to his supervisor and have the injury treated. A small cut that is not attended to can easily become infected and can cause more trouble than some injuries which at first seem more serious. It never pays to take chances.

17. According to the above passage, the one statement that is NOT true is that 17.____

    A. by being more careful, employees can reduce the number of accidents that happen
    B. women should wear shoes with open toes for comfort when working
    C. supplies should be piled so that nothing is sticking out from the pile
    D. if an employee sprains his wrist at work, he should tell his supervisor about it

18. According to the above passage, you should NOT wear loose clothing when you are 18.____

    A. in a corridor   B. storing tools
    C. opening cabinets   D. near moving machinery

19. According to the above passage, before moving a ladder you should 19.____

    A. test all the rungs
    B. get a dolly to carry the ladder at all times
    C. remove everything from the top of the ladder which might fall off
    D. remove your necktie

20. According to the above passage, an employee who gets a slight cut should 20.____

    A. have it treated to help prevent infection
    B. know that a slight cut becomes more easily infected than a big cut
    C. pay no attention to it as it can't become serious
    D. realize that it is more serious than any other type of injury

Questions 21-24.

DIRECTIONS: Questions 21 through 24 are to be answered on the basis of the following report.

TO: Thomas Smith   Date: June 14.
       Supervising Menagerie Keeper
                                         Subject:
FROM: Jay Jones
       Senior Menagerie Keeper

On June 14, a visitor to the monkey house at the zoo was noticed annoying the animals. He was frightening the animals by making loud noises and throwing stones at the animals in the cages. The visitor was asked to stop annoying the animals but did not. And he was then asked to leave the monkey house by the keeper on duty. The visitor would not leave and said that the zoo is public property and that as a citizen he has every right to be there. The keeper kept trying to pursuade the visitor to leave but was unsuccessful. The keeper finally threatened to call the police. The visitor soon left the monkey house and did not return. Fortunately, no animals were harmed in this incident.

21. The subject of the report has been left out.
Which one of these would be the BEST statement for the subject of the report?

    A. Loud noises in the monkey house
    B. Police called to monkey house
    C. Visitor annoying monkeys on June 14
    D. Monkeys unharmed by visitor

22. Which one of these is an important piece of information that should have been included in the FIRST sentence of the report?

    A. The kinds of monkeys in the monkey house
    B. Whether the visitor was a man or a woman
    C. The address of the monkey house
    D. The name of the zoo where the incident took place

23. The fourth sentence which begins with the words *And he was then asked...* is poorly written because

    A. the sentence begins with *And*
    B. the words *monkey house* should be written *Monkey House*
    C. the words *on duty* should be written *on-duty*
    D. *didn't* would be better than *did not*

24. In the sixth sentence, which begins with the words *The keeper kept trying...* , a word that is spelled wrong is

    A. trying   B. pursuade
    C. visitor   D. unsuccessful

Questions 25-27.

DIRECTIONS: Questions 25 through 27 test how well you can read and understand what you read. Read about ELEPHANTS. Then, on the basis of what you read, answer these questions.

ELEPHANTS

Elephants are peaceful animals and have very few real natural enemies. As with many other animals, when faced with danger the elephant tries to make himself look larger to his enemy. He does this by raising his head and trunk to look taller. The elephant will also extend his ears to look wider. Other threatening gestures may be made. The elephant may shift his weight from side to side, make a shrill scream, or pretend to charge with his trunk held high. If the enemy still fails to retreat, the elephant will make a serious attack.

25. When an elephant is in danger, he tries to make it appear that he is

    A. stronger   B. smaller   C. larger   D. angry

26. When he is threatened, an elephant tries to make himself look broader by 26.____

    A. taking a deep breath
    B. spreading out his ears
    C. shifting his weight from side to side
    D. holding his trunk high

27. If his enemy does not run away, the elephant will 27.____

    A. attack him
    B. run in the opposite direction
    C. hit the enemy with his trunk
    D. make a shrill scream

Questions 28-30.

DIRECTIONS: Read about PREVENTING DISEASE. Then, on the basis of what you read, answer Questions 28 through 30.

PREVENTING DISEASE

Proper feeding, housing, and handling are important in maintaining an animal's defenses against disease and parasites. The best diets are those that contain proteins, vitamins, minerals, and the other essential food elements. Proteins are especially important because they are necessary for growth. Minerals such as iron, copper, and cobalt help correct anemia. It has been shown that an animal's resistance can be decreased by improper feeding. However, it has not been proved that the use of certain types of feeds will increase the resistance of animals to infectious diseases. If animals are kept in good condition by proper diet and sanitary conditions, natural resistance to disease and parasites will be highest.

28. Food elements that are required especially for growth are 28.____

    A. minerals   B. vitamins
    C. proteins   D. carbohydrates

29. If animals are NOT fed correctly, they will 29.____

    A. have more diseases
    B. fight with each other
    C. need more proteins
    D. be able to kill parasites

30. The bodies of animals will BEST be able to fight disease naturally when they 30.____

    A. are kept warm
    B. are given immunity shots
    C. are given extra food
    D. have good diet and clean quarters

KEY (CORRECT ANSWERS)

1.	A	16.	A
2.	A	17.	B
3.	C	18.	D
4.	B	19.	C
5.	C	20.	A
6.	D	21.	C
7.	A	22.	D
8.	B	23.	A
9.	B	24.	B
10.	A	25.	C
11.	D	26.	B
12.	A	27.	A
13.	C	28.	C
14.	C	29.	A
15.	B	30.	D

READING COMPREHENSION
UNDERSTANDING AND INTERPRETING WRITTEN MATERIAL
EXAMINATION SECTION
TEST 1

DIRECTIONS: Each question or incomplete statement is followed by several suggested answers or completions. Select the one that BEST answers the question or completes the statement. *PRINT THE LETTER OF THE CORRECT ANSWER IN THE SPACE AT THE RIGHT.*

Questions 1-3.

DIRECTIONS: Questions 1 through 3 are to be answered SOLELY on the basis of the following paragraph.

The final step in an accident investigation is the making out of the police report. In the case of a traffic accident, the officer should go right from the scene to his office to write up the report. However, if a person was injured in the accident and taken to a hospital, the officer should visit him there before going to his office to prepare his report. This personal visit to the injured person does not mean that the office must make a physical examination; but he should make an effort to obtain a statement from the injured person or persons. If this is not possible, information should be obtained from the attending physician as to the extent of the injury. In any event, without fail, the name of the physician should be secured and the report should state the name of the physician and the fact that he told the officer that, at a certain stated time on a certain stated date, the injuries were of such and such a nature. If the injured person dies before the officer arrives at the hospital, it may be necessary to take the responsible person into custody at once.

1. When a person has been injured in a traffic accident, the one of the following actions which it is necessary for a police officer to take in connection with the accident report is to
    A. prepare the police report immediately after the accident, and then go to the hospital to speak to the victim
    B. do his utmost to verify the victim's story prior to preparing the official police report of the incident
    C. be sure to include the victim's statement in the police report in every case
    D. try to get the victim's version of the accident prior to preparing the police report

1.____

2. When one of the persons injured in a motor vehicle accident dies, the above paragraph provides that the police officer
    A. must immediately take the responsible person into custody, if the injured person is already dead when the officer appears at the scene of the accident
    B. must either arrest the responsible person or get a statement from him, if the injured person dies after arrival at the hospital

2.____

C. may have to immediately arrest the responsible person, if the injured person dies in the hospital prior to the officer's arrival there
D. may refrain from arresting the responsible person, but only if the responsible person is also seriously injured

3. When someone has been injured in a collision between two automobiles and is given medical treatment shortly thereafter by a physician, the one of the following actions which the police officer MUST take with regard to the physician is to
   A. obtain his name and his diagnosis of the injuries, regardless of the place where treatment was given
   B. obtain his approval of the portion of the police report relating to the injured person and the treatment given him prior to and after his arrival at the hospital
   C. obtain his name, his opinion of the extent of the person's injuries, and his signed statement of the treatment he gave the injured person
   D. set a certain stated time on a certain stated date for interviewing him, unless he is an attending physician in a hospital

Questions 4-7.

DIRECTIONS: Questions 4 through 7 are to be answered SOLELY on the basis of the following paragraph.

Because of the importance of preserving physical evidence, the patrolman should not enter a scene of a crime if it can be examined visually from one position and if no other pressing duty requires his presence there. However, there are some responsibilities that take precedence over preservation of evidence. Some examples are: rescue work, disarming dangerous persons, quelling a disturbance. However, the patrolman should learn how to accomplish these more vital tasks, while at the same time preserving as much evidence as possible. If he finds it necessary to enter upon the scene, he should quickly study the place of entry to learn if any evidence will suffer by his contact; then he should determine the routes to be used in walking to the spot where his presence is required. Every place where a foot will fall or where a hand or other part of his body will touch, should be examined with the eye. Objects should not be touched or moved unless there is a definite and compelling reason. For identification of most items of physical evidence at the initial investigation, it is seldom necessary to touch or move them.

4. The one of the following titles which is the MOST appropriate for the above paragraph is:
   A. Determining the Priority of Tasks at the Scene of a Crime
   B. The Principal Reasons for Preserving Evidence at the Scene of a Crime
   C. Precautions to Take at the Scene of a Crime
   D. Evidence to be Examined at the Scene of a Crime

3 (#1)

5. When a patrolman feels that it is essential for him to enter the immediate area where a crime has been committed, he should
   A. quickly but carefully glance around to determine whether his entering the area will damage any evidence present
   B. remove all objects of evidence from his predetermined route in order to avoid stepping on them
   C. carefully replace any object immediately if it is moved or touched by his hands or any other part of his body
   D. use only the usual place of entry to the scene in order to avoid disturbing any possible clues left on rear doors and windows by the criminal

5.____

6. The one of the following which is the LEAST urgent duty of a police officer who has just reported to the scene of a crime is to
   A. disarm the hysterical victim of the crime who is wildly waving a loaded gun in all directions
   B. give first aid to a possible suspect who has been injured while attempting to leave the scene of the crime
   C. prevent observers from attacking and injuring the persons suspected of having committed the crime
   D. preserve from damage or destruction any evidence necessary for the proper prosecution of the case against the criminals

6.____

7. A police officer has just reported to the scene of a crime in response to a phone call.
   The BEST of the following actions for him to take with respect to objects of physical evidence present at the scene is to
   A. make no attempt to enter the crime scene if his entry will disturb any vital physical evidence
   B. map out the shortest straight path to follow in walking to the spot where the physical evidence may be found
   C. move such objects of physical evidence as are necessary to enable him to assist the wounded victim of the crime
   D. quickly examine all objects of physical evidence in order to determine which objects may be touched and which may not

7.____

Questions 8-11.

DIRECTIONS: Questions 8 through 11 are to be answered SOLELY on the basis of the following paragraph.

After examining a document and comparing the characters with specimens of other specimens of other handwritings, the laboratory technician may conclude that a certain individual did write the questioned document. This opinion could be based on a large number of similar, as well as a small number of dissimilar but explainable characteristics. On the other hand, if the laboratory technician concludes that the person in question did not write the questioned document, such an opinion could be based on the large number of characteristics which are dissimilar, or even on a small number which are dissimilar provided that these are of overriding significance, and despite the presence of explainable similarities. The laboratory expert is not always able to give a positive opinion. He may state that a certain individual probably did or did not write the questioned document. Such an opinion is usually the result of insufficient material, either in the questioned document or in the specimens submitted for comparison. Finally, the expert may be unable to come to any conclusion at all because of insufficient material submitted for comparison or because of improper specimens.

8. The one of the following which is the MOST appropriate title for the above paragraph is:
   A. Similar and Dissimilar Characteristics in Handwriting
   B. The Limitations of Handwriting Analysis in Identifying the Writer
   C. The Positive Identification of Suspects Through Their Handwriting
   D. The Inability to Identify an Individual Through His Handwriting

9. When a handwriting expert compares the handwriting on two separate documents and decides that they were written by the same person, his conclusions are generally based on the fact that
   A. a large number of characteristics in both documents are dissimilar but the few similar characteristics are more important
   B. all the characteristics are alike in both documents
   C. similar characteristics need to be examined as to the cause for their similarity
   D. most of the characteristics in both documents are alike and their few differences are readily explainable

10. If a fingerprint technician carefully examines a handwritten threatening letter and compares it with specimens of handwriting made by a suspect, he would be MOST likely to decide that the suspect did NOT write the threatening letter when the handwriting specimens and the letter have
    A. a small number of dissimilarities
    B. a small number of dissimilar but explainable characteristics
    C. important dissimilarities despite the fact that these may be few
    D. some similar characteristics that are easily imitated or disguised

11. There are instances when even a trained handwriting expert cannot decide definitely whether or not a certain document and a set of handwriting specimens were written by the same person.
    This inability to make a positive decision generally arises in situations where
    A. only one document of considerable length is available for comparison with a sufficient supply of handwriting specimens
    B. the limited nature of the handwriting specimens submitted restricts their comparability with the questioned document
    C. the dissimilarities are not explainable
    D. the document submitted for comparison does not include all the characteristics included in the handwriting specimens

Questions 12-14.

DIRECTIONS: Questions 12 through 14 are to be answered SOLELY on the basis of the following paragraph.

In cases of drunken driving, or of disorderly conduct while intoxicated, too many times some person who had been completely under the influence of alcoholic liquor at the time of his arrest has walked out of court without any conviction just because an officer failed to make the proper observation. Many of the larger cities and counties make use of various scientific methods to determine the degree of intoxication of a person, such as breath, urine, and blood tests. Many of the smaller cities, however, do not have the facilities to make these various tests, and must, therefore, rely on the observation tests given at the scene. These consist, among other things, of noticing how the subject walked, talked, and acted. One test that is usually given at night is the eye reaction to light, which the officer gives by shining his flashlight into the eyes of the subject. The manner in which the pupils of the eyes react to the light helps to determine the sobriety of a person. If he is intoxicated, the pupils of his eyes are dilated more at night than the eyes of a sober person. Also, when a light is flashed into the eyes of a sober person, his pupils contract instantly, but in the case of a person under the influence of liquor, the pupils contract very slowly.

12. Many persons who have been arrested on a charge of driving while completely intoxicated have been acquitted by a judge because the arresting officer had neglected to
    A. bring the driver to court while he was still under the influence of alcohol
    B. make the required scientific tests to fully substantiate his careful personal observations of the driver's intoxicated condition
    C. submit to the court any test results showing the driver's condition or degree of drunkenness
    D. watch the driver closely for some pertinent facts which would support the officer's suspicions of the driver's intoxicated condition

12.____

13. When a person is arrested for acting in a disorderly and apparently intoxicated manner in public, the kind of test which would fit in BEST with the thought of the above statement is:
    A. In many smaller cities, a close watch on his behavior and of his reactions to various blood and body tests
    B. In many smaller cities, having him walk a straight line
    C. In most larger counties, close watch of the speed of his reactions to the flashlight test
    D. In most cities of all sizes, the application of the latest scientific techniques in the analysis of his breath

13.____

14. When a person suspected of driving a motor vehicle while intoxicated is being examined to determine whether or not he actually is intoxicated, one of the methods used is to shine the light of a flashlight into his eyes.

14.____

When this method is used, the NORMAL result is that the pupils of the suspect's eyes will
- A. expand instantly if he is fully intoxicated, and remain unchanged if he is completely sober
- B. expand very slowly if he has had only a small amount of alcohol, and very rapidly if he has had a considerable amount of alcohol
- C. grow smaller at once if he is sober, and grow smaller more slowly if he is intoxicated
- D. grow smaller very slowly if he is fully sober, and grow smaller instantaneously if he is fully intoxicated

Questions 15-17.

DIRECTIONS: Questions 15 through 17 are to be answered SOLELY on the basis of the following paragraph.

Where an officer has personal knowledge of facts, sufficient to constitute reasonable grounds to believe that a person has committed or is committing a felony, he may arrest him, and, after having lawfully placed him under arrest, may search and take into his possession any incriminating evidence. The right of an officer to make an arrest and search is not limited to cases where the officer has personal knowledge of the commission of a felony, because he may act upon information conveyed to him by third persons which he believes to be reliable. Where an officer, charged with the duty of enforcing the law, receives information from apparently reliable sources, which would induce in the mind of the prudent person a belief that a felony was being or had been committed, he may make an arrest and search the person of a defendant, but he is not justified in acting on anonymous information alone.

15. When a felony has been committed, an officer would be acting MOST properly if he arrested a man
    - A. when he, the officer, has a police report that the man is suspected of having been involved in several minor offenses
    - B. when he, the officer, has received information from a usually reliable source that the man was involved in the crime
    - C. only when he, the officer, has personal knowledge that the man has committed the felony
    - D. when he, the officer, knows for a fact that the man has associated in the past with several persons who had been seen near the scene of the felony

15.____

16. An officer would be acting MOST properly if he searched a suspect for incriminating evidence
    - A. when he has received detailed information concerning the fact that the suspect is going to commit a felony
    - B. only after having lawfully arrested the suspect and charged him with having committed a felony
    - C. when he has just received an anonymous tip that the suspect had just committed a felony and is in illegal possession of stolen goods

16.____

D. in order to find in his possession legally admissible evidence on the basis of which the officer could then proceed to arrest the suspect for having committed a felony

17. A police officer has received information from an informant that a crime has been committed. The informant has also named two persons who he says committed the crime.
The officer's decision to both arrest and search the two suspects would be
    A. *correct*, if it would not be unreasonable to assume that the crime committed is a felony, and if the informant has been trustworthy in the past
    B. *incorrect*, if the informant has no proof but his own word to offer that a felony has been committed, although he has always been trustworthy in the past
    C. *correct*, if it would be logical and prudent to assume that the information is accurate regardless of whether the offense committed is a felony or a less serious crime
    D. *incorrect*, even if the informant produces objective and seemingly convincing proof that a felony has been committed, but has a reputation of occasional past unreliability

17._____

Questions 18-20.

DIRECTIONS: Questions 18 through 20 are to be answered SOLELY on the basis of the following paragraph.

If there are many persons at the scene of a hit-and-run accident, it would be a waste of time to question all of them; the witness needed is the one who can best describe the missing auto. Usually the person most qualified to do this is a youth of fifteen or sixteen years of age. He is more likely to be able to tell the make and year of a car than most other persons. A woman may be a good witness as to how the accident occurred, but usually will be unable to tell the make of the car. As soon as any information with regard to the missing car or its description is obtained, the police officer should call or radio headquarters and have the information put on the air. This should be done without waiting for further details, for time is an important factor. If a good description of the wanted car is obtained, then the next task is to get a description of the driver. In this hunt, it is found that a woman is often a more accurate witness than a man. Usually she will be able to state the color of clothes worn by the driver. If the wanted driver is a woman, another woman will often be able to tell the color and sometimes even the material of the clothing worn.

18. A hit-and-run accident has occurred and a police officer is attempting to obtain information from persons who had witnessed the incident.
It would generally be BEST for him to question a
    A. boy in his late teens, when the officer is seeking an accurate description of the age, coloring, and physical build of the driver of the car
    B. man, when the officer is seeking an accurate description of the driver of the car and the color and material of his coat, suit, and hat

18._____

C. woman, when the officer is seeking an accurate description of the driver of the car
D. young teenage girl, when the officer is seeking an accurate description of the style and color of the clothes worn by the driver of the car

19. Time is an important factor when an attempt is being made to apprehend the guilty driver in a hit-and-run accident.
However, the EARLIEST moment when the police should broadcast a radio announcement of the crime is when a(n)
    A. description of the missing car or any facts concerning it have been obtained
    B. tentative identification of the driver of the missing car has been made
    C. detailed description of the missing car and its occupant has been obtained
    D. eyewitness account has been obtained of the accident, including the identity of the victim, the extent of injuries, and the make and license number of the car

19._____

20. The time when it would be MOST desirable to get a description of the driver of the hit-and-run car is
    A. after getting a description of the car itself
    B. before transmitting information concerning the car to headquarters for broadcasting
    C. as soon as the officer arrives at the scene of the accident
    D. as soon as the victim of the accident has been given needed medical assistance

20._____

KEY (CORRECT ANSWERS)

1.	D	11.	B
2.	C	12.	D
3.	A	13.	B
4.	C	14.	C
5.	A	15.	B
6.	D	16.	B
7.	C	17.	A
8.	B	18.	C
9.	D	19.	A
10.	C	20.	A

TEST 2

DIRECTIONS: Each question or incomplete statement is followed by several suggested answers or completions. Select the one that BEST answers the question or completes the statement. *PRINT THE LETTER OF THE CORRECT ANSWER IN THE SPACE AT THE RIGHT.*

Questions 1-4.

DIRECTIONS: Questions 1 through 4 are to be answered SOLELY on the basis of the following paragraph.

Automobile tire tracks found at the scene of a crime constitute an important link in the chain of physical evidence. In many cases, these are the only clues available. In some areas, unpaved ground adjoins the highway or paved streets. A suspect will often park his car off the paved portion of the street when committing a crime, sometimes leaving excellent tire tracks. Comparison of the tire track impressions with the tires is possible only when the vehicle has been found. However, the initial problem facing the police is the task of determining what kind of car probably made the impressions found at the scene of the crime. If the make, model, and year of the car which made the impressions can be determined, it is obvious that the task of elimination is greatly lessened.

1. The one of the following which is the MOST appropriate title for the above paragraph is:
    A. The Use of Automobiles in the Commission of Crimes
    B. The Use of Tire Tracks in Police Work
    C. The Capture of Criminals by Scientific Police Work
    D. The Positive Identification of Criminals Through Their Cars

1.____

2. When searching for clear signs left by the car used in the commission of a crime, the MOST likely place for the police to look would be on the
    A. highway adjoining unpaved streets
    B. highway adjacent to paved street
    C. paved street adjacent to the highway
    D. unpaved ground adjacent to a highway

2.____

3. Automobile tire tracks found at the scene of a crime are of value as evidence in that they are
    A. generally sufficient to trap and convict a suspect
    B. the most important link in the chain of physical evidence
    C. often the only evidence at hand
    D. circumstantial rather than direct

3.____

4. The PRIMARY reason for the police to try to find out which make, model, and year of car was involved in the commission of a crime is to
    A. compare the tire tracks left at the scene of the crime with the type of tires used on cars of that make
    B. determine if the mud on the tires of the suspected car matches the mud in the unpaved road near the scene of the crime

4.____

111

C. reduce to a large extent the amount of work involved in determining the particular car used in the commission of a crime
D. alert the police patrol forces to question the occupants of all automobiles of this type

Questions 5-8.

DIRECTIONS: Questions 5 through 8 are to be answered SOLELY on the basis of the following paragraph.

When stopping vehicles on highways to check for suspects or fugitives, the police use an automobile roadblock whenever possible. This consists of three cars placed in prearranged positions. Car number one is parked across the left lane of the roadway with the front diagonally facing toward the center line. Car number two is parked across the right lane, with the front of the vehicle also toward the center line, in a position perpendicular to car number one and approximately twenty feet to the rear. Continuing another twenty feet to the rear along the highway, car number three is parked in an identical manner to car number one. The width of the highway determines the angle or position in which the autos should be placed. In addition to the regular roadblock signs and the uses of flares at night only, there is an officer located at both the entrance and exit to direct and control traffic from both directions. This type of roadblock forces all approaching autos to reduce speed and zigzag around the police cars. Officers standing behind the parked cars can most safely and carefully view all passing motorists. Once a suspect is inside the block, it becomes extremely difficult to crash out.

5. Of the following, the MOST appropriate title for this paragraph is:
   A. The Construction of an Escape-Proof Roadblock
   B. Regulation of Automobile Traffic Through a Police Roadblock
   C. Safety Precautions Necessary in Making an Automobile Roadblock
   D. Structure of a Roadblock to Detain Suspects or Fugitives

6. When setting up a three-car roadblock, the *relative* positions of the cars should be such that
   A. the front of car number one is placed diagonally to the center line and faces car number three
   B. car number three is placed parallel to the center line and its front faces the right side of the road
   C. car number two is placed about 20 feet from car number one and its front faces the left side of the road
   D. car number three is parallel to and about 20 feet away from car number one

7. Officers can observe occupants of all cars passing through the roadblock with GREATEST safety when
   A. warning flares are lighted to illuminate the area sufficiently at night
   B. warning signs are put up at each end of the roadblock
   C. they are stationed at both the exit and the entrance of the roadblock
   D. they take up positions behind cars in the roadblock

8. The type of automobile roadblock described in the above paragraph is of value in police work because
    A. a suspect is unable to escape its confines by using force
    B. it is frequently used to capture suspects with no danger to the police
    C. it requires only two officers to set up and operate
    D. vehicular traffic within its confines is controlled as to speed and direction

8.____

Questions 9-11.

DIRECTIONS: Questions 9 through 11 are to be answered SOLELY on the basis of the following paragraph.

A problem facing the police department in one area of the city was to try to reduce the number of bicycle thefts which had been increasing at an alarming rate in the past three or four years. A new program was adopted to get at the root of the problem. Tags were printed, reminding youngsters that bicycles left unlocked can be easily stolen. The police concentrated on such places as theaters, a municipal swimming pool, an athletic field, and the local high school, and tied tags on all bicycles which were not locked. The majority of bicycle thefts took place at the swimming pool. In 2019, during the first two weeks the pool was open, an average of 10 bicycle was stolen there daily. During the same two-week period, 30 bicycles a week were stolen at the athletic field, 15 at the high school, and 11 at all theaters combined. In 2020, after tagging the unlocked bicycles, it was found that 20 bicycles a week were stolen at the pool and 5 at the high school. It was felt that the police tags had helped the most, although the school officials had helped to a great extent in this program by distributing "locking" notices to parents and children, and the use of the loudspeaker at the pool urging children to lock their bicycles had also been very helpful.

9. The one of the following which had the GREATEST effect in the campaign to reduce bicycle stealing was the
    A. distribution of "locking" notices by the school officials
    B. locking of all bicycles left in public places
    C. police tagging of bicycles left unlocked by youngsters
    D. use of the loudspeaker at the swimming pool

9.____

10. The tagging program was instituted by the police department CHIEFLY to
    A. determine the areas where most bicycle thieves operated
    B. instill in youngsters the importance of punishing bicycle thieves
    C. lessen the rising rate of bicycle thefts
    D. recover as many as possible of the stolen bicycles

10.____

11. The figures showing the number of bicycle thefts in the various areas surveyed indicate that in 2019
    A. almost as many thefts occurred at the swimming pool as at all theaters combined
    B. fewer thefts occurred at the athletic field than at both the high school and all theaters combined
    C. more than half the thefts occurred at the swimming pool
    D. twice as many thefts occurred at the high school as at the athletic field

11.____

Questions 12-13.

DIRECTIONS: Questions 12 and 13 are to be answered SOLELY on the basis of the following paragraph.

A survey has shown that crime prevention work is most successful if the officers are assigned on rotating shifts to provide for around-the-clock coverage. An officer may work days for a time and then be switched to nights. The prime object of the night work is to enable the officer to spot conditions inviting burglars. Complete lack of, or faulty locations of, night lights and other conditions that may invite burglars, which might go unnoticed during daylight hours, can be located and corrected more readily through night work. Night work also enables the officer to check local hangouts of juvenile, such as bus and railway depots, certain cafes or pool halls, the local roller rink, and the building where a juvenile dance is held every Friday night. Detectives also join patrolmen cruising in radio patrol cars to check on juveniles loitering late at night and to spot-check local bars for juveniles.

12. The MOST important purpose of assigning officers to night shifts is to make it possible for them to   12._____
   A. correct conditions which may not be readily noticed during the day
   B. discover the locations of, and replace, missing and faulty night lights
   C. locate criminal hangouts
   D. notice things at night which cannot be noticed during the daytime

13. The type of shifting of officers which BEST prevents crime is to have   13._____
   A. day-shift officers rotated to night work
   B. rotating shifts provide sufficient officers for coverage 24 hours daily
   C. an officer work around the clock on a 24-hour basis as police needs arise
   D. rotating shifts to give the officers varied experience

Questions 14-15.

DIRECTIONS: Questions 14 and 15 are to be answered SOLELY on the basis of the following paragraph.

Proper firearms training is one phase of law enforcement which cannot be ignored. No part of the training of a police officer is more important or more valuable. The officer's life and often the lives of his fellow officers depend directly upon his skill with the weapon he is carrying. Proficiency with the revolver is not attained exclusively by the volume of ammunition used and the number of hours spent on the firing line. Supervised practice and the use of training aids and techniques help make the shooter. It is essential to have a good firing range where new officers are trained and older personnel practice in scheduled firearms sessions. The fundamental points to be stressed are grip, stance, breathing, sight alignment and trigger squeeze. Coordination of thought, vision, and motion must be achieved before the officer gains confidence in his shooting ability. Attaining this ability will make the student a better officer and enhance his value to the force.

14. A police officer will gain confidence in his shooting ability only after he has
    A. spent the required number of hours on the firing line
    B. been given sufficient supervised practice
    C. learned the five fundamental points
    D. learned to coordinate revolver movement with his sight and thought

15. Proper training in the use of firearms is one aspect of law enforcement which must be given serious consideration CHIEFLY because it is the
    A. most useful and essential single factor in the training of a police officer
    B. one phase of police officer training which stresses mental and physical coordination
    C. costliest aspect of police officer training involving considerable expense for the ammunition used in target practice
    D. most difficult part of police officer training, involving the expenditure of many hour on the firing line

Questions 16-20.

DIRECTIONS: Questions 16 through 20 are to be answered SOLELY on the basis of the following paragraph.

Lifting consists of transferring a print that has been dusted with powder to a transfer medium in order to preserve the print. Chemically developed prints cannot be lifted. Proper lifting of fingerprints is difficult and should be undertaken only when other means of recording the print are neither available nor suitable. Lifting should not be attempted from a porous surface. There are two types of commercial lifting tape which are good transfer mediums: rubber adhesive lift, one side of which is gummed and covered with thin, transparent celluloid; and transparent lifting tape, made of cellophane, one side of which is gummed. A package of acetate covers, frosted on one side and used to cover and protect the lifted print, accompanies each roll. If commercial tape is not available, transparent scotch tape may be used. The investigator should remove the celluloid or acetate cover from the lifting tape; smooth the tape, gummy side down, firmly and evenly over the entire print; gently peel the tape off the surface; replace the cover; and attach pertinent identifying data to the tape. All parts of the print should come in contact with the tape; air pockets should be avoided. The print will adhere to the lifting tape. The cover permits the print to be viewed and protects it from damage. Transparent lifting tape does not reverse the print. If a rubber adhesive lift is utilized, the print is reversed. Before a direct comparison can be made, the lifted print must be photographed, the negative reversed and a positive made.

16. An investigator wishing to preserve a record of fingerprints on a highly porous surface should
    A. develop them chemically before attempting to lift them
    B. lift them with scotch tape only when no other means of recording the prints are available
    C. employ some method other than lifting
    D. dust them with powder before attempting to lift them with rubber adhesive lift

17. Disregarding all other considerations, the SIMPLEST process to use in lifting a fingerprint from a window pane is that involving the use of
    A. rubber adhesive lift, because it gives a positive print in one step
    B. dusting powder and a camera, because the photograph is less likely to break than the window pane
    C. a chemical process, because it both develops and preserves the print at the same time
    D. transparent lifting tape, because it does not reverse the print

17.____

18. When a piece of commercial lifting tape is being used by an investigator wishing to lift a clear fingerprint from a smoothly-finished metal safe-door, he should
    A. prevent the ends of the tape from getting stuck to the metal surface because of the danger of forming air-pockets and thus damaging the print
    B. make certain that the tape covers all parts of the print and no air-pocket are formed
    C. carefully roll the tape over the most significant parts of the print only to avoid forming air-pockets
    D. be especially cautious not to destroy the air-pockets since this would tend to blur the print

18.____

19. When fingerprints lifted from an object found at the scene of a crime are to be compared with the fingerprints of a suspect, the lifted print
    A. can be compared directly only if a rubber adhesive lift was used
    B. cannot be compared directly if transparent scotch tape was used
    C. can be compared directly if transparent scotch tape was used
    D. must be photographed first and a positive made if any commercial lifting tape was used

19.____

20. When a rubber adhesive lift is to be used to lift a fingerprint, the one of the following which must be gently peeled off FIRST is the
    A. acetate cover   B. celluloid strip
    C. dusted surface   D. tape off the print surface

20.____

KEY (CORRECT ANSWERS)

1.	B	11.	C
2.	D	12.	A
3.	C	13.	B
4.	C	14.	D
5.	D	15.	A
6.	C	16.	C
7.	D	17.	D
8.	D	18.	B
9.	C	19.	C
10.	C	20.	B

MAP READING
EXAMINATION SECTION
TEST 1

DIRECTIONS: Each question or incomplete statement is followed by several suggested answers or completions. Select the one that BEST answers the question or completes the Statement. *PRINT THE LETTER OF THE CORRECT ANSWER IN THE SPACE AT THE RIGHT.*

Questions 1-5.

DIRECTIONS: Questions 1 through 5 are to be answered SOLELY on the basis of the following information and map.

An employee may be required to assist civilians who seek travel directions or referral to city agencies and facilities.

The following is a map of part of a city, where several public offices and other institutions are located. Each of the squares represents one city block. Street names are as shown. If there is an arrow next to the street name, it means the street is one-way only in the direction of the arrow. If there is no arrow next to the street name, two-way traffic is allowed.

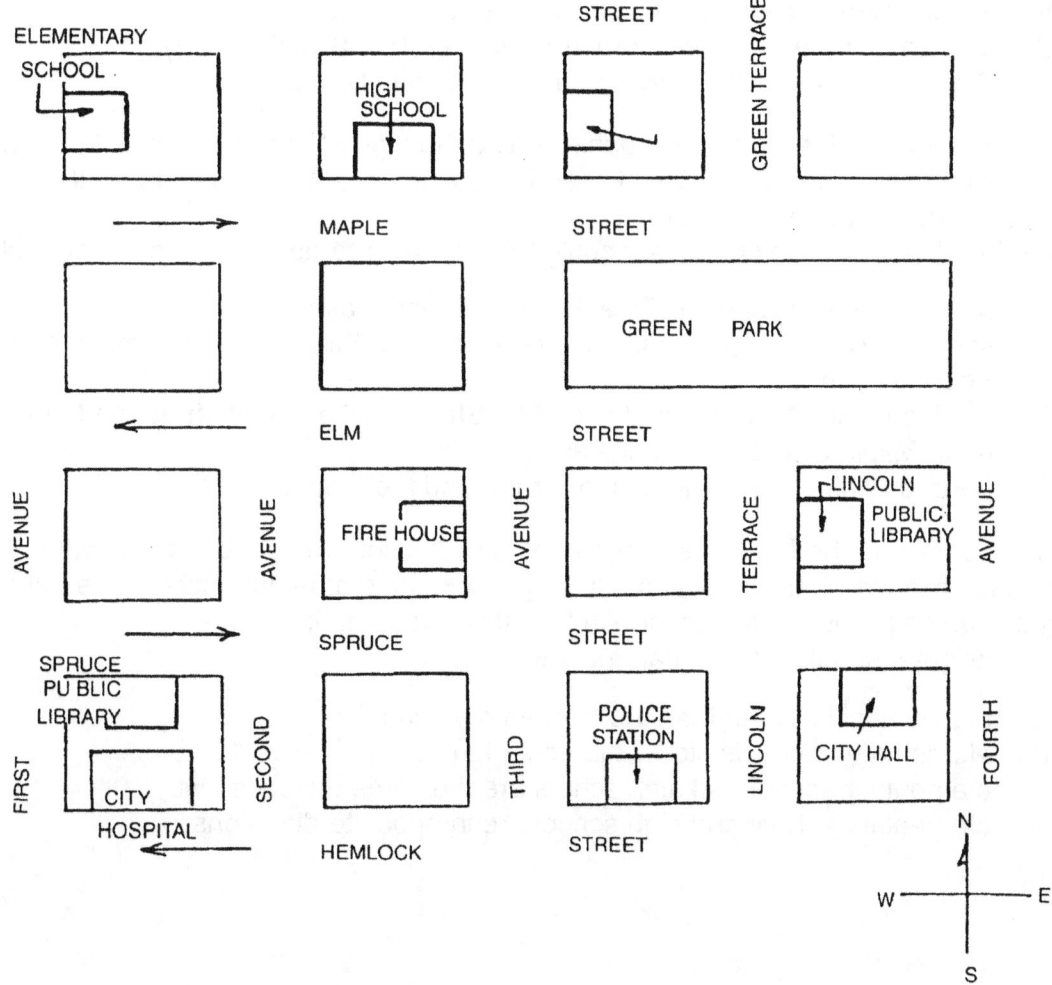

119

1. A woman whose handbag was stolen from her in Green Park asks a firefighter at the firehouse where to go to report the crime.
   The firefighter should tell the woman to go to the

   A. police station on Spruce Street
   B. police station on Hemlock Street
   C. city hall on Spruce Street
   D. city hall on Hemlock Street

2. A disabled senior citizen who lives on Green Terrace telephones the firehouse to ask which library is closest to her home.
   The firefighter should tell the senior citizen it is the

   A. Spruce Public Library on Lincoln Terrace
   B. Lincoln Public Library on Spruce Street
   C. Spruce Public Library on Spruce Street
   D. Lincoln Public Library on Lincoln Terrace

3. A woman calls the firehouse to ask for the exact location of City Hall.
   She should be told that it is on

   A. Hemlock Street, between Lincoln Terrace and Fourth Avenue
   B. Spruce Street, between Lincoln Terrace and Fourth Avenue
   C. Lincoln Terrace, between Spruce Street and Elm Street
   D. Green Terrace, between Maple Street and Pine Street

4. A delivery truck driver is having trouble finding the high school to make a delivery. The driver parks the truck across from the firehouse on Third Avenue facing north and goes into the firehouse to ask directions.
   In giving directions, the firefighter should tell the driver to go _____ to the school.

   A. north on Third Avenue to Pine Street and then make a right
   B. south on Third Avenue, make a left on Hemlock Street, and then make a right on Second Avenue
   C. north on Third Avenue, turn left on Elm Street, make a right on Second Avenue and go to Maple Street, then make another right
   D. north on Third Avenue to Maple Street, and then make a left

5. A man comes to the firehouse accompanied by his son and daughter. He wants to register his son in the high school and his daughter in the elementary school. He asks a firefighter which school is closest for him to walk to from the firehouse.
   The firefighter should tell the man that the

   A. high school is closer than the elementary school
   B. elementary school is closer than the high school
   C. elementary school and high school are the same distance away
   D. elementary school and high school are in opposite directions

Questions 6-8.

DIRECTIONS: Questions 6 through 8 are to be answered SOLELY on the basis of the following map and information. The flow of traffic is indicated by the arrows. If there is only one arrow shown, then traffic flows in the direction indicated by the arrow. If there are two arrows, then traffic flows in both directions. You must follow the flow of traffic

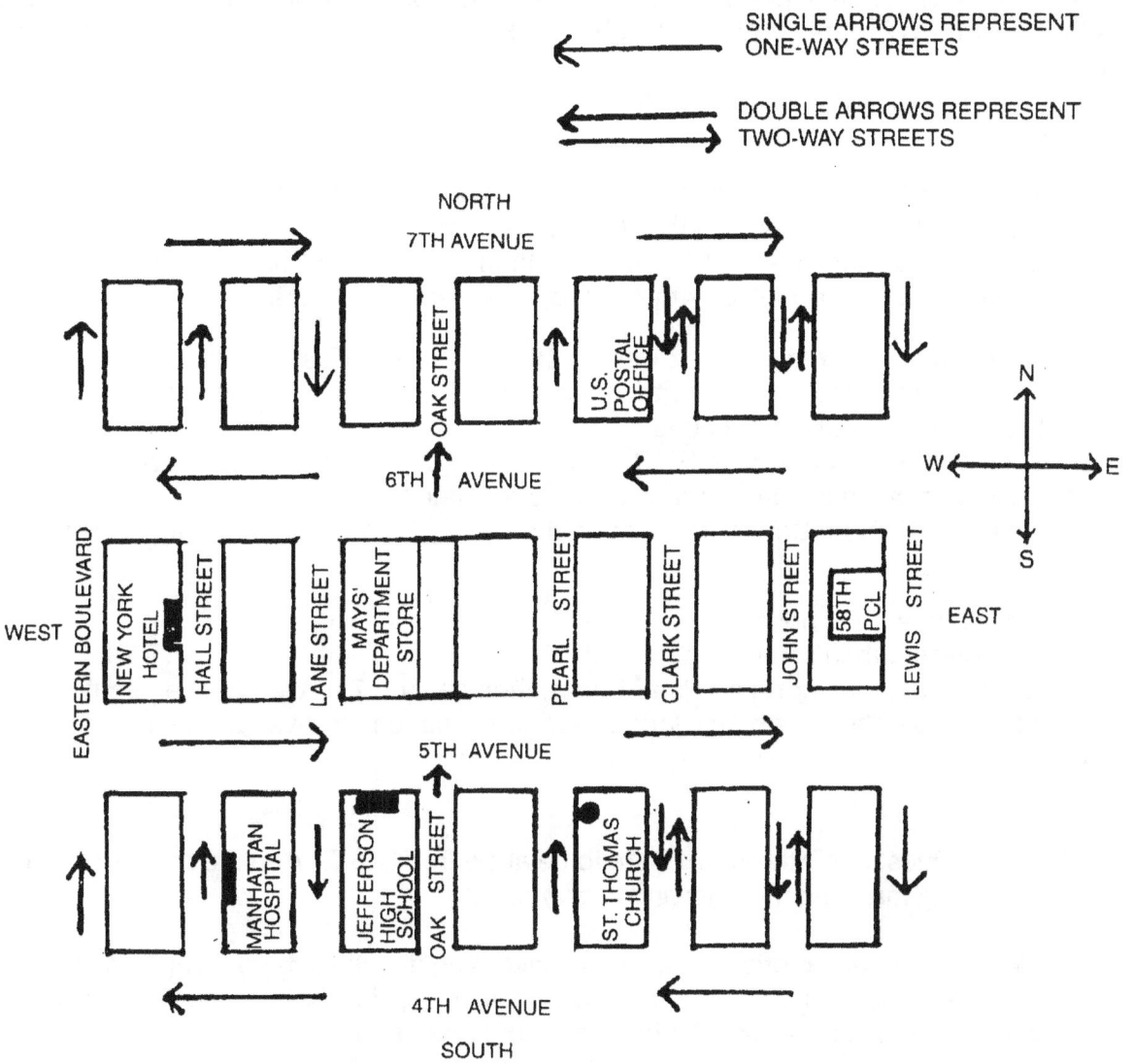

6. Traffic Enforcement Agent Fox was on foot patrol at John Street between 6th and 7th Avenues when a motorist driving southbound asked her for directions to the New York Hotel, which is located on Hall Street between 5th and 6th Avenues. Which one of the following is the SHORTEST route for Agent Fox to direct the motorist to take, making sure to obey all traffic regulations?
Travel _____ to the New York Hotel.

   A. north on John Street, then east on 7th Avenue, then north on Lewis Street, then west on 4th Avenue, then north on Eastern Boulevard, then east on 5th Avenue, then north on Hall Street
   B. south on John Street, then west on 6th Avenue, then south on Eastern Boulevard, then east on 5th Avenue, then north on Hall Street

C. south on John Street, then west on 6th Avenue, then south on Clark Street, then east on 4th Avenue, then north on Eastern Boulevard, then east on 5th Avenue, then north on Hall Street
D. south on John Street, then west on 4th Avenue, then north on Hall Street

7. Traffic Enforcement Agent Murphy is on motorized patrol on 7th Avenue between Oak Street and Pearl Street when Lt. Robertson radios him to go to Jefferson High School, located on 5th Avenue between Lane Street and Oak Street. Which one of the following is the SHORTEST route for Agent Murphy to take, making sure to obey all the traffic regulations?
Travel east on 7th Avenue, then south on _____, then east on 5th Avenue to Jefferson High School.

    A. Clark Street, then west on 4th Avenue, then north on Hall Street
    B. Pearl Street, then west on 4th Avenue, then north on Lane Street
    C. Lewis Street, then west on 6th Avenue, then south on Hall Street
    D. Lewis Street, then west on 4th Avenue, then north on Oak Street

7._____

8. Traffic Enforcement Agent Vasquez was on 4th Avenue and Eastern Boulevard when a motorist asked him for directions to the 58th Police Precinct, which is located on Lewis Street between 5th and 6th Avenues.
Which one of the following is the SHORTEST route for Agent Vasquez to direct the motorist to take, making sure to obey all traffic regulations.
Travel north on Eastern Boulevard, then east on _____ on Lewis Street to the 58th Police Precinct.

    A. 5th Avenue, then north
    B. 7th Avenue, then south
    C. 6th Avenue, then north on Pearl Street, then east on 7th Avenue, then south
    D. 5th Avenue, then north on Clark Street, then east on 6th Avenue, then south

8._____

Questions 9-13.

DIRECTIONS: Questions 9 through 13 are to be answered SOLELY on the basis of the following map and the following information.

Toll collectors answer motorists' questions concerning directions by reading a map of the metropolitan area. Although many alternate routes leading to destinations exist on the following map, you are to choose the MOST direct route of those given.

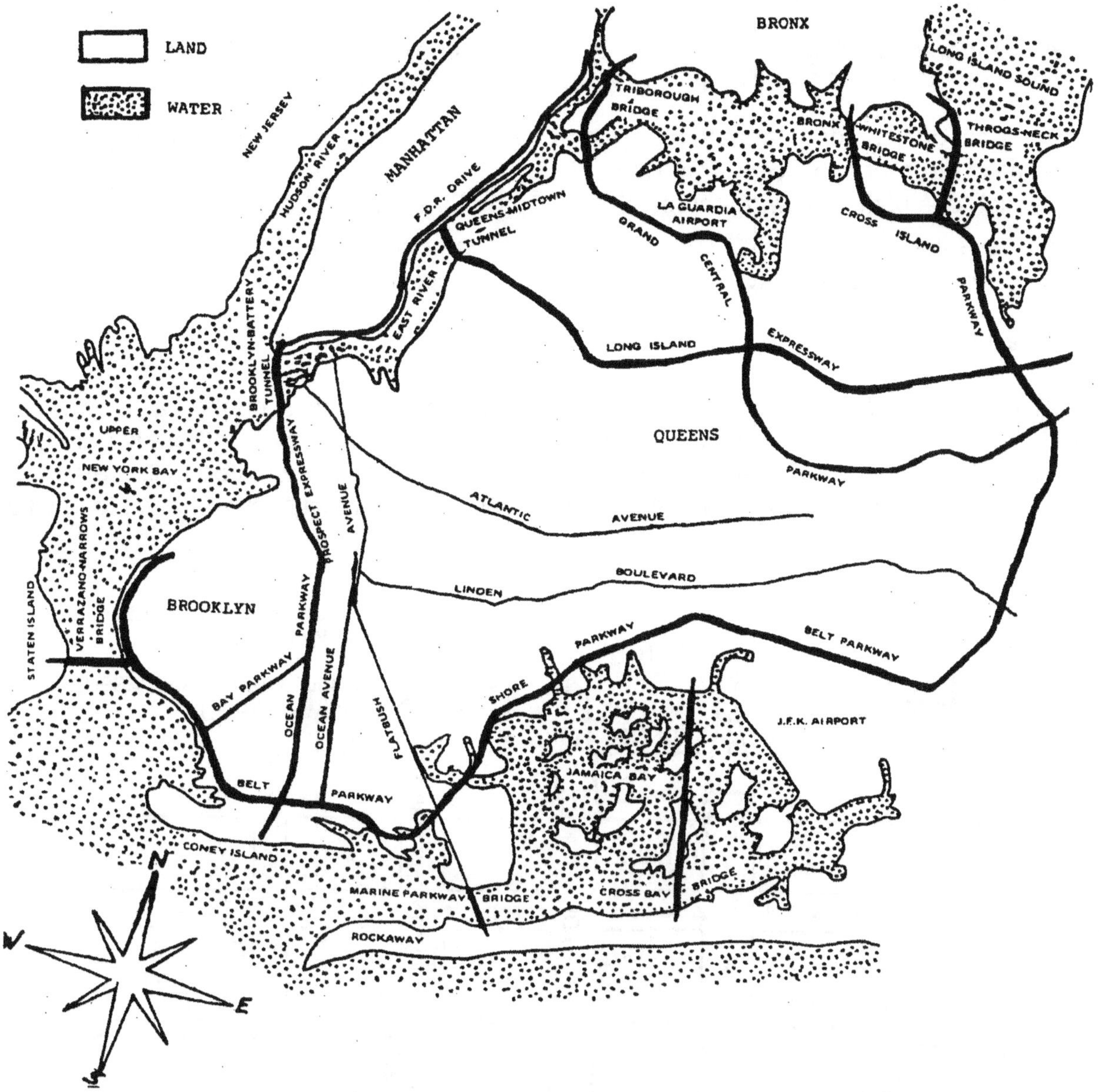

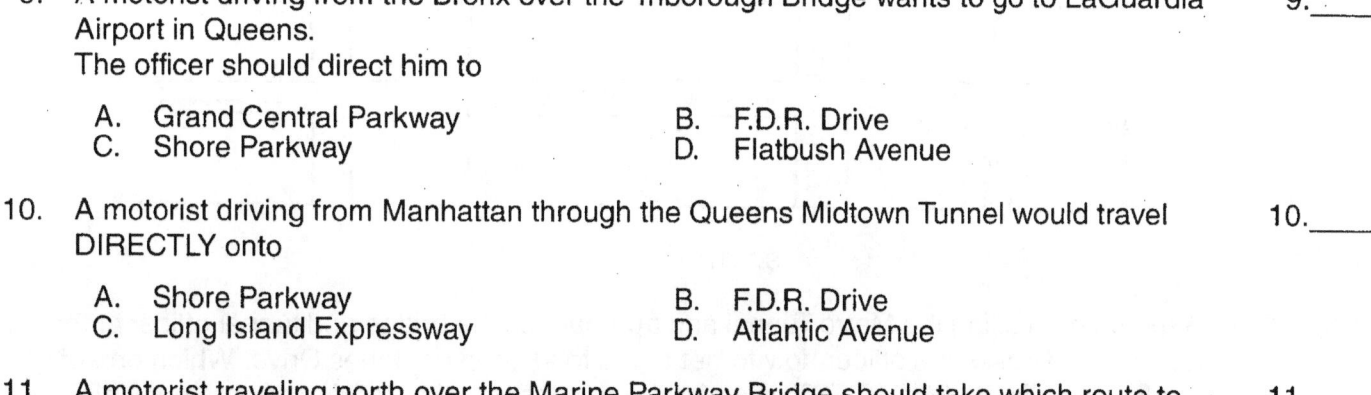

9. A motorist driving from the Bronx over the Triborough Bridge wants to go to LaGuardia Airport in Queens.
   The officer should direct him to

   A. Grand Central Parkway B. F.D.R. Drive
   C. Shore Parkway D. Flatbush Avenue

10. A motorist driving from Manhattan through the Queens Midtown Tunnel would travel DIRECTLY onto

    A. Shore Parkway B. F.D.R. Drive
    C. Long Island Expressway D. Atlantic Avenue

11. A motorist traveling north over the Marine Parkway Bridge should take which route to reach Coney Island?

    A. Shore Parkway East B. Belt Parkway West
    C. Linden Boulevard D. Ocean Parkway

12. Which facility does NOT connect the Bronx and Queens? 12.___

    A. Triborough Bridge   B. Bronx-Whitestone Bridge
    C. Verrazano-Narrows Bridge   D. Throgs-Neck Bridge

13. A motorist driving from Manhattan arrives at the toll booth of the Brooklyn-Battery Tunnel 13.___
    and asks directions to Ocean Parkway.
    To which one of the following routes should the motorist FIRST be directed?

    A. Atlantic Avenue   B. Bay Parkway
    C. Prospect Expressway   D. Ocean Avenue

Questions 14-16.

DIRECTIONS: Questions 14 through 16 are to be answered SOLELY on the basis of the following map. The flow of traffic is indicated by the arrows. If there is only one arrow shown, then traffic flows only in the direction indicated by the arrow. If there are two arrows, then traffic flows in both directions. You must follow the flow of traffic.

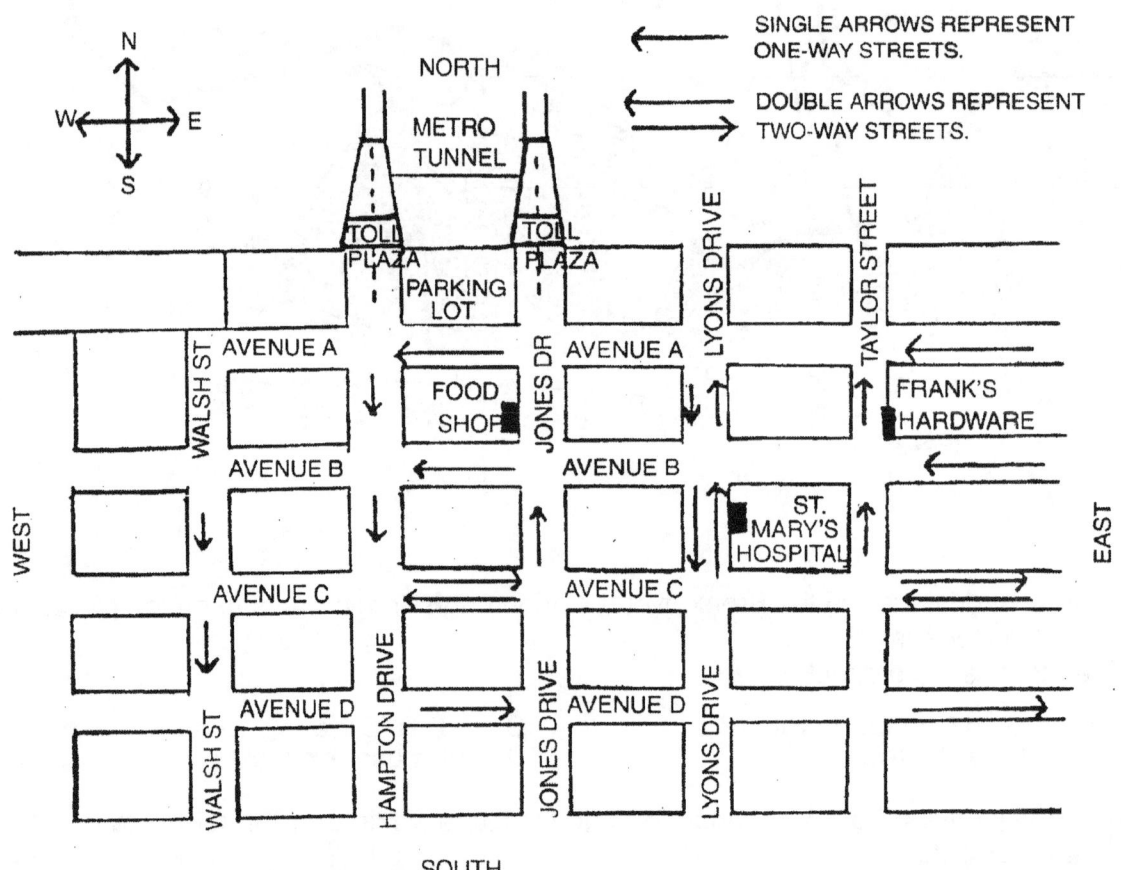

14. A motorist is exiting the Metro Tunnel and approaches the bridge and tunnel officer at the 14.___
    toll plaza. He asks the officer how to get to the food shop on Jones Drive. Which one of
    the following is the SHORTEST route for the motorist to take, making sure to obey all
    traffic regulations?
    Travel south on Hampton Drive, then left on _____ on Jones Drive to the food shop.

A. Avenue A, then right   B. Avenue B, then right
C. Avenue D, then left   D. Avenue C, then left

15. A motorist heading south pulls up to a toll booth at the exit of the Metro Tunnel and asks   15._____
    Bridge and Tunnel Officer Evans how to get to Frank's Hardware Store on Taylor Street.
    Which one of the following is the SHORTEST route for the motorist to take, making
    sure to obey all traffic regulations?
    Travel south on Hampton Drive, then east on

    A. Avenue B to Taylor Street
    B. Avenue D, then north on Taylor Street to Avenue B
    C. Avenue C, then north on Taylor Street to Avenue B
    D. Avenue C, then north on Lyons Drive, then east on Avenue B to Taylor Street

16. A motorist is exiting the Metro Tunnel and approaches the toll plaza. She asks Bridge   16._____
    and Tunnel Officer Owens for directions to St. Mary's Hospital.
    Which one of the following is the SHORTEST route for the motorist to take, making
    sure to obey all traffic regulations?
    Travel south on Hampton Drive, then _____ on Lyons Drive to St. Mary's Hospital.

    A. left on Avenue D, then left
    B. right on Avenue A, then left on Walsh Street, then left on Avenue D, then left
    C. left on Avenue C, then left
    D. left on Avenue B, then right

Questions 17-18.

DIRECTIONS: Questions 17 and 18 are to be answered SOLELY on the basis of the map
              which appears on the following page. The flow of traffic is indicated by the
              arrows. If there is only one arrow shown, then traffic flows only in the direction
              indicated by the arrow. If there are two arrows shown, then traffic flows in both
              directions. You must follow the flow of traffic.

8 (#1)

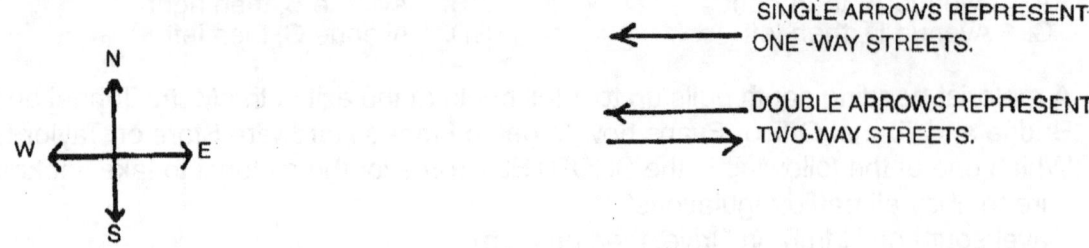

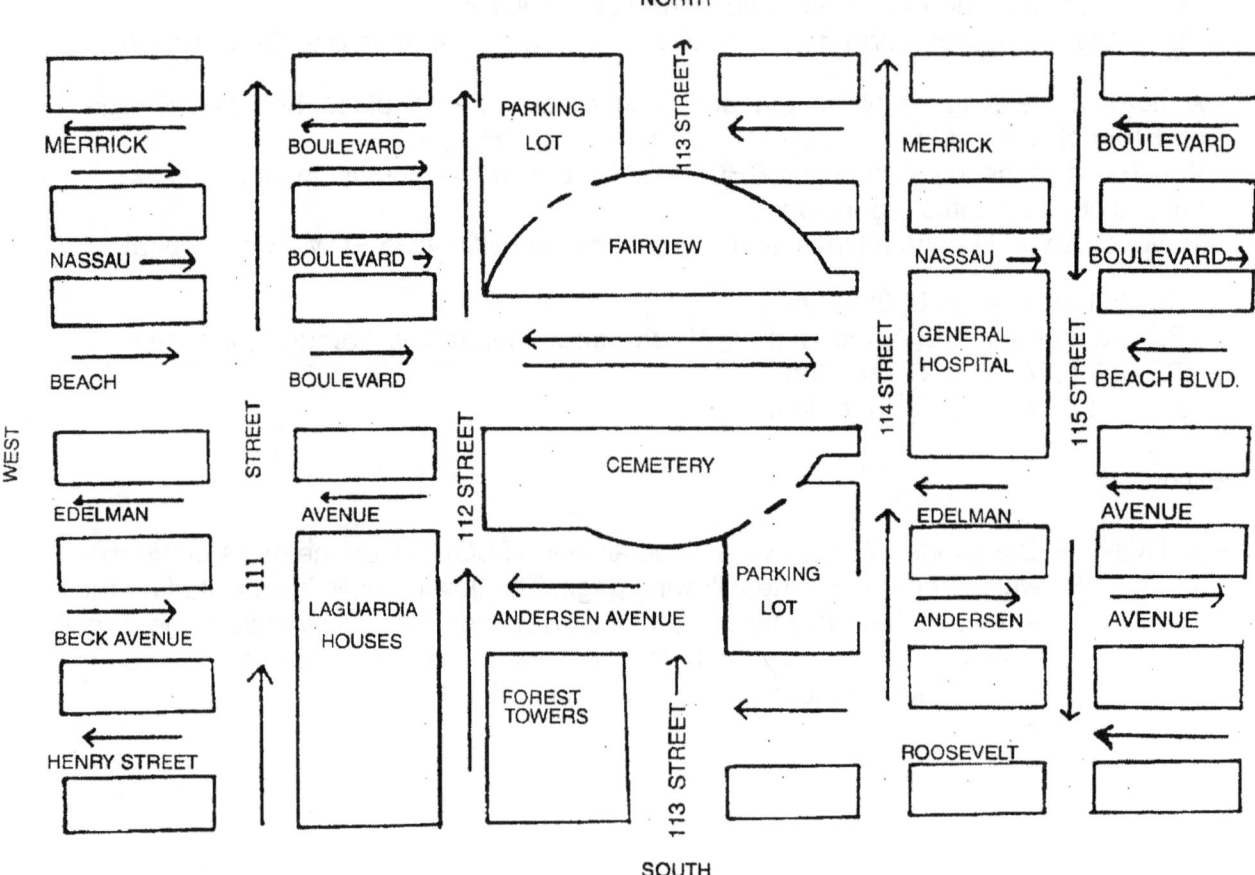

17. Police Officers Glenn and Albertson are on 111th Street at Henry Street when they are dispatched to a past robbery at Beach Boulevard and 115th Street.
Which one of the following is the SHORTEST route for the officers to follow in their patrol car, making sure to obey all traffic regulations?
Travel north on 111th Street, then east on _____ south on 115th Street.

    A. Edelman Avenue, then north on 112th Street, then east on Beach Boulevard, then north on 114th Street, then east on Nassau Boulevard, then one block
    B. Beach Boulevard, then north on 114th Street, then east on Nassau Boulevard, then one block
    C. Merrick Boulevard, then two blocks
    D. Nassau Boulevard, then south on 112th Street, then east on Beach Boulevard, then north on 114th Street, then east on Nassau Boulevard, then one block

17.____

18. Later in their tour, Officers Glenn and Albertson are driving on 114th Street. If they make a left turn to enter the parking lot at Andersen Avenue, and then make a u-turn, in what direction would they now be headed?

   A. North   B. South   C. East   D. West

Questions 19-20.

DIRECTIONS: Questions 19 and 20 are to be answered SOLELY on the basis of the following map. The flow of traffic is indicated by the arrows. If there is only one arrow shown, then traffic flows only in the direction indicated by the arrow. If there are two arrows shown, then traffic flows in both directions. You must follow the flow of traffic.

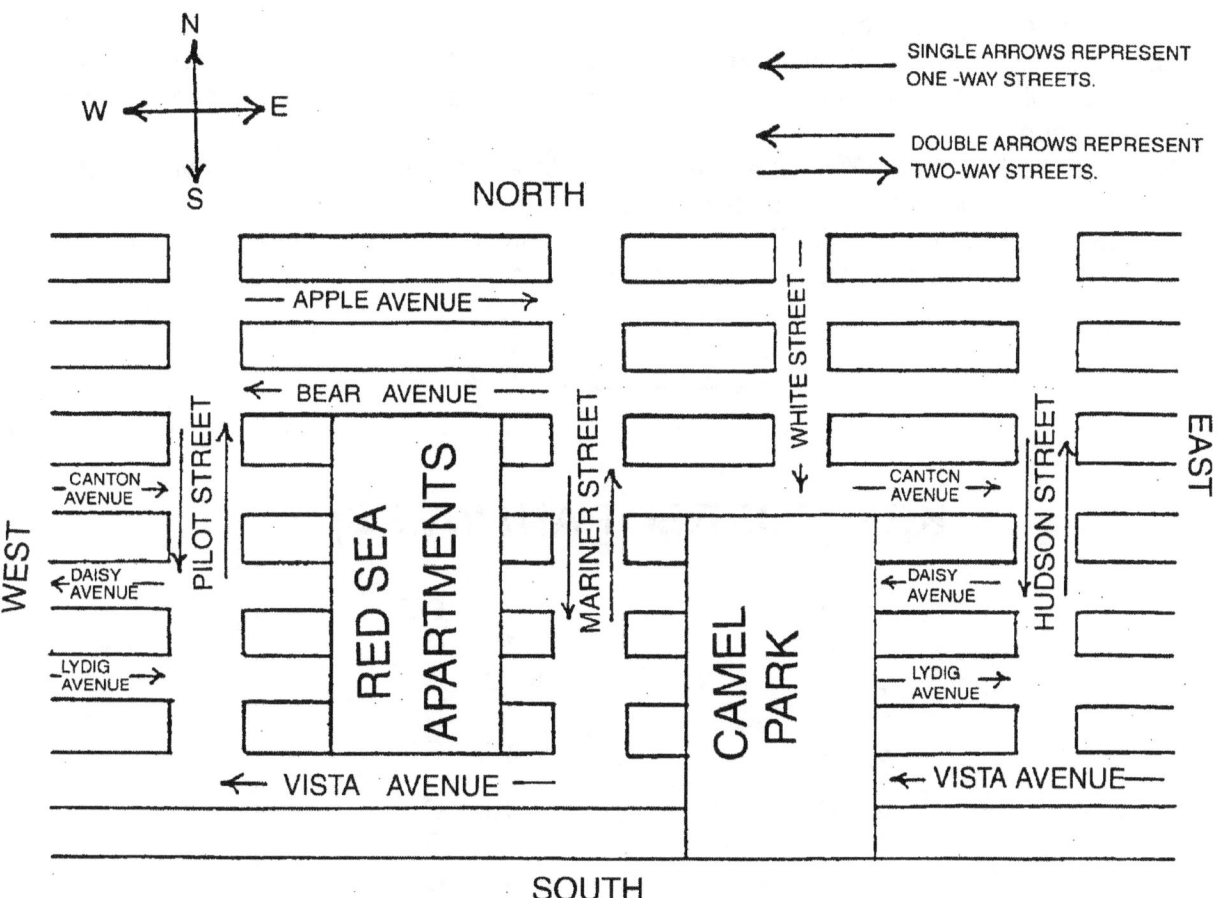

19. You are located at Apple Avenue and White Street. You receive a call to respond to the corner of Lydig Avenue and Pilot Street.
Which one of the following is the MOST direct route for you to take in your patrol car, making sure to obey all traffic regulations?
Travel _____ on Pilot Street.

   A. two blocks south on White Street, then one block east on Canton Avenue, then one block north on Hudson Street, then three blocks west on Bear Avenue, then three blocks south
   B. one block south on White Street, then two blocks west on Bear Avenue, then three blocks south

C. two blocks west on Apple Avenue, then four blocks south
D. two blocks south on White Street, then one block west on Canton Avenue, then three blocks south on Mariner Street, then one block west on Vista Avenue, then one block north

20. You are located at Canton Avenue and Pilot Street. You receive a call of a crime in progress at the intersection of Canton Avenue and Hudson Street.
Which one of the following is the MOST direct route for you to take in your patrol car, making sure to obey all traffic regulations?
Travel

    A. two blocks north on Pilot Street, then two blocks east on Apple Avenue, then one block south on White Street, then one block east on Bear Avenue, then one block south on Hudson Street
    B. three blocks south on Pilot Street, then travel one block east on Vista Avenue, then travel three blocks north on Mariner Street, then travel two blocks east on Canton Avenue
    C. one block north on Pilot Street, then travel three blocks east on Bear Avenue, then travel one block south on Hudson Street
    D. two blocks north on Pilot Street, then travel three blocks east on Apple Avenue, then travel two blocks south on Hudson Street

KEY (CORRECT ANSWERS)

1.	B	11.	B/D
2.	D	12.	C
3.	B	13.	C
4.	C	14.	D
5.	A	15.	C
6.	D	16.	C
7.	A	17.	B
8.	B	18.	C
9.	A	19.	B
10.	C	20.	D

INTERPRETING STATISTICAL DATA GRAPHS, CHARTS AND TABLES

EXAMINATION SECTION
TEST 1

DIRECTIONS: Each question or incomplete statement is followed by several suggested answers or completions. Select the one that BEST answers the question or completes the statement. *PRINT THE LETTER OF THE CORRECT ANSWER IN THE SPACE AT THE RIGHT.*

Questions 1-5.

DIRECTIONS: Questions 1 through 5 are to be answered SOLELY on the basis of the contents of the following graph.

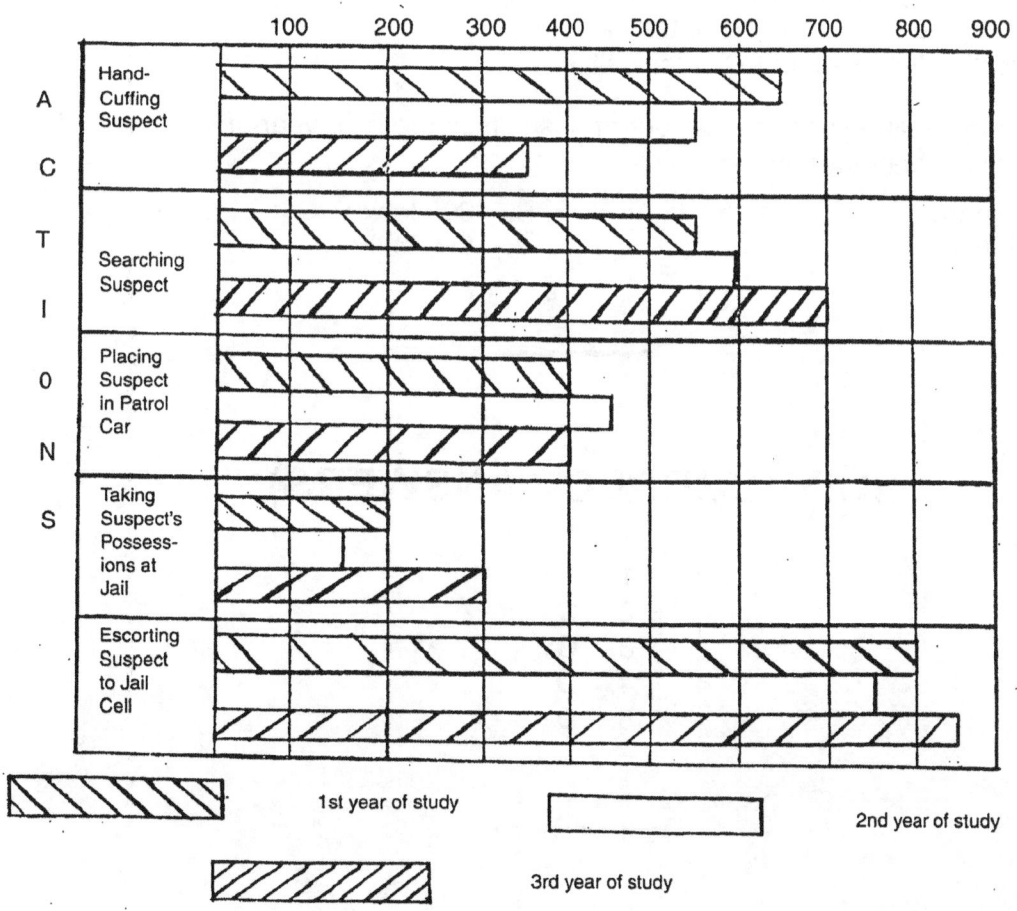

1. Which one of the following MOST closely approximates the number of assaults on Detectives/Investigators for all five actions during the second year of the study?
   A. 1850   B. 2450   C. 2500   D. 5050

2. Which one of the following conditions led to the GREATEST increase in number of assaults on Detectives/Investigators between the 2nd and 3rd years of the study?
   A. Handcuffing the suspect
   B. Searching the suspect
   C. Taking the suspect's possessions at the jail
   D. Escorting the suspect to the jail cell

3. Which one of the following MOST closely approximates the TOTAL number of Detective/Investigator injuries attributed to placing the suspect in patrol car for the three years of the study?
   A. 750   B. 1050   C. 1250   D. 1550

4. Which one of the following actions resulted in the GREATEST number of assaults on Detectives/Investigators throughout the three years of the study?
   A. Taking the suspect's possessions at the jail
   B. Handcuffing the suspect
   C. Placing the suspect in the patrol car
   D. Escorting the suspect to the jail cell

5. Compared to the first year, the number of assaults in the third year of the study attributable to all five situations was
   A. 300 more   B. 300 fewer
   C. 600 more   D. the same

KEY (CORRECT ANSWERS)

1. C
2. C
3. C
4. D
5. D

TEST 2

Questions 1-5.

DIRECTIONS: Questions 1 through 5 are to be answered SOLELY on the basis of the information given in the table below. The numbers which have been omitted from the table can be calculated from the other numbers which are given.

NUMBER OF DWELLING UNITS CONSTRUCTED

Year	Private one-family houses	In private apt. houses	In public housing	Total dwelling units
2006	4,500	500	600	5,600
2007	9,200	5,300	2,800	17,300
2008	8,900	12,800	6,800	28,500
2009	12,100	15,500	7,100	34,700
2010	?	12,200	14,100	39,200
2011	10,200	26,000	8,600	44,800
2012	10,300	17,900	7,400	35,600
2013	11,800	18,900	7,700	38,400
2014	12,700	22,100	8,400	43,200
2015	13,300	24,300	8,100	45,700
TOTALS	105,900	?	?	?

1. According to this table, the AVERAGE number of public housing units constructed yearly during the period 2006 through 2015 was

   A. 7,160 B. 6,180 C. 7,610 D. 6,810

2. Of the following, the two years in which the number of private one-family homes constructed was GREATEST for the two years together is

   A. 2008 and 2009 B. 2007 and 2013
   C. 2008 and 2014 D. 2011 and 2012

3. For the entire period of 2006 through 2015, the TOTAL of all private one-family houses constructed exceeded the total of all public housing units constructed by

   A. 34,300 B. 45,700 C. 50,000 D. 83,900

4. Of the total number of private apartment house dwelling units constructed in the ten years given in the table, the percentage which was constructed in 2012 was MOST NEARLY

   A. 5% B. 11% C. 16% D. 21%

5. Considering dwelling units of all types, the average number constructed annually in the period from 2011 through 2015 was greater than the average number constructed annually in the period from 2006 through 2010 by

   A. 16,480 B. 33,320 C. 79,300 D. 82,400

KEY (CORRECT ANSWERS)

1. A
2. C
3. A
4. B
5. A

TEST 3

Questions 1-5.

DIRECTIONS: Questions 1 through 5 are to be answered SOLELY on the basis of the information contained in the two tables shown below.

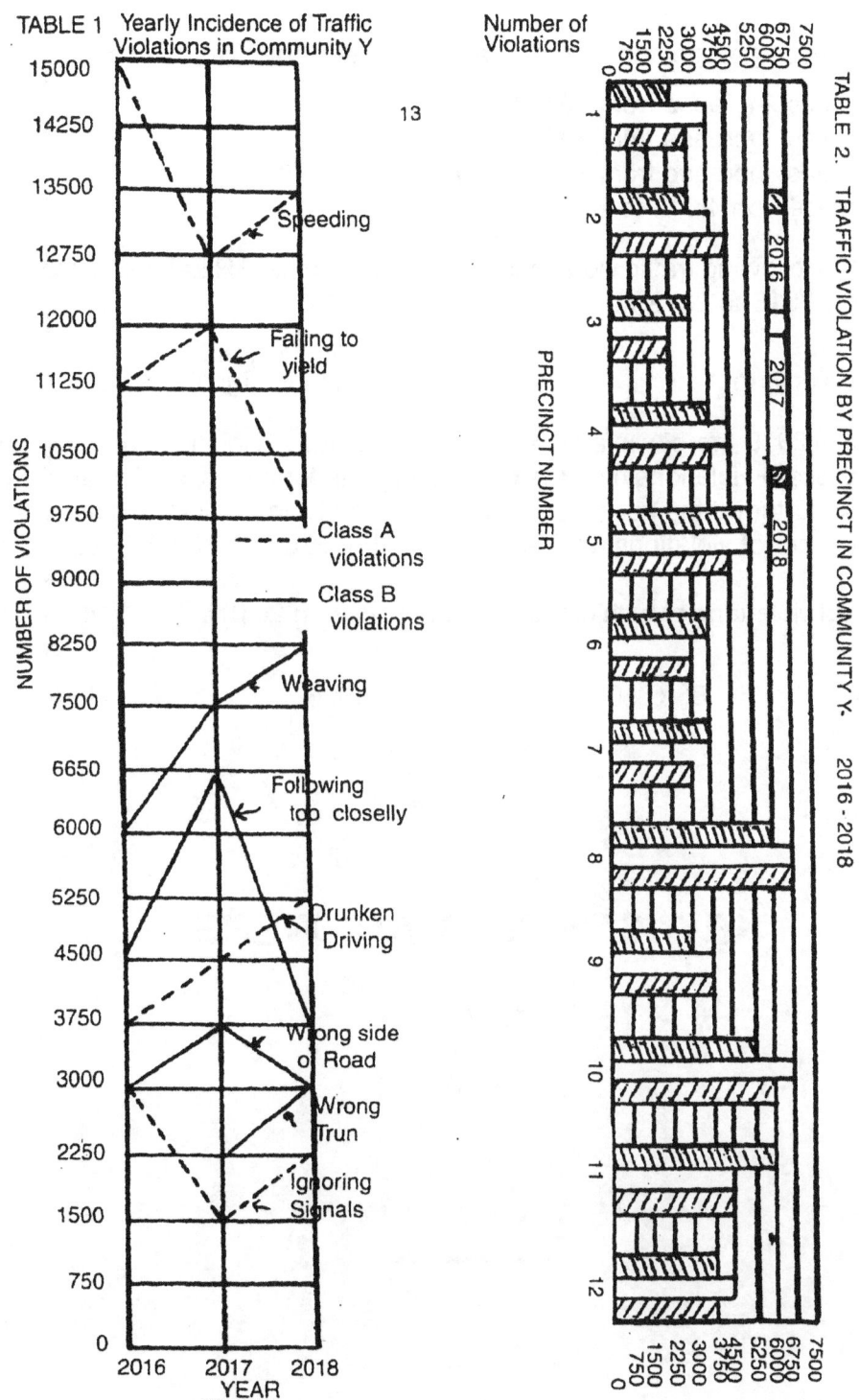

1. Of the total number of traffic violations that occurred in Community Y during 2017, the percentage that occurred in Precinct 10 was MOST NEARLY

   A. 13.2% B. 14.8% C. 35.3% D. 132%

2. Of the following traffic violations, the one for which the number occurring in 2018 exceeded the average of the preceding two years by the GREATEST amount was

   A. speeding
   C. ignoring signals
   B. drunken driving
   D. weaving

3. According to these groups, the ratio of Class B violations to Class A violations showed

   A. the greatest increase from 2016 to 2017
   B. the greatest increase from 2017 to 2018
   C. the greatest increase from 2016 to 2018
   D. a decrease from 2016 to 2018

4. The one of the following traffic violations which showed the GREATEST percentage decrease from 2016 to 2018 was

   A. speeding
   C. drunken driving
   B. failing to yield
   D. ignoring signals

5. Assume that in 2019 there was a 10% increase in Class A violations and the same 10% increase in Class B violations over the preceding year, for each violation and in each precinct. Assume further that Precincts 11 and 12 were eliminated in 2019 and that their areas and number of violations were equally distributed among the 8th, 9th, and 10th Precincts.
   The number of violations of both classes that did occur in 2019 in Precinct 10 is MOST NEARLY

   A. 9,025 B. 350 C. 9,625 D. 15,075

KEY (CORRECT ANSWERS)

1. C
2. D
3. A
4. D
5. A

TEST 4

Questions 1-5.

DIRECTIONS: Questions 1 through 5 are to be answered SOLELY on the basis of the information contained in the graph on the following page.

MONTHLY INCIDENCE FOR ROBBERY AND BURGLARY FOR 2015
AND MONTHLY AVERAGES FOR THESE CRIMES FOR THE PRECEDING 5 YEARS

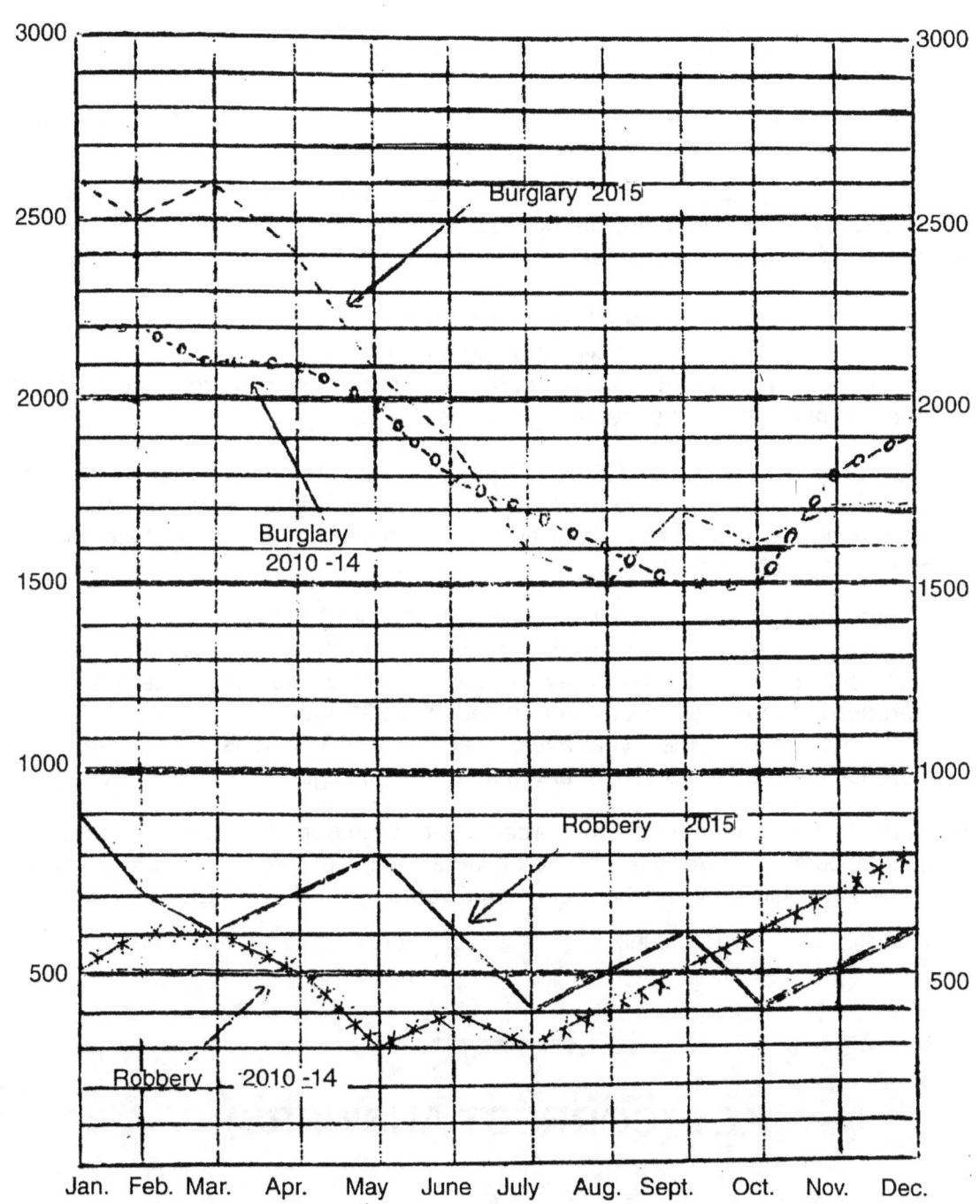

2 (#4)

1. Of the total number of burglaries committed during the first half of 2015, the percentage which occurred during March was MOST NEARLY

   A. 15%   B. 17%   C. 18%   D. 21%

2. The one of the following months for which the percentage increase in the 2015 incidence of crime over the previous five-year average incidence of crime for the same month is GREATEST is

   A. robbery during January
   B. burglary during March
   C. burglary during January
   D. robbery during May

3. A consideration of the data presented for robbery in the graph would justify the statement that the number of robberies committed during

   A. January of each of the years from 2010 through 2014 was less than the number of robberies committed during January 2015
   B. March of 2015 was the same as the number of robberies committed during March of 2014
   C. April of 2015 was 200 more than the total number of robberies committed during April of all of the preceding five years combined
   D. August of 2015 exceeded the average number of robberies committed during the months of August of the preceding 5 years

4. Assume that during December 2008 and December 2009 there was a combined total of 900 robberies committed. A seven-year average (2008-2014) can now be obtained. Of the following, it would be MOST correct to state that for the month of December, in connection with robberies, the

   A. 7-year average is less than the 5-year average by 100
   B. 7-year average is less than the 5-year average by 300
   C. difference between the 7-year average and the 2015 figure is greater than the difference between the 5-year average and the 2005 figure
   D. difference between the 7-year average and the 2015 figure is the same as the difference between the 5-year average and the 2005 figure

5. The month in 2015 during which the percentage decline from the preceding month in incidence of burglaries exceeded the percentage decline in average incidence of burglaries for the same period during the preceding 5 years by the GREATEST amount was

   A. May   B. June   C. July   D. August

KEY (CORRECT ANSWERS)

1. C
2. D
3. D
4. A
5. C

TEST 5

Questions 1-5.

DIRECTIONS: Questions 1 through 5 are to be answered on the basis of the information given in the table below. The numbers which have been omitted can be calculated from the other numbers which are given.

NUMBER OF VEHICLE ACCIDENTS IN GREAT CITY
FOR THE PERIOD 2011 TO 2016

County	2011	2012	2013	2014	2015	2016	TOTAL
A	8,141	8,680	8,554	8,213	8,822	8,753	?
B	3,301	3,836	3,623	4,108	4,172	3,735	22,775
C	6,480	7,562	7,275	7,872	8,554	8,341	46,084
D	3,366	3,801	3,715	3,740	4,473	4,390	23,485
E	259	272	?	252	255	457	1,741
TOTAL	21,547	24,151	23,413	24,185	26,276	25,676	145,248

1. For the total period covered by the table, the average number of vehicle accidents per year in County A exceeded the average number per year in County D by APPROXIMATELY

   A. 4,550   B. 5,450   C. 8,520   D. 27,000

2. In comparing the years 2015 and 2016, the one of the following statements which is MOST accurate is that the

   A. number of accidents in County E and County B combined increased
   B. number of accidents decreased in each of the five counties
   C. number of accidents in County D and County E combined increased
   D. decrease in the number of accidents in County C amounted to more than one-half of the decrease in the total number of accidents for the entire city

3. The percentage increase in 2016 over 2011 in vehicle accidents was LARGEST in County

   A. A   B. B   C. C   D. D

4. If the counties are ranked for each year according to the number of accidents (largest number to rank first), a county which will NOT have the same rank each year is County

   A. A   B. D   C. C   D. E

5. The LARGEST increase in the number of vehicle accidents from any one year to the next was in County

   A. C   B. B   C. A   D. D

137

KEY (CORRECT ANSWERS)

1. A
2. C
3. D
4. B
5. A

TEST 6

Questions 1-4.

DIRECTIONS: Questions 1 through 4 are to be answered on the basis of the following graph.

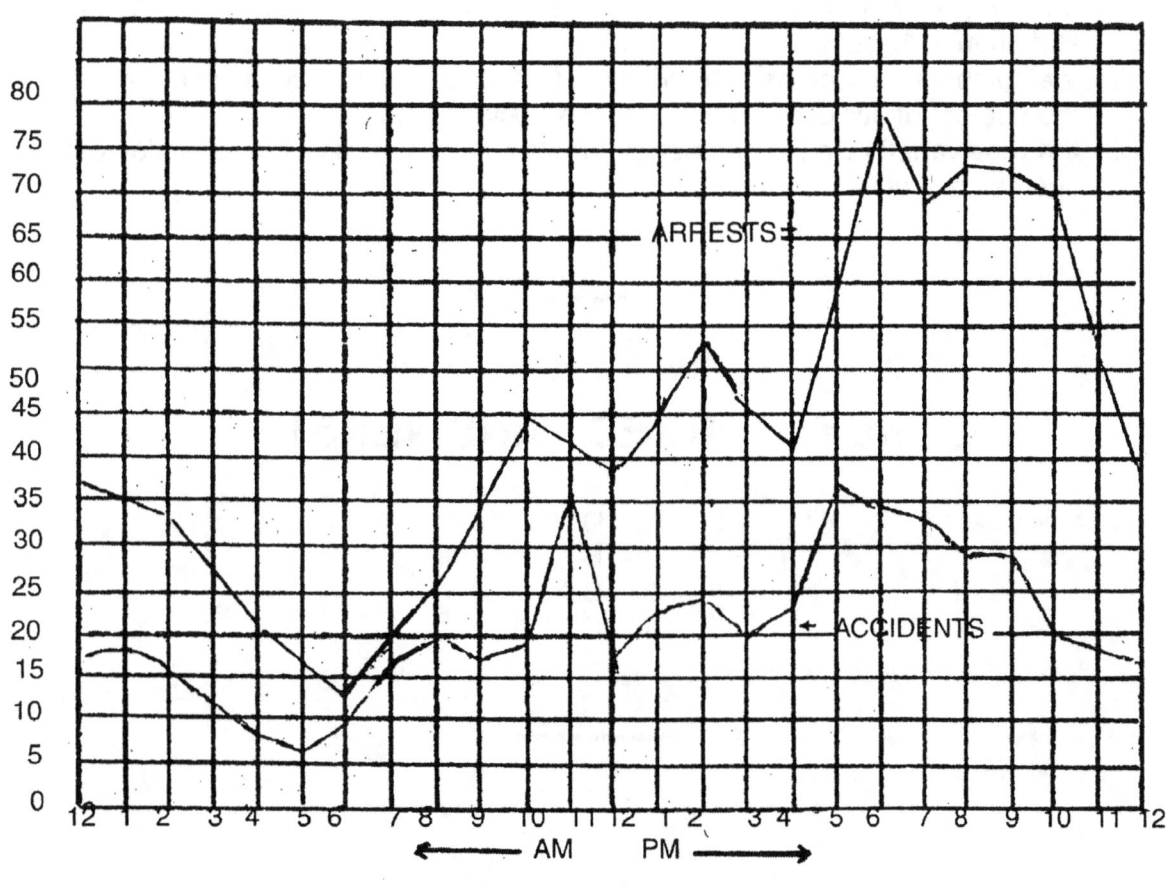

AVERAGE HOURLY INCIDENCE OF ARRESTS AND ACCIDENTS
FOR COMMUNITY X

(Hourly figures represent total number of occurrences in the immediately preceding hour)

HOURS OF THE DAY

1. According to this graph, of the following hours of the day, the hour which shows the HIGHEST ratio of arrests to accidents is

   A. 2 P.M.   B. 6 P.M.   C. 8 P.M.   D. 10 P.M.

2. According to the above graph, the LEAST average hour-to-hour variation, during the following time periods, was in the number of

A. arrests during the 4 P.M. through 8 P.M. period
B. accidents during the 12 Noon through 4 P.M. period
C. arrests during the 8 P.M. through 12 Midnight period
D. accidents during the 8 A.M. through 12 Noon period

3. According to the above graph, of all the accidents occurring from 12 Noon through Midnight, the percentage which occurred from 12 Noon through 4 P.M. was MOST NEARLY

A. 26%   B. 30%   C. 34%   D. 38%

4. On the basis of the above graph,
A. an equal number of accidents was recorded daily at 8 A.M. and 3 P.M.
B. on any given day, during the year covered, there were more arrests recorded at 2 P.M. than at 10 A.M.
C. the number of accidents entered in the first 12 o'clock column must always equal the number of accidents in the last 12 o'clock column
D. the wide variation in the number of arrests makes statistical interpretation of the figures unreliable

KEY (CORRECT ANSWERS)

1. D
2. B
3. B
4. C

TEST 7

Questions 1-5.

DIRECTIONS: Questions 1 through 5 are to be answered on the basis of the following two statements and the diagram shown on the following page.

Statement 1: Room G will be the public intake room from which persons will be directed to Room F or Room H; under no circumstances are they to enter the wrong room, and they are not to move from Room F to Room H or vice-versa. A minimum of two officers must be in each room frequented by the public at all times, and they are to keep unauthorized individuals from going to the second floor or into restricted areas. All usable entrances or exits must be covered.

Statement 2: The senior officer can lock any door except the main entrance and stairway doors. He has a staff of five officers to carry out these operations.

NOTE: The senior officer is available for guard duty. Room J is an active office.

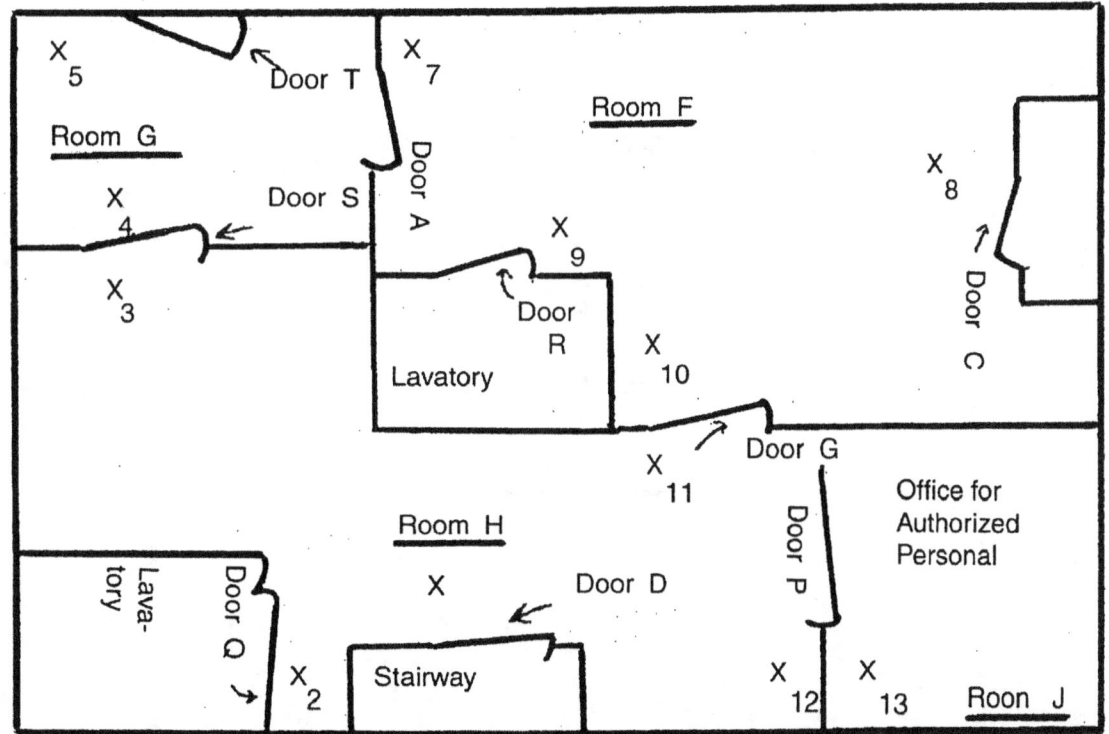

1. According to the instructions, how many officers should be assigned inside the office for authorized personnel (Room J)?

   A. 0   B. 1   C. 2   D. 3

141

2. In order to keep the public from moving between Room F and Room H, which door(s) can be locked without interfering with normal office operations?
Door(s)

   A. G   B. P   C. R and Q   D. S

3. When placing officers in Room H, the only way the senior officer can satisfy the agency's objectives and his manpower limitations is by placing men at locations _____ and _____.

   A. 1; 3   B. 1; 12   C. 3; 11   D. 11; 12

4. In accordance with the instructions, the LEAST effective locations to place officers in Room F are locations _____ and _____.

   A. 7; 9   B. 7; 10   C. 8; 9   D. 9; 10

5. In which room is it MOST difficult for each of the officers to see all the movements of the public? Room

   A. G   B. F   C. H   D. J

KEY (CORRECT ANSWERS)

1. A
2. A
3. B
4. D
5. C

TEST 8

Questions 1-4.

DIRECTIONS: Questions 1 through 4 are to be answered SOLELY on the basis of the following graph relating to the Burglary Rate in the City, 2013 to 2018, inclusive.

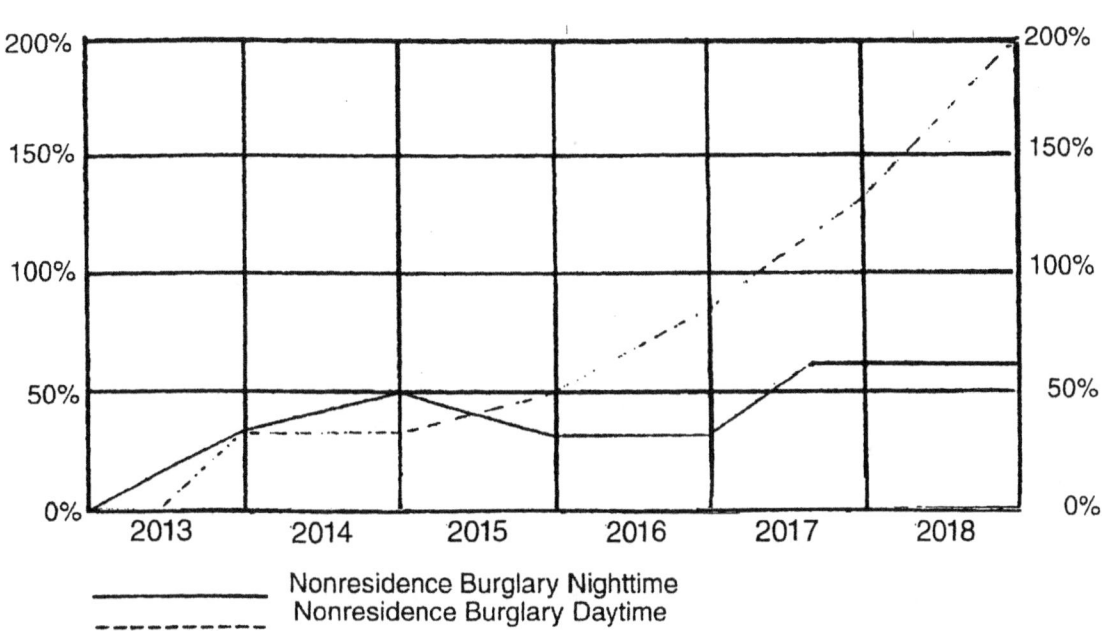

1. At the beginning of what year was the percentage increase in daytime and nighttime burglaries the SAME?

   A. 2013   B. 2015   C. 2016   D. 2018

2. In what year did the percentage of nighttime burglaries DECREASE?

   A. 2013   B. 2015   C. 2016   D. 2018

3. In what year was there the MOST rapid increase in the percentage of daytime non-residence burglaries?

   A. 2014   B. 2016   C. 2017   D. 2018

4. At the end of 2017, the actual number of nighttime burglaries committed

   A. was about 20%
   B. was 40%
   C. was 400
   D. cannot be determined from the information given

KEY (CORRECT ANSWERS)

1. A
2. B
3. D
4. D

TEST 9

Questions 1-4.

DIRECTIONS: Questions 1 through 4 are to be answered SOLELY on the basis of the following graphs.

BUDGETS FOR POLICE
IN MILLIONS OF DOLLARS
(ACTUAL DOLLARS)
2012-2016

BUDGETS FOR OTHER
CRIMINAL JUSTICE EXPENDITURES
IN MILLIONS OF DOLLARS
ACTUAL DOLLARS)
2012-2016

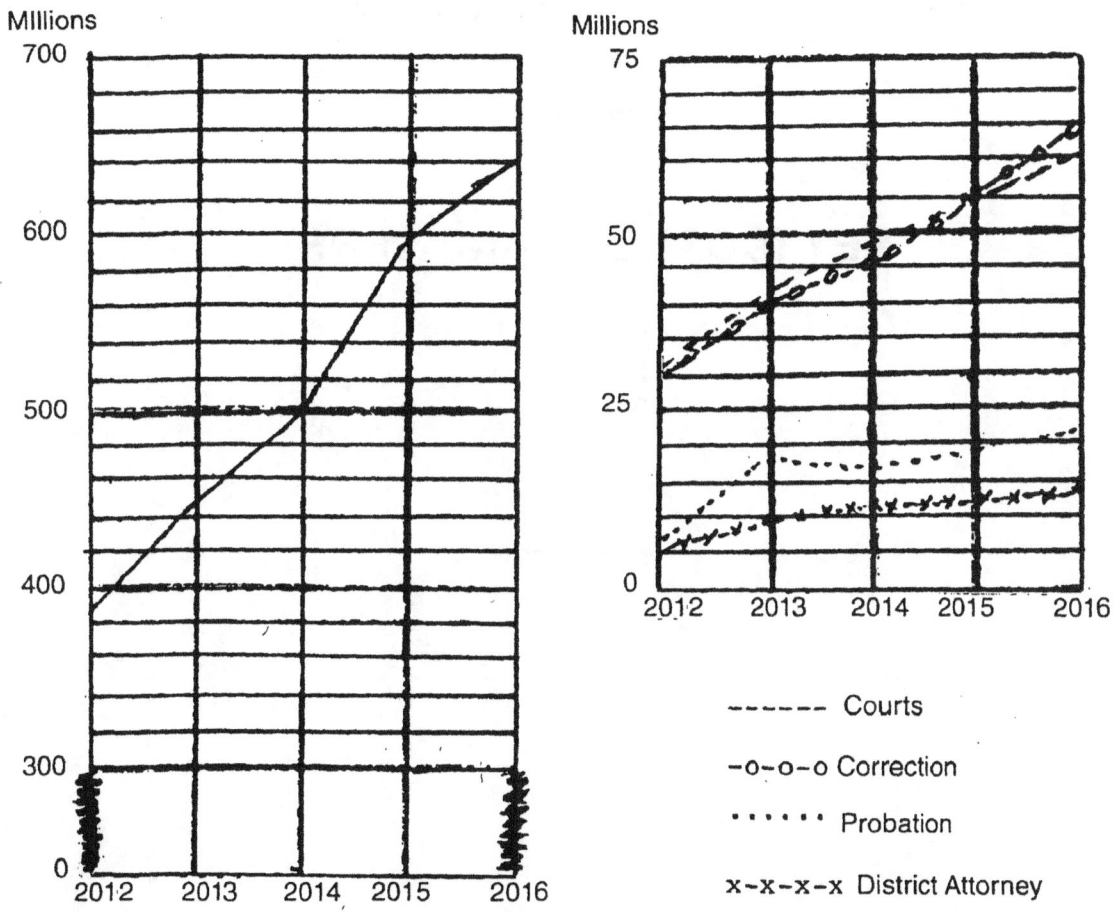

------ Courts
-o-o-o Correction
• • • • • • Probation
x-x-x-x District Attorney

1. In 2016, the amount of money budgeted for courts amounted to APPROXIMATELY what percentage of the amount of money budgeted for police?   1._____

   A. 10% B. 20% C. 30% D. 40%

145

2. In 2015, the police budget exceeded the sum of amounts budgeted for the four other criminal justice expenditures MOST NEARLY by

   A. $410,000,000
   B. $459,000,000
   C. $475,000,000
   D. $487,000,000

3. Between which of the following years did the amount of money budgeted for one category of criminal justice decrease by about one million dollars?

   A. 2012-2013
   B. 2013-2014
   C. 2014-2015
   D. 2015-2016

4. If the 2013 dollar was worth 96% of the 2012 dollar and the 2014 dollar was worth 90% of the 2012 dollar, the increase in the budget for Correction from 2013 to 2014, in terms of the 2012 dollar, amounted to

   A. $2,100,000
   B. $4,200,000
   C. $4,320,000
   D. $4,700,000

KEY (CORRECT ANSWERS)

1. A
2. B
3. B
4. A

TEST 10

Questions 1-4.

DIRECTIONS: Questions 1 through 4 are to be answered SOLELY on the basis of the following table.

STOLEN AND RECOVERED PROPERTY IN COMMUNITY IN 2018 AND 2019

Type of Property	Value of Property Stolen		Value of Property Recovered	
	2018	2019	2018	2019
Currency	$ 264,925	$ 204,534	$ 10,579	$ 13,527
Jewelry	165,317	106,885	2-0,913	20,756
Furs	10,007	24,028	105	1,620
Clothing	62,265	49,219	4,322	15,821
Automobiles	740,719	606,062	736,701	558,442
Miscellaneous	356,901	351,064	62,077	103,117
TOTAL	$ 1,600,134	$1,341,792	$834,697	$713,283

5. Of the following types of property, the one which shows the HIGHEST ratio of *value of property recovered* to *value of property stolen* is

   A. clothing for 2018
   B. currency for 2018
   C. jewelry for 2019
   D. miscellaneous for 2019

6. Of the types of property which show a decrease from 2018 to 2019 in the value of property stolen, the one which shows the GREATEST percentage decrease in the value of the property recovered is

   A. automobiles
   B. currency
   C. furs
   D. jewelry

7. According to the above table, the total value of currency and jewelry stolen in 2019, as compared to 2018, decreased APPROXIMATELY by

   A. 3%   B. 20%   C. 28%   D. 38%

8. According to the above table, the TOTAL value of all types of property recovered was

   A. a slightly lower percentage of the value of property stolen for 2018 than for 2019
   B. less for the year 2018 than the value of any individual type of property recovered for the year 2019
   C. approximately 60% of the value of all property stolen in 2018 and approximately 70% in 2019
   D. greater for the year 2019 than the value of any individual type of property recovered for the year 2018

KEY (CORRECT ANSWERS)

1. D
2. A
3. C
4. A

PREPARING WRITTEN MATERIAL

PARAGRAPH REARRANGEMENT
COMMENTARY

The sentences that follow are in scrambled order. You are to rearrange them in proper order and indicate the letter choice containing the correct answer at the space at the right.

Each group of sentences in this section is actually a paragraph presented in scrambled order. Each sentence in the group has a place in that paragraph; no sentence is to be left out. You are to read each group of sentences and decide upon the best order in which to put the sentences so as to form a well-organized paragraph.

The questions in this section measure the ability to solve a problem when all the facts relevant to its solution are not given.

More specifically, certain positions of responsibility and authority require the employee to discover connection between events sometimes, apparently, unrelated. In order to do this, the employee will find it necessary to correctly infer that unspecified events have probably occurred or are likely to occur. This ability becomes especially important when action must be taken on incomplete information.

Accordingly, these questions require competitors to choose among several suggested alternatives, each of which presents a different sequential arrangement of the events. Competitors must choose the MOST logical of the suggested sequences.

In order to do so, they may be required to draw on general knowledge to infer missing concepts or events that are essential to sequencing the given events. Competitors should be careful to infer only what is essential to the sequence. The plausibility of the wrong alternatives will always require the inclusion of unlikely events or of additional chains of events which are NOT essential to sequencing the given events.

It's very important to remember that you are looking for the best of the four possible choices, and that the best choice of all may not even be one of the answers you're given to choose from.

There is no one right way to solve these problems. Many people have found it helpful to first write out the order of the sentences, as they would have arranged them, on their scrap paper before looking at the possible answers. If their optimum answer is there, this can save them some time. If it isn't, this method can still give insight into solving the problem. Others find it most helpful to just go through each of the possible choices, contrasting each as they go along. You should use whatever method feels comfortable and works for you.

While most of these types of questions are not that difficult, we've added a higher percentage of the difficult type, just to give you more practice. Usually there are only one or two questions on this section that contain such subtle distinctions that you're unable to answer confidently. And you then may find yourself stuck deciding between two possible choices, neither of which you're sure about.

EXAMINATION SECTION
TEST 1

DIRECTIONS: The sentences that follow are in scrambled order. You are to rearrange them in proper order and indicate the letter choice containing the CORRECT answer. *PRINT THE LETTER OF THE CORRECT ANSWER IN THE SPACE AT THE RIGHT.*

1. Fire Marshal Adams has arrested a man for pulling a false alarm. He has recorded the following items of information about the incident in his notebook for use in his subsequent report:

    I. I was on surveillance at a frequently pulled false alarm box located at Edison Street and Harvard Road.
    II. At 1605 hours, I observed the white male, with long brown hair and a mustache, wearing black pants and a red shirt, pull the fire alarm box.
    III. I interviewed the officer of the first due ladder company, Lt. Morgan - L-37, who informed me that a search of the area disclosed no cause for an alarm to be transmitted.
    IV. A man wearing a red shirt, black pants, with long brown hair and a mustache came out of Ryan's Pub, located at Edison Street and Harvard Road, and walked directly to the alarm box.
    V. I stopped the man about five blocks away at 33rd Street and Harvard Road and asked him why he pulled the fire alarm box, and he replied, *Because I felt like it.*

    The MOST logical order for the above sentences to appear in the report is

    A. I, IV, II, III, V   B. I, II, III, IV, V
    C. I, IV, III, II, V   D. I, IV, V, II, III

    1.____

2. A fire marshal is preparing a report regarding Tom Jones, who was a witness to an arson fire at his apartment building. Following are five sentences which will be included in the report:

    I. On July 16, I responded to the fire building, address 2020 Elm Street, to interview Tom Jones.
    II. Tom Jones described the *super* (name unknown) as a middle-aged male with beard, six feet tall, wearing a blue jumpsuit.
    III. Tom Jones stated that he saw the *super* of the building next door set the fire.
    IV. After being advised of his constitutional rights at the 44th Precinct detective's squad room, the *super* confessed.
    V. I interviewed the *super* and took him to the precinct for further investigation.

    The MOST logical order for the above sentences to appear in the report is

    A. I, II, III, V, IV   B. I, II, III, IV, V
    C. I, III, II, IV, V   D. I, III, II, V, IV

    2.____

3. A fire marshal is preparing a report on a shooting incident which will include the following five sentences:
    I. I ran around the corner and observed a man pointing a gun at another man.
    II. I informed the man I was a police officer and that he should drop his gun.
    III. I was on the corner of 4th Avenue and 43rd Street when I heard a gunshot coming from around the corner.
    IV. The man turned around and pointed his gun at me.
    V. I fired once, shooting him in the chest and causing him to fall to the ground.
  The MOST logical order for the above sentences to appear in the report is

   A. I, III, IV, II, V
   B. IV, V, II, I, III
   C. III, I, II, IV, V
   D. III, I, V, II, IV

4. Fire Marshal Smith is writing a report. The report will include the following five sentences:
    I. I asked the woman for a description of the man and his location in the building.
    II. When I said, *Don't move, Five Marshal,* the man dropped the can containing a flammable liquid.
    III. I transmitted on my handie-talkie for fire companies to respond.
    IV. A woman approached our car and said there was a man pouring a liquid, which she thought to be gasoline, on a staircase at 123 East Street.
    V. Upon entering that location, I observed a man spilling a liquid on the floor.
  The MOST logical order for the above sentences to appear on the interview sheet is

   A. IV, I, V, II, III
   B. I, IV, III, V, II
   C. V, II, IV, I, III
   D. IV, III, I, V, II

5. Fire Marshal Fox is completing an interview report for a fire in the kitchen of an apartment at 1700 Clayton Road. The following five sentences will be included in the interview report:
    I. This is the first fire in which Mrs. Brown has ever been involved.
    II. A neighbor smelled the food burning and called the Fire Department.
    III. Mrs. Brown has been a tenant in Apt. 4C for 7 years.
    IV. Mrs. Brown was very tired and laid down to rest and fell asleep.
    V. Mrs. Brown was cooking beef stew in the kitchen after coming home from work.
  The MOST logical order for the above sentences to appear in the report is

   A. II, III, I, IV, V
   B. III, V, IV, II, I
   C. I, III, II, V, IV
   D. III, V, I, IV, II

6. A fire marshal is completing a report of an arson fire. The report will contain the following five statements made by a witness:
    I. I heard the sound of breaking glass; and when I looked out my window, I saw orange flames coming from the building across the street.
    II. I saw two young men on bicycles rapidly riding away, one with long blond hair, the other had long brown hair.
    III. He made a threat to get even when he was being evicted.
    IV. The young man with long blond hair was evicted from the fire building last week.
    V. The two young men rode in the direction of Flowers Avenue.
  The MOST logical order for the above statements to appear in the report is

A. I, II, V, IV, III B. I, II, IV, V, III
C. III, I, V, II, IV D. III, I, II, IV, V

7. A fire marshal is preparing a report regarding an eleven-year-old who was burned in a fire at the Midtown School for Boys. The report will include the following five sentences:
    I. The child described the fire-setter as a male with glasses, five feet tall, wearing a blue uniform.
    II. On December 12, I responded to Hill Top Hospital to interview a child who was burned in a fire at the Midtown School for Boys.
    III. The male perpetrator made a full confession in front of the Assistant District Attorney at the precinct.
    IV. I responded to the school, after interviewing the boy, and found a security guard who fit the description.
    V. I interviewed the security guard and took him to the precinct for further questioning.

    The MOST logical order for the above sentences to appear in the fire report is

    A. I, IV, V, II, III   B. IV, III, II, I, V
    C. II, I, IV, V, III   D. II, IV, I, V, III

8. A fire marshal is preparing a report concerning a fire in an auto body shop. The report will contain the following five sentences:
    I. The shop owner stated that he argued with a customer about the cost of a repair job.
    II. The shop owner will be the complainant in the arson case.
    III. While on surveillance, my partner and I saw the fire and called it in over the Department radio.
    IV. The customer paid the bill and left saying, *I'll fix you for charging so much.*
    V. According to witnesses, the customer returned to the shop and threw a Molotov cocktail on the floor.

    The MOST logical order for the above sentences to appear in the report is

    A. I, IV, V, II, III   B. III, I, IV, V, II
    C. V, I, IV, III, II   D. III, V, I, IV, II

9. Security Officer Mace is completing an entry in her memo-book. The entry has the following five sentences:
    I. I observed the defendant removing a radio from a facility vehicle.
    II. I placed the defendant under arrest and escorted him to the patrolroom.
    III. I was patrolling the facility parking lot.
    IV. I asked the defendant to show identification. V. I determined that the defendant was not authorized to remove the radio.

    The MOST logical order for these sentences to be entered in Officer Mace's memo-book is

    A. I, III, II, IV, V   B. II, V, IV, I, III
    C. III, I, IV, V, II   D. IV, V, II, I, III

10. Security Officer Riley is completing an entry in his memo-book. The entry has the following five sentences:
    I. Anna Jones admitted that she stole Mary Green's wallet.
    II. I approached the women and asked them who they were and why they were arguing.
    III. I arrested Anna Jones for stealing Mary Green's wallet.
    IV. They identified themselves and Mary Green accused Anna Jones of stealing her wallet.
    V. I was in the lobby area when I observed two women arguing about a wallet.

    The MOST logical order for these sentences to be entered in Officer Riley's memo-book is

    A. II, IV, I, III, V
    B. III, I, IV, V, II
    C. IV, I, V, II, III
    D. V, II, IV, I, III

11. Assume that Security Officer John Ryan is completing an entry in his memobook. The entry has the following five sentences:
    I. I then cleared the immediate area of visitors and staff.
    II. I noticed smoke coming from a broom closet outside Room A71.
    III. Sergeant Mueller arrived with other officers to assist in clearing the area.
    IV. Upon investigation, I determined the smoke was due to burning material in the broom closet.
    V. I pulled the corridor fire alarm and notified Sergeant Mueller of the fire.

    The MOST logical order for these sentences to be entered in Officer Ryan's memo-book is

    A. II, III, IV, V, I
    B. II, IV, V, I, III
    C. IV, I, II, III, V
    D. V, III, II, I, IV

12. Security Officer Hernandez is completing an entry in his memobook. The entry has the following five sentences:
    I. I asked him to leave the premises immediately.
    II. A visitor complained that there was a strange man loitering in Clinic B hallway.
    III. I went to investigate and saw a man dressed in rags sitting on the floor of the hallway.
    IV. As he walked out, he started yelling that he had no place to go.
    V. I asked to see identification, but he said that he did not have any.

    The MOST logical order for these sentences to be entered in Officer Hernandez's memobook is

    A. II, III, V, I, IV
    B. III, I, II, IV, V
    C. IV, I, V, II, III
    D. III, I, V, II, IV

13. Officer Hogan is completing an entry in his memobook. The entry has the following five sentences:
    I. When the fighting had stopped, I transmitted a message requesting medical assistance for Mr. Perkins.
    II. Special Officer Manning assisted me in stopping the fight,
    III. When I arrived at the scene, I saw a client, Adam Finley, strike a facility employee, Peter Perkins.
    IV. As I attempted to break up the fight, Special Officer Manning came on the scene.
    V. I received a radio message from Sergeant Valez to investigate a possible fight in progress in the waiting room.

    The MOST logical order for these sentences to be entered in Officer Hogan's memobook is

    A. II, I, IV, V, III
    B. III, V, II, IV, I
    C. IV, V, III, I, II
    D. V, III, IV, II, I

14. Police Officer White is preparing a crime report concerning the burglary of Mr. Smith's home. The report will contain the following five sentences:
    I. Upon entering the house, Mr. Smith noticed that the mortgage money, which had been left on the kitchen table, had been taken.
    II. An investigation by the reporting Officer determined that the burglar had left the house through the first floor rear door.
    III. Further investigation revealed that there were no witnesses to the burglary.
    IV. In addition, several pieces of jewelry were missing from a first floor bedroom.
    V. After arriving at home, Mr. Smith discovered that someone had broken into the house by jimmying the front door.

    The MOST logical order for the above sentences to appear in the report is

    A. V, IV, II, III, I
    B. V, I, III, IV, II
    C. V, I, IV, II, III
    D. V, IV, II, I, III

15. Police Officer Jenner responds to the scene of a burglary at 2106 La Vista Boulevard. He is approached by an elderly man named Richard Jenkins, whose account of the incident includes the following five sentences:
    I. I saw that the lock on my apartment door had been smashed and the door was open.
    II. My apartment was a shambles; my belongings were everywhere and my television set was missing.
    III. As I walked down the hallway toward the bedroom, I heard someone opening a window.
    IV. I left work at 5:30 P.M. and took the bus home.
    V. At that time, I called the police.

    The MOST logical order for the above sentences to appear in the report is

    A. I, V, IV, II, III
    B. IV, I, II, III, V
    C. I, V, II, III, IV
    D. IV, III, II, V, I

16. Police Officer LaJolla is writing an Incident Report in which back-up assistance was required. The report will contain the following five sentences:
    I. The radio dispatcher asked what my location was and he then dispatched patrol cars for back-up assistance.
    II. At approximately 9:30 P.M., while I was walking my assigned footpost, a gunman fired three shots at me.
    III. I quickly turned around and saw a White male, approximately 5'10", with black hair, wearing blue jeans, a yellow T-shirt, and white sneakers, running across the avenue carrying a handgun.
    IV. When the back-up officers arrived, we searched the area but could not find the suspect.
    V. I advised the radio dispatcher that a gunman had just fired a gun at me, and then I gave the dispatcher a description of the man.

    The MOST logical order for the above sentences to appear in the report is

    A. III, V, II, IV, I
    B. II, III, V, I, IV
    C. III, II, IV, I, V
    D. II, V, I, III, IV

17. Police Officer Engle is completing a Complaint Report of a burglary which occurred at Monty's Bar. The following five sentences will be included in the Complaint Report:
    I. The owner said that approximately $600 was taken, along with eight bottles of expensive brandy.
    II. The burglar apparently gained entry to the bar through the window and exited through the front door.
    III. When Mr. Barrett returned to reopen the bar at 1:00 P.M., he found the front door open and items thrown all over the bar.
    IV. Mr. Barrett, the owner of Monty's Bar, said he closed the bar at 4:00 M. and locked all the doors.
    V. After interviewing the owner, I conducted a search of the bar and found that a window in the back of the bar was broken.

    The MOST logical order for the above sentences to appear in the report is

    A. II, IV, III, V, I
    B. IV, III, I, V, II
    C. IV, II, III, I, V
    D. II, V, IV, III, I

18. Police Officer Revson is writing a report concerning a vehicle pursuit. His report will include the following five sentences:
    I. I followed the vehicle for several blocks and then motioned to the driver to pull the car over to the curb and stop.
    II. I informed the radio dispatcher that I was in a high-speed pursuit.
    III. When the driver ignored me, I turned on my siren and the driver increased his speed.
    IV. The vehicle hit a tree, and I was able to arrest the driver.
    V. While on patrol in Car #4135, I observed a motorist driving suspiciously.

    The MOST logical order for the above sentences to appear in the report is

    A. V, I, III, II, IV
    B. II, V, III, I, IV
    C. V, I, II, IV, III
    D. II, I, V, IV, III

19. Crime Reports are completed by Police Officers. One section of a report contains the following five sentences:
    I. The man, seeing that the woman had the watch, pushed Mr. Lugano to the ground.
    II. Frank Lugano was walking into the Flame Diner on Queens Boulevard when he was jostled by a man in front of him.
    III. A few minutes later, Mr. Lugano told a police officer on foot patrol about a man and a woman taking his watch.
    IV. As soon as he was jostled, a woman reached toward Mr. Lugano's wrist and removed his expensive watch.
    V. The man and woman, after taking Mr. Lugano's watch, ran around the corner.

    The MOST logical order for the above sentences to appear in the report is

    A. II, IV, I, III, V
    B. II, IV, I, V, III
    C. IV, I, III, II, V
    D. IV, II, I, V, III

20. Detective Adams completed a Crime Report which includes the following five sentences:
    I. I arrived at the scene of the crime at 10:20 A.M. and began to question Mr. Sands about the security devices he had installed.
    II. Several clearly identifiable fingerprints were found.
    III. A Fingerprint Unit specialist arrived at the scene and immediately began to dust for fingerprints.
    IV. After questioning Mr. Sands, I called the Fingerprint Unit.
    V. On Friday morning at 10 A.M., Mr. Sands, the owner of the High Fashion Fur Store on Fifth Avenue, called the precinct to report that his safe had been broken into.

    The MOST logical order for the above sentences to appear in the Crime Report is

    A. I, V, IV, III, II
    B. I, V, III, IV, II
    C. V, I, IV, II, III
    D. V, I, IV, III, II

KEY (CORRECT ANSWERS)

1.	A	11.	B
2.	D	12.	A
3.	C	13.	D
4.	A	14.	C
5.	B	15.	B
6.	A	16.	B
7.	C	17.	B
8.	B	18.	A
9.	C	19.	B
10.	D	20.	D

TEST 2

DIRECTIONS: The sentences that follow are in scrambled order. You are to rearrange them in proper order and indicate the letter choice containing the CORRECT answer. *PRINT THE LETTER OF THE CORRECT ANSWER IN THE SPACE AT THE RIGHT.*

1. Police Officer Ling is preparing a Complaint Report of a missing person. His report will contain the following five sentences:
    I. I was greeted by Mrs. Miah Ali, who stated her daughter Lisa, age 17, did not return from school.
    II. I questioned Mrs. Ali as to what time her daughter left for school and what type of clothing she was wearing.
    III. I notified the Patrol Sergeant, searched the building and area, and prepared a Missing Person Complaint Report.
    IV. I received a call from the radio dispatcher to respond to 9 Maple Street, Apartment 1H, on a missing person complaint.
    V. Mrs. Ali informed me that Lisa was wearing a grey suit and black shoes, and departed for school at 7:30 A.M.

    The MOST logical order for the above sentences to appear in the report is

    A. IV, I, V, II, III
    B. I, IV, V, III, II
    C. IV, I, II, V, III
    D. III, I, IV, II, V

2. Police Officer Dunn is preparing a Complaint Report which will include the following five sentences:
    I. Mrs. Field screamed and fought with the man.
    II. A man wearing a blue ski mask grabbed Mrs. Field's purse.
    III. Mrs. Field was shopping on 34th Street and Broadway at 1 o'clock in the afternoon.
    IV. The man then ran around the corner.
    V. The man was white, five feet six inches tall with a medium build.

    The MOST logical order for the above sentences to appear in the report is

    A. I, V, II, IV, III
    B. III, II, I, IV, V
    C. III, IV, V, I, II
    D. V, IV, III, I, II

3. Police Officer Davis is preparing a written report concerning child abuse. The report will include the following five sentences:
    I. I responded to the scene and was met by an adult and a child who was approximately four years old.
    II. I was notified by an unidentified pedestrian of a possible case of child abuse at 325 Belair Terrace.
    III. The adult told me that the child fell and that the police were not needed.
    IV. I felt that this might be a case of child abuse, and I requested that a Sergeant respond to the scene.
    V. The child was bleeding from the head and had several bruises on the face.

    The MOST logical order for the above sentences to appear in the report is

    A. II, I, V, III, IV
    B. I, II, IV, III, V
    C. I, III, IV, II, V
    D. II, IV, I, V, III

4. The following five sentences will be part of a memobook entry concerning found property:

   I. Mr. Gustav said that while cleaning the lobby he found six credit cards and a passport.
   II. The credit cards and passport were issued to Manuel Gomez.
   III. I went to the precinct to give the property to the Desk Officer.
   IV. I prepared a receipt listing the property, gave the receipt to Mr. Gustav, and had him sign my memobook.
   V. While on foot patrol, I was approached by Mr. Gustav, the superintendent of 50-12 Maiden Parkway.

   The MOST logical order for the above sentences to appear in the memobook is

   A. V, I, II, IV, III
   B. I, II, IV, III, V
   C. V, I, III, IV, II
   D. I, IV, III, II, V

5. Police Officer Thomas is making a memobook entry that will include the following five sentences:

   I. My partner obtained a brief description of the suspects and the direction they were heading when they left the store.
   II. Edward Lemkin was asked to come with us to search the immediate area.
   III. I transmitted this information over the radio.
   IV. At the corner of 72nd Street and Broadway, our patrol car was stopped by Edward Lemkin, the owner of PJ Records.
   V. He told us that a group of teenagers stole some merchandise from his record store.

   The MOST logical order for the above sentences to appear in the report is

   A. V, IV, I, III, II
   B. IV, V, I, III, II
   C. V, I, III, II, IV
   D. IV, I, III, II, V

6. Police Officer Caldwell is completing a Complaint Report. The report will include the following five sentences:

   I. When I yelled, *Don't move, Police,* the taller man dropped the bat and ran.
   II. I asked the girl for a description of the two men.
   III. I called for an ambulance.
   IV. A young girl approached me and stated that a man with a baseball bat was beating another man in front of 1700 Grande Street.
   V. Upon approaching the location, I observed the taller man hitting the other man with the bat.

   The MOST logical order for the above sentences to appear in the report is

   A. IV, V, I, II, III
   B. V, IV, II, III, I
   C. V, I, III, IV, II
   D. IV, II, V, I, III

7. Police Officer Moore is writing a memobook entry concerning a summons he issued. The entry will contain the following five sentences:
   I. As I was walking down the platform, I heard music coming from a radio that a man was holding on his shoulder.
   II. I asked the man for some identification.
   III. I was walking in the subway when a passenger complained about a man playing a radio loudly at the opposite end of the station.
   IV. I then gave the man a summons for playing the radio. V. As soon as the man saw me approaching, he turned the radio off.
   The MOST logical order for the above sentences to appear in the memobook entry is

   A. III, V, II, I, IV
   B. I, II, V, IV, III
   C. III, I, V, II, IV
   D. I, V, II, IV, III

8. Police Officer Kashawahara is completing an Incident Report regarding fleeing suspects he had pursued earlier. The report will include the following five sentences:
   I. I saw two males attempting to break into a store through the front window.
   II. On Myrtle Avenue, they ran into an alley between two abandoned buildings.
   III. I yelled to them, Hey, what are you guys doing by that window?
   IV. At that time, I lost sight of the suspects and I returned to the station house.
   V. They started to run south on Wycoff Avenue heading towards Myrtle Avenue.
   The MOST logical order for the above sentences to appear in the report is

   A. I, V, II, IV, III
   B. III, V, II, IV, I
   C. I, III, V, II, IV
   D. III, I, V, II, IV

9. Police Officer Bloom is completing an entry in his memo-book regarding a confession made by a perpetrator. The entry will include the following five sentences:
   I. I went towards the dresser and took $400 in cash and a jewelry box with rings, watches, and other items in it.
   II. There in the bedroom, lying on the bed, a woman was sleeping.
   III. It was about 1:00 A.M. when I entered the apartment through an opened rear window.
   IV. I spun around, punched her in the face with my free hand, and then jumped out the window into the street.
   V. I walked back to the window carrying the money and the jewelry box and was about to go out when all of a sudden I heard the woman scream.
   The MOST logical order for the above sentences to appear in the memobook entry is

   A. I, III, II, V, IV
   B. I, V, IV, III, II
   C. III, II, I, V, IV
   D. III, V, IV, I, II

10. Police Officer Webster is preparing an Arrest Report which will include the following five sentences:
    I. I noticed that the robber had a knife placed at the victim's neck.
    II. I told the robber to drop the knife.
    III. While on patrol, I observed a robbery which was in progress.
    IV. I grabbed the robber, placed him in handcuffs, and took him to the precinct.
    V. The robber dropped the knife and tried to flee.
    The MOST logical order for the above sentences to appear in the report is

    A. I, II, V, IV, III
    B. III, I, II, V, IV
    C. III, II, IV, I, V
    D. I, III, IV, V, II

11. Police Officer Lee is preparing a report regarding someone who apparently attempted to commit suicide with a gun. The report will include the following five sentences:
    I. At the location, the woman pointed to the open door of Apartment 7L.
    II. I called for an ambulance to respond.
    III. The male had a gun in his hand and a large head wound.
    IV. A call was received from the radio dispatcher regarding a woman who heard a gunshot at 936 45th Avenue.
    V. Upon entering Apartment 7L, I saw the body of a male on the kitchen floor.

    The MOST logical order for the above sentences to appear in the report is

    A. IV, I, V, III, II
    B. I, III, V, IV, II
    C. I, V, III, II, IV
    D. IV, V, III, II, I

12. Police Officer Modrak is completing a memobook entry which will include the following five sentences:
    I. The victim, a male in his thirties, told me that the robbery occurred a few minutes ago.
    II. My partner and I jumped out of the patrol car and arrested the suspect.
    III. We responded to an armed robbery in progress at Billings Avenue and 59th Street.
    IV. On Chester Avenue and 68th Street, the victim spotted and identified the suspect.
    V. I told the victim to get into the patrol car and that we would drive him around the area.

    The MOST logical order for the above sentences to appear in the memobook is

    A. III, I, V, IV, II
    B. I, III, V, II, IV
    C. I, IV, III, V, II
    D. III, V, I, II, IV

13. Police Officer Rodriguez is preparing a report concerning an incident in which she used her revolver. Her report will include the following five sentences:
    I. Upon seeing my revolver, the robber dropped his gun to the ground.
    II. At about 10:55 P.M., I was informed by a passerby that several people were being robbed at gunpoint on 174th Street and Walton Avenue.
    III. I was assigned to patrol on 174th Street and Ghent Avenue during the evening shift.
    IV. I saw a man holding a gun on three people, took out my revolver, and shouted, *Police, don't move!*
    V. After calling for assistance, I went to 174th Street and Walton Avenue and took cover behind a car.

    The MOST logical order for the above sentences to appear in the report is

    A. II, III, IV, V, I
    B. IV, V, I, III, II
    C. III, II, V, IV, I
    D. II, IV, I, V, III

14. Police Officer Davis is completing an Activity Log entry which will include the following five sentences:
    I. A radio car was dispatched and the male was taken to Greenville Hospital.
    II. Several people saw him and called the police.
    III. A naked man was running down the street waving his arms above his head and screaming, *Insects are all over me!*
    IV. I arrived on the scene and requested an ambulance.
    V. The dispatcher informed me that no ambulances were available.

    The MOST logical order for the above sentences to appear in the Activity Log is

    A. III, IV, V, I, II
    B. II, III, V, I, IV
    C. III, II, IV, V, I
    D. II, IV, III, V, I

15. Police Officer Peake is completing an entry in his Activity Log. The entry contains the following five sentences:
    I. He went to his parked car only to find he was blocked in.
    II. The owner of the vehicle refused to move the van until he had finished his lunch.
    III. Approximately 30 minutes later, I arrived on the scene and ordered the owner of the van to remove the vehicle.
    IV. Mr. O'Neil had an appointment and was in a hurry to keep it.
    V. Mr. O'Neil entered a nearby delicatessen and asked if anyone in there drove a dark blue van, license plate number BUS 265.

    The MOST logical order for the above sentences to appear in the Activity Log is

    A. II, III, I, IV, V
    B. IV, I, V, II, III
    C. V, IV, I, III, II
    D. II, I, III, IV, V

16. Police Officer Harrison is preparing a report regarding a 10-year-old who was sexually abused at school. The report will include the following five sentences:
    I. The child described the perpetrator as a white male with a mustache, six feet tall, wearing a green uniform.
    II. On September 10, I responded to General Hospital to interview a child who was sexually abused.
    III. He later confessed at the station house.
    IV. After I interviewed the child, I responded to the school and found a janitor who fit the description.
    V. I interviewed the janitor and took him to the station house for further investigation.

    The MOST logical order for the above sentences to appear in the report is

    A. II, IV, I, V, III
    B. I, IV, V, II, III
    C. II, I, IV, V, III
    D. V, III, II, I, IV

17. Police Officer Madden is completing a report of a theft. The report will include the following five sentences:
    I. I followed behind the suspect for two blocks.
    II. I saw a man pass by the radio car carrying a shopping bag.
    III. I looked back in the direction he had just come from and noticed that the top of a parking meter was missing.
    IV. As he saw me, he started to walk faster, and I noticed a red piece of metal with the word *violation* drop out of the shopping bag.
    V. When I saw a parking meter in the shopping bag, I apprehended the suspect and placed him under arrest.
    The MOST logical order for the above sentences to appear in the report is

    A. I, IV, II, III, V
    B. II, I, IV, V, III
    C. II, IV, III, I, V
    D. III, II, IV, I, V

18. Police Officer McCaslin is preparing a report of disorderly conduct which will include the following five sentences:
    I. Police Officer Kenny and I were on patrol in a radio car when we received a dispatch to go to the Hard Rock Disco on Third Avenue.
    II. We arrived at the scene and found three men arguing loudly and obviously intoxicated.
    III. The dispatcher had received a call from a bartender regarding a dispute.
    IV. Two of the men left the disco shortly before we did.
    V. We calmed the men down after managing to separate them.
    The MOST logical order for the above sentences to appear in the report is

    A. I, II, V, III, IV
    B. III, I, IV, II, V
    C. II, I, III, IV, V
    D. I, III, II, V, IV

19. Police Officer Langhorne is completing a report of a murder. The report will contain the following five statements made by a witness:
    I. The noise created by the roar of a motorcycle caused me to look out of my window.
    II. I ran out of the house and realized the man was dead, which is when I called the police.
    III. I saw a man driving at high speed down the dead-end street on a motorcycle, closely followed by a green BMW.
    IV. The motorcyclist then parked the bike and approached the car, which was occupied by two males.
    V. Two shots were fired and the cyclist fell to the ground; then the car made a u-turn and sped down the street.
    The MOST logical order for the above sentences to appear in the report is

    A. I, II, IV, III, V
    B. V, II, I, IV, III
    C. I, III, IV, V, II
    D. III, IV, I, II, V

20. Police Officer Murphy is preparing a report of a person who was assaulted. The report will include the following five sentences:
      I. I responded to the scene, but Mr. Jones had already fled.
      II. She was bleeding profusely from a cut above her right eye.
      III. Mr. and Mrs. Jones apparently were fighting in the street when Mr. Jones punched his wife in the face.
      IV. I then applied pressure to the cut to control the bleeding.
      V. I called the dispatcher on the radio to send an ambulance to respond to the scene.

   The MOST logical order for the above sentences to appear in the report is

   A. III, II, IV, I, V
   B. III, I, II, IV, V
   C. I, V, II, III, IV
   D. II, V, IV, III, I

KEY (CORRECT ANSWERS)

1.	C	11.	A
2.	B	12.	A
3.	A	13.	C
4.	A	14.	C
5.	B	15.	B
6.	D	16.	C
7.	C	17.	C
8.	C	18.	D
9.	C	19.	C
10.	B	20.	B

PREPARING WRITTEN MATERIAL
EXAMINATION SECTION
TEST 1

DIRECTIONS: Each question or incomplete statement is followed by several suggested answers or completions. Select the one that BEST answers the question or completes the statement. *PRINT THE LETTER OF THE CORRECT ANSWER IN THE SPACE AT THE RIGHT.*

1. The one of the following sentences which is LEAST acceptable from the viewpoint of correct usage is:
   A. The police thought the fugitive to be him.
   B. The criminals set a trap for whoever would fall into it.
   C. It is ten years ago since the fugitive fled from the city.
   D. The lecturer argued that criminals are usually cowards.
   E. The police removed four bucketfuls of earth from the scene of the crime.

1.____

2. The one of the following sentences which is LEAST acceptable from the viewpoint of correct usage is:
   A. The patrolman scrutinized the report with great care.
   B. Approaching the victim of the assault, two bruises were noticed by the patrolman.
   C. As soon as I had broken down the door, I stepped into the room.
   D. I observed the accused loitering near the building, which was closed at the time.
   E. The storekeeper complained that his neighbor was guilty of violating a local ordinance.

2.____

3. The one of the following sentences which is LEAST acceptable from the viewpoint of correct usage is:
   A. I realized immediately that he intended to assault the woman, so I disarmed him.
   B. It was apparent that Mr. Smith's explanation contained many inconsistencies.
   C. Despite the slippery condition of the street, he managed to stop the vehicle before injuring the child.
   D. Not a single one of them wish, despite the damage to property, to make a formal complaint.
   E. The body was found lying on the floor.

3.____

4. The one of the following sentences which contains NO error in usage is:
   A. After the robbers left, the proprietor stood tied in his chair for about two hours before help arrived.
   B. In the cellar I found the watchman's hat and coat.
   C. The persons living in adjacent apartments stated that they had heard no unusual noises.

4.____

D. Neither a knife or any firearms were found in the room.
E. Walking down the street, the shouting of the crowd indicated that something was wrong.

5. The one of the following sentences which contains NO error in usage is:
   A. The policeman lay a firm hand on the suspect's shoulder.
   B. It is true that neither strength nor agility are the most important requirement for a good patrolman.
   C. Good citizens constantly strive to do more than merely comply the restraints imposed by society.
   D. No decision was made as to whom the prize should be awarded.
   E. Twenty years is considered a severe sentence for a felony.

6. Which of the following sentences is NOT expressed in standard English usage?
   A. The victim reached a pay-phone booth and manages to call police headquarters.
   B. By the time the call was received, the assailant had left the scene.
   C. The victim has been a respected member of the community for the past eleven years.
   D. Although the lighting was bad and the shadows were deep, the storekeeper caught sight of the attacker.
   E. Additional street lights have since been installed, and the patrols have been strengthened.

7. Which of the following sentences is NOT expressed in standard English usage?
   A. The judge upheld the attorney's right to question the witness about the missing glove.
   B. To be absolutely fair to all parties is the jury's chief responsibility.
   C. Having finished the report, a loud noise in the next room startled the sergeant.
   D. The witness obviously enjoyed having played a part in the proceedings.
   E. The sergeant planned to assign the case to whoever arrived first.

8. In which of the following sentences is a word misused?
   A. As a matter of principle, the captain insisted that the suspect's partner be brought for questioning.
   B. The principle suspect had been detained at the station house for most of the day.
   C. The principal in the crime had no previous criminal record, but his closest associate had been convicted of felonies on two occasions.
   D. The interest payments had been made promptly, but the firm had been drawing upon the principal for these payments.
   E. The accused insisted that his high school principal would furnish him a character reference.

9. Which of the following statements is ambiguous?
   A. Mr. Sullivan explained why Mr. Johnson had been dismissed from his job.
   B. The storekeeper told the patrolman he had made a mistake.
   C. After waiting three hours, the patients in the doctor's office were sent home.
   D. The janitor's duties were to maintain the building in good shape and to answer tenants' complaints.
   E. The speed limit should, in my opinion, be raised to sixty miles an hour on that stretch of road.

9._____

10. In which of the following is the punctuation or capitalization faulty?
    A. The accident occurred at an intersection in the Kew Gardens section of Queens, near the bus stop.
    B. The sedan, not the convertible, was struck in the side.
    C. Before any of the patrolmen had left the police car received an important message from headquarters.
    D. The dog that had been stolen was returned to his master, John Dempsey, who lived in East Village.
    E. The letter had been sent to 12 Hillside Terrace, Rutland, Vermont 05702.

10._____

Questions 11-25.

DIRECTIONS: Questions 11 through 25 are to be answered in accordance with correct English usage; that is, standard English rather than nonstandard or substandard. Nonstandard and substandard English includes words or expressions usually classified as slang, dialect, illiterate, etc., which are not generally accepted as correct in current written communication. Standard English also requires clarity, proper punctuation and capitalization and appropriate use of words. Write the letter of the sentence NOT expressed in standard English usage in the space at the right.

11. A. There were three witnesses to the accident.
    B. At least three witnesses were found to testify for the plaintiff.
    C. Three of the witnesses who took the stand was uncertain about the defendant's competence to drive.
    D. Only three witnesses came forward to testify for the plaintiff.
    E. The three witnesses to the accident were pedestrians.

11._____

12. A. The driver had obviously drunk too many martinis before leaving for home.
    B. The boy who drowned had swum in these same waters many times before.
    C. The petty thief had stolen a bicycle from a private driveway before he was apprehended.
    D. The detectives had brung in the heroin shipment they intercepted.
    E. The passengers had never ridden in a converted bus before.

12._____

13.
- A. Between you and me, the new platoon plan sounds like a good idea.
- B. Money from an aunt's estate was left to his wife and he.
- C. He and I were assigned to the same patrol for the first time in two months.
- D. Either you or he should check the front door of that store.
- E. The captain himself was not sure of the witness's reliability.

14.
- A. The alarm had scarcely begun to ring when the explosion occurred.
- B. Before the firemen arrived at the scene, the second story had been destroyed.
- C. Because of the dense smoke and heat, the firemen could hardly approach the now-blazing structure.
- D. According to the patrolman's report, there wasn't nobody in the store when the explosion occurred.
- E. The sergeant's suggestion was not at all unsound, but no one agreed with him.

15.
- A. The driver and the passenger they were both found to be intoxicated.
- B. The driver and the passenger talked slowly and not too clearly.
- C. Neither the driver nor his passengers were able to give a coherent account of the accident.
- D. In a corner of the room sat the passenger, quietly dozing.
- E. the driver finally told a strange and unbelievable story, which the passenger contradicted.

16.
- A. Under the circumstances I decided not to continue my examination of the premises.
- B. There are many difficulties now not comparable with those existing in 1960.
- C. Friends of the accused were heard to announce that the witness had better been away on the day of the trial.
- D. The two criminals escaped in the confusion that followed the explosion.
- E. The aged man was struck by the considerateness of the patrolman's offer.

17.
- A. An assemblage of miscellaneous weapons lay on the table.
- B. Ample opportunities were given to the defendant to obtain counsel.
- C. The speaker often alluded to his past experience with youthful offenders in the armed forces.
- D. The sudden appearance of the truck aroused my suspicions.
- E. Her studying had a good affect on her grades in high school.

18.
- A. He sat down in the theater and began to watch the movie.
- B. The girl had ridden horses since she was four years old.
- C. Application was made on behalf of the prosecutor to cite the witness for contempt.
- D. The bank robber, with his two accomplices, were caught in the act.
- E. His story is simply not credible.

19. A. The angry boy said that he did not like those kind of friends.
    B. The merchant's financial condition was so precarious that he felt he must avail himself of any offer of assistance.
    C. He is apt to promise more than he can perform.
    D. Looking at the messy kitchen, the housewife felt like crying.
    E. A clerk was left in charge of the stolen property.

20. A. His wounds were aggravated by prolonged exposure to sub-freezing temperatures.
    B. The prosecutor remarked that the witness was not averse to changing his story each time he was interviewed.
    C. The crime pattern indicated that the burglars were adapt in the handling of explosives.
    D. His rigid adherence to a fixed plan brought him into renewed conflict with his subordinates.
    E. He had anticipated that the sentence would be delivered by noon.

21. A. The whole arraignment procedure is badly in need of revision.
    B. After his glasses were broken in the fight, he would of gone to the optometrist if he could.
    C. Neither Tom nor Jack brought his lunch to work.
    D. He stood aside until the quarrel was over.
    E. A statement in the psychiatrist's report disclosed that the probationer vowed to have his revenge.

22. A. His fiery and intemperate speech to the striking employees fatally affected any chance of a future reconciliation.
    B. The wording of the statute has been variously construed.
    C. The defendant's attorney, speaking in the courtroom, called the official a demagogue who contempuously disregarded the judge's orders.
    D. The baseball game is likely to be the most exciting one this year.
    E. The mother divided the cookies among her two children.

23. A. There was only a bed and a dresser in the dingy room.
    B. John was one of the few students that have protested the new rule.
    C. It cannot be argued that the child's testimony is negligible; it is, on the contrary, of the greatest importance.
    D. The basic criterion for clearance was so general that officials resolved any doubts in favor of dismissal.
    E. Having just returned from a long vacation, the officer found the city unbearably hot.

24. A. The librarian ought to give more help to small children.
    B. The small boy was criticized by the teacher because he often wrote careless.
    C. It was generally doubted whether the women would permit the use of her apartment for intelligence operations.
    D. The probationer acts differently every time the officer visits him.
    E. Each of the newly appointed officers has 12 years of service.

25. A. The North is the most industrialized region in the country.
    B. L. Patrick Gray 3d, the bureau's acting director, stated that, while "rehabilitation is fine" for some convicted criminals, "it is a useless gesture for those who resist every such effort."
    C. Careless driving, faulty mechanism, narrow or badly kept roads all play their part in causing accidents.
    D. The childrens' books were left in the bus.
    E. It was a matter of internal security; consequently, he felt no inclination to rescind his previous order.

KEY (CORRECT ANSWERS)

1.	C	11.	C
2.	B	12.	D
3.	D	13.	B
4.	C	14.	D
5.	E	15.	A
6.	A	16.	C
7.	C	17.	E
8.	B	18.	D
9.	B	19.	A
10.	C	20.	C

21.	B
22.	E
23.	B
24.	B
25.	D

TEST 2

DIRECTIONS: Each question or incomplete statement is followed by several suggested answers or completions. Select the one that BEST answers the question or completes the statement. *PRINT THE LETTER OF THE CORRECT ANSWER IN THE SPACE AT THE RIGHT.*

Questions 1-6.

DIRECTIONS: Each of Questions 1 through 6 consists of a statement which contains a word (one of those underlined) that is either incorrectly used because it is not in keeping with the meaning the quotation is evidently intended to convey, or is misspelled. There is only one INCORRECT word in each quotation. Of the four underlined words, determine if the first one should be replaced by the word lettered A, the second replaced by the word lettered B, the third replaced by the word lettered C, or the fourth replaced by the word lettered D.

1. Whether one depends on fluorescent or artificial light or both, adequate standards should be maintained by means of systematic tests.
   A. natural   B. safeguards   C. established   D. routine

2. A police officer has to be prepared to assume his knowledge as a social scientist in the community.
   A. forced   B. role   C. philosopher   D. street

3. It is practically impossible to indicate whether a sentence is too long simply by measuring its length.
   A. almost   B. tell   C. very   D. guessing

4. Strong leaders are required to organize a community for delinquency prevention and for dissemination of organized crime and drug addiction.
   A. tactics   B. important   C. control   D. meetings

5. The demonstrators who were taken to the Criminal Courts building in Manhattan (because it was large enough to accommodate them), contended that the arrests were unwarranted.
   A. demonstraters   B. Manhatten
   C. accomodate   D. unwarranted

6. They were guaranteed a calm atmosphere, free from harassment, which would be conducive to quiet consideration of the indictments.
   A. guarenteed   B. atmspher
   C. harassment   D. inditements

Questions 7-11.

DIRECTIONS: Each of Questions 7 through 11 consists of a statement containing four words in capital letters. One of these words in capital letters is not in keeping with the meaning which the statement is evidently intended to carry. The four words in capital letters in each statement are reprinted after the statement. Print the capital letter preceding the one of the four words which does MOST to spoil the true meaning of the statement in the space at the right.

7. Retirement and pension systems are essential not only to provide employees with with a means of support in the future, but also to prevent longevity and CHARITABLE considerations from UPSETTING the PROMOTIONAL opportunities RETIRED members of the career service. 7.____
   A. charitable   B. upsetting   C. promotional   D. retired

8. Within each major DIVISION in a properly set up public or private organization, provision is made so that each NECESSARY activity is CARED for and lines of authority and responsibility are clear-cut and INFINITE. 8.____
   A. division   B. necessary   C. cared   D. infinite

9. In public service, the scale of salaries paid must be INCIDENTAL to the services rendered, with due CONSIDERATION for the attraction of the desired MANPOWER and for the maintenance of a standard of living COMMENSURATE with the work to be performed. 9.____
   A. incidental   B. consideration
   C. manpower   D. commensurate

10. An understanding of the AIMS of an organization by the staff will AID greatly in increasing the DEMAND of the correspondence work of the office, and will to a large extent DETERMINE the nature of the correspondence. 10.____
   A. aims   B. aid   C. demand   D. determine

11. BECAUSE the Civil Service Commission strongly feels that the MERIT system is a key factor in the MAINTENANCE of democratic government, it has adopted as one of its major DEFENSES the progressive democratization of its own procedures in dealing with candidates for positions in the public service. 11.____
   A. Because   B. merit   C. maintenance   D. defenses

Questions 12-14.

DIRECTIONS: Questions 12 through 14 consist of one sentence each. Each sentence contains an incorrectly used word. First, decide which is the incorrectly used word. Then, from among the options given, decide which word, when substituted for the incorrectly used word, makes the meaning of the sentence clear.
EXAMPLE:
The U.S. national income exhibits a pattern of long term deflection.
   A. reflection   B. subjection   C. rejoicing   D. growth

The word *deflection* in the sentence does not convey the meaning the sentence evidently intended to convey. The word *growth* (Answer D), when substituted for the word *deflection*, makes the meaning of the sentence clear. Accordingly, the answer to the question is D.

12. The study commissioned by the joint committee fell compassionately short of the mark and would have to be redone.
    A. successfully
    B. insignificantly
    C. experimentally
    D. woefully

13. He will not idly exploit any violation of the provisions of the order.
    A. tolerate   B. refuse   C. construe   D. guard

14. The defendant refused to be virile and bitterly protested service.
    A. irked   B. feasible   C. docile   D. credible

Questions 15-25.

DIRECTIONS: Questions 15 through 25 consist of short paragraphs. Each paragraph contains one word which is INCORRECTLY used because it is NOT in keeping with the meaning of the paragraph. Find the word in each paragraph which is INCORRECTLY used and then select as the answer the suggested word which should be substituted for the incorrectly used word.

SAMPLE QUESTION:
In determining who is to do the work in your unit, you will have to decide just who does what from day to day. One of your lowest responsibilities is to assign work so that everybody gets a fair share and that everyone can do his part well.
A. new   B. old   C. important   D. performance

EXPLANATION:
The word which is NOT in keeping with the meaning of the paragraph is *lowest*. This is the INCORRECTLY used word. The suggested word *important* would be in keeping with the meaning of the paragraph and should be substituted for *lowest*. Therefore, the CORRECT answer is choice C.

15. If really good practice in the elimination of preventable injuries is to be achieved and held in any establishment, top management must refuse full and definite responsibility and must apply a good share of its attention to the task.
    A. accept   B. avoidable   C. duties   D. problem

16. Recording the human face for identification is by no means the only service performed by the camera in the field of investigation. When the trial of any issue takes place, a word picture is sought to be distorted to the court of incidents, occurrences, or events which are in dispute.
    A. appeals   B. description   C. portrayed   D. deranged

17. In the collection of physical evidence, it cannot be emphasized too strongly that a haphazard systematic search at the scene of the crime is vital. Nothing must be overlooked. Often the only leads in a case will come from the results of this search.
    A. important
    B. investigation
    C. proof
    D. thorough

17._____

18. If an investigator has reason to suspect that the witness is mentally stable, or a habitual drunkard, he should leave no stone unturned in his investigation to determine if the witness was under the influence of liquor or drugs, or was mentally unbalanced either at the time of the occurrence to which he testified or at the time of the trial.
    A. accused
    B. clue
    C. deranged
    D. question

18._____

19. The use of records is a valuable step in crime investigation and is the main reason every department should maintain accurate reports. Crimes are not committed through the use of departmental records alone but from the use of all records, of almost every type, wherever they may be found and whenever they give any incidental information regarding the criminal.
    A. accidental
    B. necessary
    C. reported
    D. solved

19._____

20. In the years since passage of the Harrison Narcotic Act of 1914, making the possession of opium amphetamines illegal in most circumstances, drug use has become a subject of considerable scientific interest and investigation. There is at present a voluminous literature on drug use of various kinds.
    A. ingestion
    B. derivatives
    C. addiction
    D. opiates

20._____

21. Of course, the fact that criminal laws are extremely patterned in definition does not mean that the majority of persons who violate them are dealt with as criminals. Quite the contrary, for a great many forbidden acts are voluntarily engaged in within situations of privacy and go unobserved and unreported.
    A. symbolic
    B. casual
    C. scientific
    D. broad-gauged

21._____

22. The most punitive way to study punishment is to focus attention on the pattern of punitive action: to study how a penalty is applied, too study what is done to or taken from an offender.
    A. characteristic
    B. degrading
    C. objective
    D. distinguished

22._____

23. The most common forms of punishment in times past have been death, physical torture, mutilation, branding, public humiliation, fines, forfeits of property, banishment, transportation, and imprisonment. Although this list is by no means differentiated, practically every form of punishment has had several variations and applications.
    A. specific
    B. simple
    C. exhaustive
    D. characteristic

23._____

24. There is another important line of inference between ordinary and professional criminals, and that is the source from which they are recruited. The professional criminal seems to be drawn from legitimate employment and, in many instances, from parallel vocations or pursuits.
    A. demarcation   B. justification   C. superiority   D. reference

24.____

25. He took the position that the success of the program was insidious on getting additional revenue.
    A. reputed   B. contingent   C. failure   D. indeterminate

25.____

KEY (CORRECT ANSWERS)

1.	A		11.	D
2.	B		12.	D
3.	B		13.	A
4.	C		14.	C
5.	D		15.	A
6.	C		16.	C
7.	D		17.	D
8.	D		18.	C
9.	A		19.	D
10.	C		20.	B

21. D
22. C
23. C
24. A
25. B

TEST 3

DIRECTIONS: Each question or incomplete statement is followed by several suggested answers or completions. Select the one that BEST answers the question or completes the statement. *PRINT THE LETTER OF THE CORRECT ANSWER IN THE SPACE AT THE RIGHT.*

Questions 1-5.

DIRECTIONS: Questions 1 through 5 are to be answered on the basis of the following.

You are a supervising officer in an investigative unit. Earlier in the day, you directed Detectives Tom Dixon and Sal Mayo to investigate a reported assault and robbery in a liquor store within your area of jurisdiction.

Detective Dixon has submitted to you a preliminary investigative report containing the following information:

- At 1630 hours on 2/20, arrived at Joe's Liquor Store at 350 SW Avenue with Detective Mayo to investigate A & R.
- At store interviewed Rob Ladd, store manager, who stated that he and Joe Brown (store owner) had been stuck up about ten minutes prior to our arrival.
- Ladd described the robbers as male whites in their late teens or early twenties. Further stated that one of the robbers displayed what appeared to be an automatic pistol as he entered the store, and said, *Give us the money or we'll kill you.* Ladd stated that Brown then reached under the counter where he kept a loaded .38 caliber pistol. Several shots followed, and Ladd threw himself to the floor.
- The robbers fled, and Ladd didn't know if any money had been taken.
- At this point, Ladd realized that Brown was unconscious on the floor and bleeding from a head wound.
- Ambulance called by Ladd, and Brown was removed by same to General Hospital.
- Personally interviewed John White, 382 Dartmouth Place, who stated he was inside store at the time of occurrence. White states that he hid behind a wine display upon hearing someone say, *Give us the money.* He then heard shots and saw two young men run from the store to a yellow car parked at the curb. White was unable to further describe auto. States the taller of the two men drove the car away while the other sat on passenger side in front.
- Recovered three spent .38 caliber bullets from premises and delivered them to Crime Lab.
- To General Hospital at 1800 hours but unable to interview Brown, who was under sedation and suffering from shock and a laceration of the head.
- Alarm #12487 transmitted for car and occupants.
- Case Active.

Based solely on the contents of the preliminary investigation submitted by Detective Dixon, select one sentence from the following groups of sentences which is MOST accurate and is grammatically correct.

1. A. Both robbers were armed.
    B. Each of the robbers were described as a male white.
    C. Neither robber was armed.
    D. Mr. Ladd stated that one of the robbers was armed.

2. A. Mr. Brown fired three shots from his revolver.
    B. Mr. Brown was shot in the head by one of the robbers.
    C. Mr. Brown suffered a gunshot wound of the head during the course of the robbery.
    D. Mr. Brown was taken to General Hospital by ambulance.

3. A. Shots were fired after one of the robbers said, *Give us the money or we'll kill you.*
    B. After one of the robbers demanded the money from Mr. Brown, he fired a shot.
    C. The preliminary investigation indicated that although Mr. Brown did not have a license for the gun, he was justified in using deadly physical force.
    D. Mr. Brown was interviewed at General Hospital.

4. A. Each of the witnesses were customers in the store at the time of occurrence.
    B. Neither of the witnesses interviewed was the owner of the liquor store.
    C. Neither of the witnesses interviewed were the owner of the store.
    D. Neither of the witnesses was employed by Mr. Brown.

5. A. Mr. Brown arrived at General Hospital at about 5:00 P.M.
    B. Neither of the robbers was injured during the robbery.
    C. The robbery occurred at 3:30 P.M. on February 10.
    D. One of the witnesses called the ambulance.

Questions 6-10.

DIRECTIONS: Each of Questions 6 through 10 consists of information given in outline form and four sentences labeled A, B, C, and D. For each question, choose the one sentence which CORRECTLY expresses the information given in outline form and which also displays PROPER English usage.

6. Client's Name: Joanna Jones
    Number of Children: 3
    Client's Income: None
    Client's Marital Status: Single

    A. Joanna Jones is an unmarried client with three children who have no income.
    B. Joanna Jones, who is single and has no income, a client she has three children.
    C. Joanna Jones, whose three children are clients, is single and has no income.
    D. Joanna Jones, who has three children, is an unmarried client with no income.

7. Client's Name: Bertha Smith
   Number of Children: 2
   Client's Rent: $1050 per month
   Number of Rooms: 4

   A. Bertha Smith, a client, pays $1050 per month for her four rooms with two children.
   B. Client Bertha Smith has two children and pays $1050 per month for four rooms.
   C. Client Bertha Smith is paying $1050 per month for two children with four rooms.
   D. For four rooms and two children client Bertha Smith pays $1050 per month.

7._____

8. Name of Employee: Cynthia Dawes
   Number of Cases Assigned: 9
   Date Cases were Assigned: 12/16
   Number of Assigned Cases Completed: 8

   A. On December 16, employee Cynthia Dawes was assigned nine cases; she has completed eight of these cases.
   B. Cynthia Dawes, employee on December 16, assigned nine cases, completed eight.
   C. Being employed on December 16, Cynthia Dawes completed eight of nine assigned cases.
   D. Employee Cynthia Dawes, she was assigned nine cases and completed eight, on December 16.

8._____

9. Place of Audit: Broadway Center
   Names of Auditors: Paul Cahn, Raymond Perez
   Date of Audit: 11/20
   Number of Cases Audited: 41

   A. On November 20, at the Broadway Center 41 cases was audited by auditors Paul Cahn and Raymond Perez.
   B. Auditors Raymond Perez and Paul Cahn has audited 41 cases at the Broadway Center on November 20.
   C. At the Broadway Center, on November 20, auditors Paul Cahn and Raymond Perez audited 41 cases.
   D. Auditors Paul Cahn and Raymond Perez at the Broadway Center, on November 20, is auditing 41 cases.

9._____

10. Name of Client: Barbra Levine
    Client's Monthly Income: $2100
    Client's Monthly Expenses: $4520

    A. Barbra Levine is a client, her monthly income is $2100 and her monthly expenses is $4520.
    B. Barbra Levine's monthly income is $2100 and she is a client, with whose monthly expenses are $4520.

10._____

C. Barbra Levine is a client whose monthly income is $2100 and whose monthly expenses are $4520.
D. Barbra Levine, a client, is with a monthly income which is $2100 and monthly expenses which are $4520.

Questions 11-13.

DIRECTIONS: Questions 11 through 13 involve several statements of fact presented in a very simple way. These statements of fact are followed by 4 choices which attempt to incorporate all of the facts into one logical statement which is properly constructed and grammatically correct.

11. I. Mr. Brown was sweeping the sidewalk in front of his house.
    II. He was sweeping it because it was dirty.
    III. He swept the refuse into the street.
    IV. Police Officer gave him a ticket.

    Which one of the following BEST presents the information given above?
    A. Because his sidewalk was dirty, Mr. Brown received a ticket from Officer Green when he swept the refuse into the street.
    B. Police Officer Green gave Mr. Brown a ticket because his sidewalk was dirty and he swept the refuse into the street.
    C. Police Officer Green gave Mr. Brown a ticket for sweeping refuse into the street because his sidewalk was dirty.
    D. Mr. Brown, who was sweeping refuse from his dirty sidewalk into the street, was given a ticket by Police Officer Green.

11.____

12. I. Sergeant Smith radioed for help.
    II. The sergeant did so because the crowd was getting larger.
    III. It was 10:00 A.M. when he made his call.
    IV. Sergeant Smith was not in uniform at the time of occurrence.

    Which one of the following BEST presents the information given above?
    A. Sergeant Smith, although not on duty at the time, radioed for help at 10 o'clock because the crowd was getting uglier.
    B. Although not in uniform, Sergeant Smith called for help at 10:00 A.M. because the crowd was getting uglier.
    C. Sergeant Smith radioed for help at 10:00 A.M. because the crowd was getting larger.
    D. Although he was not in uniform, Sergeant Smith radioed for help at 10:00 A.M. because the crowd was getting larger.

12.____

13. I. The payroll office is open on Fridays.
    II. Paychecks are distributed from 9:00 A.M. to 12 Noon.
    III. The office is open on Fridays because that's the only day the payroll staff is available.
    IV. It is open for the specified hours in order to permit employees to cash checks at the bank during lunch hour.

13.____

The choice below which MOST clearly and accurately presents the above idea is:
  A. Because the payroll office is open on Fridays from 9:00 A.M. to 12 Noon, employees can cash their checks when the payroll staff is available.
  B. Because the payroll staff is only available on Fridays until noon, employees can cash their checks during their lunch hour.
  C. Because the payroll staff is available only on Fridays, the office is open from 9:00 A.M. to 12 Noon to allow employees to cash their checks.
  D. Because of payroll staff availability, the payroll office is open on Fridays. It is open from 9:00 A.M. to 12 Noon so that distributed paychecks can be cashed at the bank while employees are on their lunch hour.

Questions 14-16.

DIRECTIONS: In each of Questions 14 through 6, the four sentences are from a paragraph in a report. They are not in the right order. Which of the following arrangements is the BEST one?

14. I. An executive may answer a letter by writing his reply on the face of the letter itself instead of having a return letter typed.
    II. This procedure is efficient because it saves the executive's time, the typist's time, and saves office file space.
    III. Copying machines are used in small offices as well as large offices to save time and money in making brief replies to business letters.
    IV. A copy is made on a copy machine to go into the company files, while the original is mailed back to the sender.

    The CORRECT answer is:
      A. I, II, IV, III   B. I, IV, II, III   C. III, I, IV, II   D. III, IV, II, I

15. I. Most organizations favor one of the types but always include the others to a lesser degree.
    II. However, we can detect a definite trend toward greater use of symbolic control.
    III. We suggest that our local police agencies are today primarily utilizing material control.
    IV. Control can be classified into three types: physical, material, and symbolic.

    The CORRECT answer is:
      A. IV, II, III, I   B. II, I, IV, III   C. III, IV, II, I   D. IV, I, III, II

16. I. They can and do take advantage of ancient political and geographical boundaries, which often give them sanctuary from effective policy activity.
    II. This country is essentially a country of small police forces, each operating independently within the limits of its jurisdiction.
    III. The boundaries that define and limit police operations do not hinder the movement of criminals, of course.
    IV. The machinery of law enforcement in America is fragmented, complicated, and frequently overlapping.

6 (#3)

The CORRECT answer is:
A. III, I, IV B. II, IV, I, III C. IV, II, III, I D. IV, III, II, I

17. Examine the following sentence, and then choose from below the words which should be inserted in the blank spaces to produce the best sentence.
The unit has exceeded _____ goals and the employees are satisfied with _____ accomplishments.
A. their, it's B. it's; it's C. its, there D. its, their

17._____

18. Examine the following sentence, and then choose from below the words which should be inserted in the blank spaces to produce the best sentence.
Research indicates that employees who _____ no opportunity for close social relationships often find their work unsatisfying, and this _____ of satisfaction often reflects itself in low production.
A. have; lack B. have; excess C. has; lack D. has; excess

18._____

19. Words in a sentence must be arranged properly to make sure that the intended meaning of the sentence is clear.
The sentence below that does NOT make sense because a clause has been separated from the word on which its meaning depends is:
A. To be a good writer, clarity is necessary.
B. To be a good writer, you must write clearly.
C. You must write clearly to be a good writer.
D. Clarity is necessary to good writing.

19._____

Questions 20-21.

DIRECTIONS: Each of Questions 20 and 21 consists of a statement which contains a word (one of those underlined) that is either incorrectly used because it is not in keeping with the meaning the quotation is evidently intended to convey, or is misspelled. There is only one INCORRECT word in each quotation. Of the four underlined words, determine if the first one should be replaced by the word lettered A, the second one replaced by the word lettered B, the third one replaced by the word lettered C, or the fourth one replaced by the word lettered D.

20. The alleged killer was occasionally permitted to excercise in the corridor.
A. alledged B. ocasionally C. permited D. exercise

20._____

21. Defense counsel stated, in affect, that their conduct was permissible under the First Amendment.
A. council B. effect C. there D. permissable

21._____

Question 22.

DIRECTIONS: Question 22 consists of one sentence. This sentence contains an incorrectly used word. First, decide which is the incorrectly used word. Then, from among the options given, decide which word, when substituted for the incorrectly used word, makes the meaning of the sentence clear.

22. As today's violence has no single cause, so its causes have no single scheme. 22._____
 A. deference B. cure C. flaw D. relevance

23. In the sentence, *A man in a light-grey suit waited thirty-five minutes in the ante-room for the all-important document*, the word IMPROPERLY hyphenated is 23._____
 A. light-grey B. thirty-five
 C. ante-room D. all-important

24. In the sentence, *The candidate wants to file his application for preference before it is too late*, the word *before* is used as a(n) 24._____
 A. preposition B. subordinating conjunction
 C. pronoun D. adverb

25. In the sentence, *The perpetrators ran from the scene*, the word *from* is a 25._____
 A. preposition B. pronoun C. verb D. conjunction

KEY (CORRECT ANSWERS)

1.	D		11.	D
2.	D		12.	D
3.	A		13.	D
4.	B		14.	C
5.	D		15.	D
6.	D		16.	C
7.	B		17.	D
8.	A		18.	A
9.	C		19.	A
10.	C		20.	D

21. B
22. B
23. C
24. B
25. A

www.ingramcontent.com/pod-product-compliance
Lightning Source LLC
Chambersburg PA
CBHW082036300426
44117CB00015B/2508